The Prince of Kirbos

Elia Awekel

Feb 25, 2018

Probing China's Soul

For Allen T. Lambert,

In admiration & with thanks,

Julia Ching

December 1, 1990

PROBING CHINA'S SOUL

Religion, Politics, and Protest
in the People's Republic

Julia Ching

1817

Harper & Row, Publishers, San Francisco

New York, Grand Rapids, Philadelphia, St. Louis
London, Singapore, Sydney, Tokyo, Toronto

FIRST EDITION

Library of Congress Cataloging-in-Publication Data

Ching, Julia.
    Probing China's soul : religion, politics, and protest in the
People's Republic / Julia Ching.—1st ed.
        p.   cm.
    Includes bibliographical references.
    ISBN 0-06-250139-9
    1. Freedom of religion—China.   2. China—Intellectual life—1976–
3. China—Politics and government—1976–   I. Title.
    BV741.C5   1990
323.44′2′0951—dc20   89–40631
                                                                                                        CIP

90 91 92 93 94 RINAM 10 9 8 7 6 5 4 3 2 1

This edition is printed on acid-free paper that
meets the American National Standards Institute Z39.48 Standard.

To a brighter future in China

The dragon is a kind of being whose miraculous changes are inscrutable.

—E. T. C. WERNER, 1924

The paradox of totalitarianism in power is that the possession of all instruments of governmental power and violence in one country is not an unmixed blessing for a totalitarian movement. Its disregard for facts, its strict adherence to the rules of a fictitious world, becomes steadily more difficult to maintain, yet remains as essential as it was before. Power means a direct confrontation with reality, and totalitarianism in power is constantly concerned with overcoming this challenge. Propaganda and organization no longer suffice to assert that the impossible is possible, that the incredible is true, that an insane consistency rules the world; the chief psychological support of totalitarian fiction—the active resentment of the status quo, which the masses refused to accept as the only possible world—is no longer there; every bit of factual information that leaks through the iron curtain, set up against the ever-threatening flood of reality from the other, nontotalitarian side, is a greater menace to totalitarian domination than counter-propaganda has been to totalitarian movements.

—HANNAH ARENDT, 1968

Contents

Acknowledgments

I did not expect to write this book. The Tian'anmen Incident shocked the world and changed many people's lives. In the aftermath, I felt that I should meditate on some of the things that led up to it, as well as what one may yet hope for the future. I also felt that I had to put everything else aside to write this, before resuming my usual work.

Mine is not an eyewitness account. It is based on the excellent reporting already done, while going back into the recent history of the last forty years, and going forward a bit into the future. By so doing, I trust that I have done a more profound probing of China's soul: namely, of its ideology, of its religious situation, and of its political protests and their significance.

To assume responsibility, I am using my real name, although assuming a pen name was my original intent. I know that there will be many books on the incident itself; this one seeks to probe deeper politically and ideologically, while also giving an account of religious developments.

Acknowledging help received is in order. I would like especially to thank Will Oxtoby for his tremendous help in clarifying the form and content of this manuscript, and for help in preparing the maps and the tables. Without him this manuscript might never have been ready on time. I would also like to thank my niece, Alice Bridget Ching, who put to good use a cartographer's skills, and my brother Frank Ching, the professional China-watcher of the family, who looked over the manuscript and offered corrections and advice.

Several people outside the family took the trouble to read it and give advice. I should like to mention in particular Margaret Atwood, Nien Cheng, and Harrison Salisbury, who took time out to read the text and offer words of support; John Fraser, who also contributed the foreword; Benjamin Schwartz and Wilfred Cantwell Smith, whose scholarship I have always admired; and Richard Teleky, who encouraged me from the beginning. I also wish to thank the editors of Harper & Row, San Francisco, for their kind collaboration, and Michael McLaughlin for his work on the index. To them, and to many others, I am most grateful.

Julia Ching

■

A Note on Pronunciation

Transliterations from Chinese are usually rendered according to the *pinyin* system, which is derived from the International Phonetic Alphabet. Exceptions are made for those proper names that are better known, such as Confucius, Mencius, Kuomintang (Chinese Nationalists), Sun Yat-sen.

A full description of the ins and outs of *pinyin* is more than should be attempted in a general book, but here are a few of the points at which the *pinyin* system appears counterintuitive to speakers of English.

Consonants:

    Q is like the *ch* in "cheese" (example: Qing)

    X is like the *sh* in "sheep" (example: Xiaoping)

    C is like the *ts* in "nuts" (example: *baicai*, a vegetable)

    ZH is like the *j* in "junk" (example: Zhao)

Vowels:

    E is like the *oo* in "book" (example: Hebei), except before *n*, when it is like the *u* in "sun" (example: Deng)

    I is like the *i* in "machine" (example: Xi'an), except after *c, ch, r, s, sh, z, zh*, when it is like the *i* in "sir" (example: Laozi)

    U is like the *u* in "true" (example: Chengdu), except after *j, q, x, y*, when it is like German "ü" (example: Yunnan)

Vowel Combinations:

    IA is like the *ia* in "California" (example: Jiangsu), except before *n*, when it is like *ye* in "yen" (example: Tian'anmen)

    UA is like the *ua* in "Guam" (example: Guangzhou), except before *n*, when it is like *we* in "went" (example: Yuan)

    OU is like the *ow* in "show" (example: Guangzhou)

    IU is like the *yeo* in "yeoman" (example: Liu)

    UI is like the *way* in "waylay" (example: Anhui)

Important Dates in
Modern Chinese History

1949	October 1	Founding of the Chinese People's Republic
1957		Anti-rightist campaign
1958–62		"Great Leap Forward" followed by nationwide famine
1966–76		Cultural Revolution
1968		Fall of Liu Shaoqi and rise of Lin Biao
1971		China admitted to United Nations Visit of Henry Kissinger Fall of Lin Biao
1972		Visit of Richard Nixon
1976	January July September	Death of Zhou Enlai Earthquake at Tangshan Death of Mao Zedong
1977		Fall of the Gang of Four
1978		Reemergence of Deng Xiaoping Xidan Democracy Movement
1979		U.S. (under Jimmy Carter) normalizes relations with China Deng Xiaoping visits the U.S.
1986	December	Nationwide student demonstrations begin
1987	January	Fall of Hu Yaobang and anti-liberalization campaign
1988	July–October	Economic crisis: currency fall, inflation, price rises
1989	April 16 June 3–4	Nationwide student demonstrations begin Military crackdown and massacre in Beijing

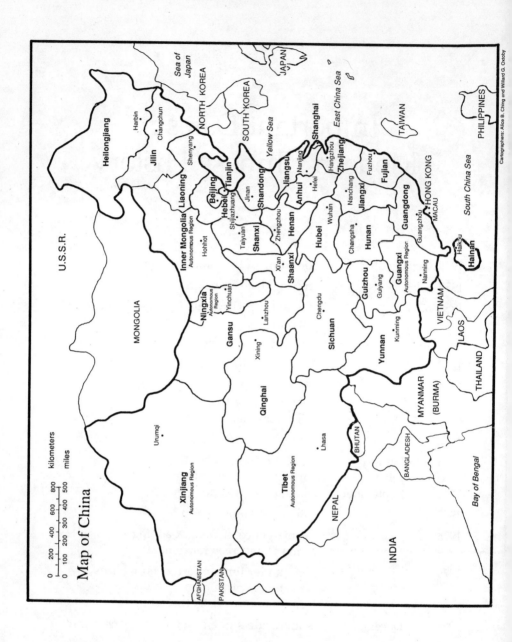

Map of China

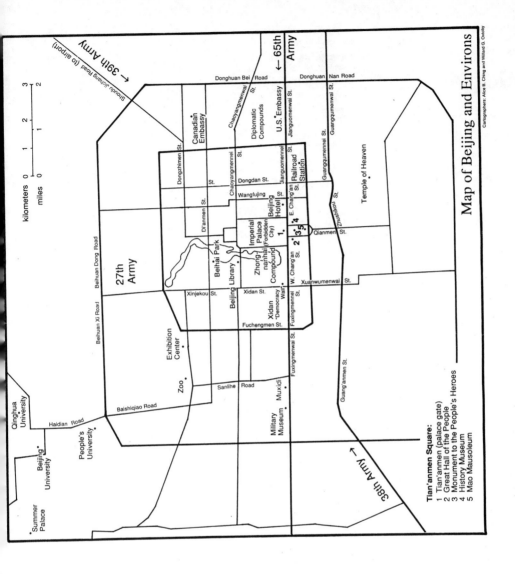

Map of Beijing and Environs

Tian'anmen Square:

1 Tian'anmen (palace gate)
2 Great Hall of the People
3 Monument to the People's Heroes
4 History Museum
5 Mao Mausoleum

Cartographers: Alice B. Ching and Willard G. Oxtoby

A Chronology of Events
April 15 to June 24, 1989

April 15   Death of Hu Yaobang.

April 16   Crowds begin to gather at Tian'anmen Square.

April 17   University students demonstrate in Beijing, Shanghai, Tianjin, and Xi'an.

April 18   Mass rally of students at Tian'anmen Square.

April 19   Student petitions at Xinhuamen, in front of Zhongnanhai.

April 20   Petitions once more at Xinhuamen meet with police brutality.

April 21   Student strike to protest police brutality; demonstrations and sit-in at Tian'anmen. Forty-seven intellectuals write joint letter to the government to support student action.

April 22   Official memorial service honoring Hu Yaobang in the Great Hall of the People. Students' rally outside, and petition for dialogue.

April 23   Unrest also reported in Xi'an, Changsha, Wuhan, Shanghai, Tianjin.

Beijing students formally organize an autonomous alliance.

April 24   Student strike to continue indefinitely in Beijing. *World Economic Herald* forbidden to publish special issue on Hu Yaobang.

April 26   *People's Daily* editorial calls student protest a "riot."

April 27   Half a million demonstrate in Beijing streets. (Several thousand in Changsha.)

April 28   Beijing students' autonomous alliance raises seven
            demands. Demonstrations in Tianjin, Changsha, Hefei,
            and Shanghai.

April 29   Conversation between State Council officials (Yuan Mu,
            He Dongchang) and some students. Demonstrations in
            Lanzhou (Gansu) and Harbin.

April 30   Beijing party secretary Li Ximing and mayor Chen Xitong
            meet with twenty-nine students.

May 1   Beijing students hold press conference.

May 2   Beijing students start public broadcasts. Shanghai
            students demonstrate.

May 3   State Council refuses dialogue with students'
            representatives. Yuan Mu and others hold press
            conference. Students respond with their own press
            conference.

May 4   † Asian Development Bank meets in Beijing with Taiwan
            participation (May 4–6).
            Student demonstrations in Beijing and at least twenty-
            five other cities. Five hundred journalists take to
            Beijing streets for freedom of the press.

May 9   Several thousand journalists petition for a free press,
            with student support. Students elect representatives
            for dialogue with government.

May 10   Tens of thousands demonstrate on bicycles to support a
            free press.

May 11   Students decide to demonstrate at the time of
            Gorbachev's visit. Demonstrations in Shanghai,
            Taiyuan (Shanxi), and Haikou (Hainan).

May 13   Mass hunger strike begins at the Tian'anmen sit-in to
            press for dialogue with the government.

May 14   Several officials visit Tian'anmen to request end to
            hunger strike, but in vain. Demonstrations in Qingdao,
            Liaoning, Yan'an, Shanghai, Nanjing, Tianjin.

May 15   † Gorbachev visits Beijing for a summit meeting with
            Deng Xiaoping and others. Western journalists
            assemble there.
            800,000 at Tian'anmen rally to support the students.
            Protests throughout the country. Hong Kong students
            begin hunger strike in support.

May 16	Hunger strikers refuse liquids; middle school students demonstrate. Demonstrations also in over twenty other cities, including Hangzhou, Shenyang, Guangzhou, Hohhot.
May 17	Zhao Ziyang promises no reprisals. Demonstrations in twenty-seven other cities.
May 18	† Gorbachev leaves Beijing for Shanghai. Zhao Ziyang and others visit students at hospitals. Li Peng meets with some student representatives and issues a warning. Demonstrations in over thirty cities, including Lhasa (Tibet), Kunming.
May 19	Zhao Ziyang and Li Peng at Tian'anmen at dawn. Students stop hunger strike. Workers' autonomous alliance posts notices to support students.
May 20	Martial law declared by Li Peng for parts of Beijing. News blackout declared. Students, workers, and hunger strikers demand removal of Li Peng and Yang Shangkun, and oppose martial law as unconstitutional.
May 21	Beijing residents begin work of stopping the army from entering the city. A million demonstrate in Hong Kong to support Chinese students. Demonstrations in many Chinese cities call for fall of Li Peng and Deng Xiaoping.
May 23	A million demonstrate in Beijing, asking for Li Peng's resignation. News blackout lifted. Beijing intellectuals organize an alliance and publish a statement asking for repeal of martial law.
May 24	Wan Li leaves the U.S. early to return to China. Demonstrations continue in many parts of China asking for extraordinary session of People's Congress to meet and lift martial law.
May 25	News blackout imposed once more. Demonstrations continue.
May 26	Students decide to remain at Tian'anmen. But many are from other parts of China than Beijing.
May 27	Hong Kong marathon concert raises a fund to support the students' movement. Wan Li declares his support of government.

May 28   Worldwide Chinese demonstrate in support of democracy movement: 100,000 in Beijing, 1.5 million in Hong Kong, many in United States, Canada, Australia and Europe, as well as in many Chinese cities.

May 29   Students continue sit-in. Hong Kong–donated tents appear at Tian'anmen Square.

May 30   Statue of the Goddess of Democracy (seven meters high) placed at Tian'anmen Square.

Security forces arrest three workers illegally. Thousands protest outside their office building.

May 31   Workers released. Government-organized demonstrations in Beijing suburbs supporting Li Peng.

June 2   Four intellectuals (Hou Dejian, Liu Shaobo, Gao Xin, Zhou To) begin seventy-two-hour hunger strike at Tian'anmen.

June 3   Soldiers begin march to Tian'anmen beginning at dawn; tens of thousands of citizens try to stop them. At 10 P.M. soldiers begin shooting civilians.

June 4   At 2:45 A.M. government broadcasts warn crowds to leave Tian'anmen.

At 4–5 A.M. troops force their way into Tian'anmen.

News of the massacre spreads in country, as crowds take to streets in Tianjin, Qingdao, Nanjing, Shanghai, Xi'an, Wuhan, Changsha, Chengdu, Guangzhou and elsewhere to protest atrocities.

Foreign governments condemn the massacre. Chinese in Hong Kong, Macau, and elsewhere protest the massacre with demonstrations.

June 5   Killings continue in Beijing. Skirmishes reported between troops for and against the crackdown.

June 6   Confusion continues in Beijing. Clashes reported in Chengdu between troops and civilians. Shanghai paralyzed by protests.

Railways paralyzed. Unrest reported in many cities.

Government spokesman Yuan Mu holds press conference.

June 7   Beijing remains in crisis. Foreigners depart. Students return home. Troops invite journalists to see Tian'anmen.

June 8	Beijing city authorities and the military declare students' union illegal, student leaders on wanted list.
	Li Peng, Wang Zhen reported as visiting some troops.
	Protests continue in Shanghai, Changsha, Shenyang, Lanzhou and elsewhere. Train from Beijing crushes six protesters in Shanghai, and is burned by crowds.
June 9	Deng Xiaoping addresses higher military cadres in Beijing, calling the massacre a crackdown on a "counterrevolutionary uprising." Protests continue in Shanghai and elsewhere.
June 10	"White terror" envelops China.
June 23–24	Fourth Plenum of Thirteenth Party Central Committee meets in Beijing.
June 24	Jiang Zemin replaces Zhao Ziyang as party general secretary.

† Indicates international events

A Note on Sources: This chronology has been made especially with the help of two published chronologies. One is in *Ming Pao Monthly,* June 1989, p. 21, and July 1989, p. 45. The other, in *Cheng-ming,* July 1989, pp. 90–92 (also pp. 19–21). *Hongkong Economic Journal Monthly,* July 1989, p. 18, also has a good summary of the events of June 4.

Jinxin dongpode wushiliu tian (The shocking fifty-six days) (Beijing: Dadi, 1989) is a full chronicle of events compiled by the state commission on education's political thought working group. It covers each day from April 15 through June 9, 1989. The book is meant for circulation within China only.

There is a Chinese-language chronicle published in Taiwan by journalists from *China Times: Beijing xueyun wushiri* (Taipei: China Times, 1989). This covers the period from April 15 to June 4, 1989.

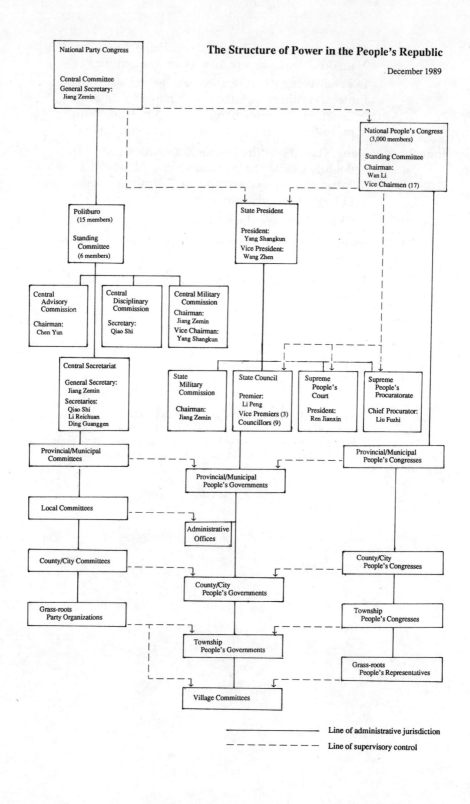

The Structure of Power in the People's Republic

December 1989

National Party Congress

Central Committee
General Secretary:
Jiang Zemin

National People's Congress
(3,000 members)

Standing Committee
Chairman:
Wan Li
Vice Chairmen (17)

Politburo
(15 members)

Standing
Committee
(6 members)

State President

President:
Yang Shangkun
Vice President:
Wang Zhen

Central
Advisory
Commission

Chairman:
Chen Yun

Central
Disciplinary
Commission

Secretary:
Qiao Shi

Central Military
Commission

Chairman:
Jiang Zemin
Vice Chairman:
Yang Shangkun

Central Secretariat

General Secretary:
Jiang Zemin
Secretaries:
Qiao Shi
Li Reichuan
Ding Guanggen

State
Military
Commission

Chairman:
Jiang Zemin

State Council

Premier:
Li Peng
Vice Premiers (3)
Councillors (9)

Supreme
People's
Court

President:
Ren Jianxin

Supreme
People's
Procuratorate

Chief Procurator:
Liu Fuzhi

Provincial/Municipal
Committees

Provincial/Municipal
People's Governments

Provincial/Municipal
People's Congresses

Local Committees

Administrative
Offices

County/City Committees

County/City
People's Governments

County/City
People's Congresses

Grass-roots
Party Organizations

Township
People's Governments

Township
People's Congresses

Grass-roots
People's Representatives

Village Committees

———————————— Line of administrative jurisdiction

– – – – – – – – – Line of supervisory control

Foreword

by John Fraser

For many people in the West, China and the Chinese remain a conundrum. It is not so much that we feel a great distance from this vast clod of earth and humanity as it is that we feel the Chinese destiny to be set apart from our own. During the era of Western imperialist ascendancy, for example, this apartness was often manifested with brutal cynicism. The world saw a combination of gunboats, forced participation in the opium trade, and extraterritorial demands. A common factor in the journals and accounts by Westerners traveling or living in China during this period was the sense that the Chinese, partly because of their very numerousness and partly because "life was cheap," are destined from birth to endure an unchangeable fate.

The magazine I edit in Canada, *Saturday Night*, is 102 years old. Some of its earlier issues reflect clearly the then prevailing view of the Chinese, especially the turn-of-the-century obsession with "the yellow peril." Canada imported indentured Chinese men to build the most difficult sections of its transcontinental railway. According to my magazine (September 1906), this was not a healthy development:

> We don't want Chinamen in Canada. . . . This is a white man's country and white men will keep it so. The slant-eyed Asiatic, with his yellow skin, his unmanly humility, his cheap wants, would destroy the whole equilibrium of industry. Turn these people loose in a country like ours and they would make progress like a pestilence. . . . Let them swarm in once and the yellow stain on the country will be one that cannot be rubbed out. We cannot assimilate them. They are an honest, industrious, but hopelessly inferior race.

Time passes, but do perceptions really improve? We can now wince, or snicker, at the stupidity of the foregoing sentiments. But how much better were the "sympathetic" views of the Chinese from dozens of academics and journalists who made the holy trek to Chairman Mao

Zedong's socialist paradise during the heyday of the Great Proletarian Cultural Revolution in the 1960s and early seventies? Weren't all those miracle tales—of selfless devotion to the Revolution and the altruistic subordination of personal ambition and desires to the collective good—merely an update to the notion of apartness and a separate fate? In this more benign, but no less harmful, guise of racism, the Chinese in China were seen as being not much more than grains of sand in the Great Helmsman's hands, waiting for the appropriate moment to be placed in a grand structure that would shake the world.

Common sense and common decency were the first casualties in much of the Western analysis of China during this hateful period. We were told that it was wrong to impose Western cultural and philosophical notions on the Chinese, that they were different from us, and that this difference constituted a barrier that could be bridged only if we left behind all the baggage of our own experience. We were told that our arrogant Western individualism and obsession with human rights were little more than a product of Western economic aggrandizement. Once shorn of such, we would presumably be able to understand clearly all sorts of things that hitherto we might have seen in a negative light, things like ruthless political suppression, special privileges for self-appointed high officials, permanent war psychosis, and the elevation of neighborhood snoops and informers into national heroes.

Two decades later, after the "opening" of China to the West by Deng Xiaoping and his colleagues, we can hear the same continuous voice in its latest guise: hard realism. Following the tragic events surrounding the Tian'anmen massacre, it was merely a matter of weeks before Western businessmen, diplomats, and academics cautioned us to try to understand that the Chinese were different from everyone else. In my country, a typical opinion was expressed by the president of a vast international firm when he spoke to a special parliamentary committee on the question of retaining full trading links with China in the aftermath of Tian'anmen:

"You cannot expect the Chinese to have a democracy within five years," said Marcel Dufour, head of Lavalin International. "It might never happen. The Chinese have their own way to settle matters . . . and what they did, they've been doing for the last thousand years."

Thus today, as always, the variety and complexity of the human condition have been deployed as a noose around the necks of the Chinese who have aspired to better their lot and those of their fellow citizens. The feeble-mindedness of much that has been said and written about the Chinese in the West during this century is sufficiently awesome in its ignorance that it is sometimes difficult to figure out how to begin rebutting it. Take the notion that Chinese culture is so profoundly different from our own that it is nonsense to try to graft Western concepts onto it. This is a classic concept in exposing the foolhardiness of the Christian missionary movement in China before the Communists put an end to all such endeavors in 1949. But where on earth did these earnest interpreters think Marxism got invented? In the musical instrument room of the Confucian temple in the ancient Kingdom of Lu?

Abandoning notions of apartness is not only an altruistic goal. It also allows us to see how the Chinese experience can influence the rest of the world. Transfixed as we all were at the end of 1989 by the earth-shaking events in Marxist Eastern Europe, no thinking person who follows world events closely could fail to see that the crumbling structure of totalitarianism had a specific Chinese context. When the dictators and rulers in Moscow, in Prague, in Berlin, in Budapest, and in Sofia had to summon up strategies to deal with massive people's protests so similar to the ones in Tian'anmen Square, they already had a practical example of the horrific consequences of one kind of approach.

In this sense, the martyrs of Tian'anmen can be said to have died for a cause far wider than that of their own country. Their blood, which looked distinctly red and much like our own, symbolizes both the hard practicality and the spiritual aspiration that the concept of sacrifice evokes among all races and creeds and political cultures. One corpse on Beijing's Avenue of Heavenly Peace redeems not only the Chinese soul but also a persecuted student in Czechoslovakia or a cultural and racial myopic in Toronto.

The first pleasure, then, of Julia Ching's look into the interior of this Chinese soul starts right here. The book you are about to read is shorn of the twin curses of Western arrogance and Western guilt when looking into the Chinese condition. It takes as its premise a simple but radical notion: that the Chinese people have the same right to aspire to freedom and political civility as any other people; that their capacity for error is no less—and certainly no greater—than anyone else's. In this way, along with Ching's impeccable scholarship and her sense of the Chinese culture she sprang from and the Western culture she now lives in, we are brought to a greater understanding of a crucial truth: that the variety of the human condition and the inequality of historical fate can never be used as a means to deny the Chinese their presiding humanity or their aspirations to change that fate.

As usual, an old Chinese saying puts it all in more eloquent and succinct form: "Under heaven, all are one."

Probing China's Soul

Introduction: On Being Human and Being Chinese

A specter is going around in China's intellectual circles—the specter of humanism . . .!

—WANG RUOSHUI, 1983

Which is more important: to be human or to be Chinese? To many people, this will appear a rhetorical question. And the answer should be obvious even if we are to change "Chinese" (whether the designation be ethnic or national or ideological) to "American" or "Canadian," "German" or "Japanese," "communist" or "capitalist." It is folly indeed to think that being human is *less* important than being this or that *kind* of human being, whether male or female, Chinese or European, revolutionary or conservative. It is unnatural and unreasonable to make people choose between *being human* and being this or that kind of human being.

Coming from those of Chinese origin, the question seems all the stranger, since many associate humanistic wisdom with the Chinese tradition. But the question is actually burning in the hearts of millions of people in China. It may be understood on different levels. "Being human" primarily means belonging to the human race, a fact of nature rather than a matter of choice. It may also mean enjoying human rights, that is, being accorded the dignity of a human being. And it can have a third meaning: that of being humane, of *regarding* others humanely. Being this or that kind of human being, for example, being Chinese, is usually not a matter of choice. In China, however, the importance of being Chinese refers to a loyalty that the state commands, which is to take priority over all other loyalties. And the state also defines *how* this loyalty is to be exercised.

I am writing this book to answer this deceptively simple question. I want to put in no uncertain terms that I consider it (and I trust most people are with me here) much more important to be human than to be anything else. To extend this to ideological categories, I also consider it much more important to be human than to be Christian or communist (or "revolutionary") or capitalist. In fact, I believe that ideologies like Marxism and capitalism, or Christianity and Confucianism, should be judged by their fruits: do they make us more human, or less?

The Chinese dissident writer Wang Ruoshui got into serious trouble for asserting just what I have asserted. In posing some questions about the meaning of being human, he had first asked, Is humanism only the ideology of the capitalist class? His answer was no.

His second question was, Is revolution an end in itself? And his answer was again no.

> In the past, the prevalent way of speaking is that . . . everything we do is for the revolution. But then, what is revolution for? Revolution is a means, not an end. We work for socialism and communism, to realize the welfare and happiness of the people, to liberate the whole human race. This is the inherent meaning of revolutionary humanism.

In light of what happened on June 3–4, 1989, when tanks rolled over bodies of unarmed civilians in Beijing, and gunshots and bayonets added to the number of casualties, we can all the more understand his predicament, and the predicament of countless others. The dehumanization of an entire people is not just isolated to the ten years of the Cultural Revolution (1966–76). It has its roots in an ideology that opposes "humanism" (*rendao zhuyi*) in principle. It can recur at any time, and appears to have done so lately.

"We want to be human beings." The statement reminds us of the humanism of *old* China, the China of Confucius. Indeed, the sage who lived over two-and-a-half millennia ago taught about human-heartedness as a virtue that governs relationships between human beings, including family as well as sociopolitical relationships. But the Communist regime did not inherit Confucian virtues, even if it does make use of Confucian respect for authority to maintain its own power. The *dehumanization* that we have witnessed in China over the past decades, and especially over the more recent past, cannot be blamed on Confucianism. This does not mean that Confucius's teachings are perfect. Confucius taught *benevolent* government. A regime that kills peaceful demonstrators cannot be considered benevolent, not even in terms of a benevolent dictatorship.

"We want to be human beings" is actually a slogan of the student demonstrations supporting freedom and democratization. In Gu Hua's novel (and film) *Hibiscus Town*, when the so-called madman Qin is refused permission by the authorities to marry his fellow victim of political repression, the tofu girl, he cries out: "But this is a right that even beasts have! Why not us?" Later, when condemned to imprisonment for his "illegal" marriage, he tells his wife: "Live on like a beast, live on!" True, the humanity of these characters shines out especially in their courage to live on (albeit like "beasts") when they are singled out for humiliation. The humanity of all who are unjustly persecuted, who are being reduced to the state of being "subhuman," shines out, even as they are being trampled upon.

"We want to be human beings." When the Chinese say this, they are not indicating that they do not want to be Chinese as well. The student demonstrators asserted quite adamantly that theirs was a "patriotic" as well as "democratic" movement. What is affirmed is the greater importance of one over the other, and the injustice of the state to judge people according to its own standard of how one should be, above all, "Chinese"–defined also as being loyal to the Revolution. In that context, it really means being "slavish," remaining in bondage to the state. In Communist China, as we have all learned of late, "the state" really means the Communist party, or more specifically, the party leader or regime of the moment.

"We want to be human beings." In the minds of the Chinese who say this, it also means that they want their country to join the larger world, and they want themselves to become citizens of this larger world while remaining citizens of China. They want to be like everybody else more than to be different from everybody else. This has surprised many in the West, accustomed to thinking of China as "a world apart," with its own values and preferences. Of course, historically speaking, China has been a world apart; and for much of the last forty years, China has been a closed country. Indeed, for much of the last four thousand years, the Chinese considered theirs the only world.

"We want to be human beings." This is also a call for peace, for peaceful co-existence with other peoples of the world, and for peaceful collaboration with other peoples. People have commented at times on the latent anti-foreign hostility among the Chinese people. The most recent facts have demonstrated that the greatest hostility is directed not so much at outsiders, but at a regime that frustrates the people's most basic wishes. Although through so much of the country's history, China has been a world apart, the people of China do not want it to remain this way. They want to be integrated into the world community. But they, as citizens, chafe under the restraint of a country whose political leaders forcibly keep the population apart from the rest of the world. The Berlin Wall came tumbling down in November 1989, but the Bamboo Curtain has grown thicker than the iron one.

A World Apart

True, for most people in the "larger" world, China is and has been a world apart. For many, the impression of China initially is that of a different civilization. For those unacquainted with Mao Zedong and Deng Xiaoping, the name of Confucius (as a wise man with a humanistic teaching) has some vague connotation. But for others, with some familiarity with *Communist* China, the image of Mao and his Red Guards comes to mind, together with the other image — of a mass of humanity in drab uniforms. However, in the last few years, the outside world began to witness an increasing openness, and started fancying that China was not that different after all. Many Chinese were exchanging their blue-gray Mao jackets for beige or blue trench coats, looking more like an army of "yuppies" getting ready to take over a high-tech universe. China, the Big Dragon, appeared poised to take off on a course that would make it the ultimate leader of the Four Little Dragons, the economically prosperous Asia-Pacific regions of South Korea, Taiwan, Hong Kong, and Singapore.

But then came the seven weeks of April to June 1989. The Chinese students' hunger strike, the sight of tanks and soldiers and citizens blocking them, followed by the military crackdown, changed everything. The days of the Cultural Revolution appeared to have returned; we saw televised arrests and confessions, one of the most memorable being the obviously forced confession of rumor-mongering by an eyewitness to the massacre. Today's China is again different.

I spent some of my formative years in mainland China, but have never felt at home on my many visits there since. I have frequently asked myself the reasons for my feelings of estrangement. The language is no problem. The difference in lifestyle (that is, in the abundance or lack of creature comforts) is not so much at issue, since it was expected. Besides, I have been to other developing countries in both South and Southeast Asia, where living conditions are similar to or worse than what I have seen in China. Rather, the reason is an all-pervading, and very different, sociopolitical system. Hence my feelings about China were corroborated by my brief visits to East Germany and the Soviet Union (long before *glasnost*). I remember a postcard sent from Moscow by an American describing the sights he had seen in that big country, on a corner of which someone (not himself), probably a local, had scribbled in English: "This is a vast prison." I find this feeling confirmed every time I leave China, as I go through tightly controlled airport exits, leaving behind the people who cannot come out.

These are impressions probably shared by many people. One fact brings home such impressions even more: the lack of a free press within Communist China. The news blackout imposed by the authorities as of the military crackdown has "frozen" our image of China. We now rely upon reading between the lines of official pronouncements, or listening to occasional reports of persons leaving the country. But in fact, there has always been a news blackout within the country—even if it was sometimes less than total. Basically, for the people living there, China *is* a world apart, where the population is subjected to official pronouncements of truth, rather than the truth itself. There are outlets to outside reports of world events, such as the *Reference News* (*Chankao Xiaoxi*) with its translations of excerpts from the outside press. But these are all controlled—carefully selected, and for a limited readership.

The eighties has seen a flood of students coming to the West and Japan from China, as well as many tourists and scholars going to China. The bamboo curtain was lifted in the seventies, some thought forever, but it has once more come down where freedom of speech is concerned. Western visitors, including businessmen now traveling to China, are treated to the official version of what happened during the student protests of April and May, and especially what led to the conclusion of these protests. Even Chinese scholars now visiting the West are toeing the party line: the soldiers fired in self-defense against a crowd of hooligans; hardly any students were killed on that fateful June 4; and blood did not flow at Tian'anmen Square. However, Chinese students overseas accept the Western version of the facts, as do more than twenty diplomats in the United States and Canada who have defected. Many students are now too frightened to go home.

I am not saying that China is entirely different from the rest of the world. China has had much in common with the rest of the communist world—a fact we should not forget. For a while, China even appeared to be setting an example of openness to the rest of the communist world, though only on the level of economic exchange, not political *glasnost*. China also shares a lot with the developing world, where many developing countries have their own dictatorships, whether in Africa, Latin America, the Middle East or elsewhere in Asia. But China, with 1.1 billion people, a quarter of the human race, has unmasked itself lately as a world apart from the free world. "The dictatorship of the proletariat" is the term with which Chinese Communist leaders themselves represent their regime. The "proletariat" here refers, of course, to those in power, rather than to the masses. China is a world apart especially because it is, and has been, a country divided—divided on the level of the people and their rulers.

China: A Changed Field

As a sinologist (or a "China scholar"), but not professionally a journalist or a political scientist, that is, not till now a "China-watcher," I have a sincere respect for the latter and sympathize with their dilemma as they confront the hard realities of political repression. I am not saying that the military crackdown of June 4, 1989, and all its brutality could have been predicted. That would have been impossible, even for the population of Beijing. I am dealing here with certain stereotypes in the way China has been treated by professional China-watchers. And I believe that major adjustments in attitude are called for after this Beijing massacre. At the same time, I realize that much of the dilemma experienced by "the pros" comes from their love of China, their desire to discern the best in the country. Besides, to give the best analysis, what is required is a combination of factors: the outsider's access to information, the insider's sensitivity and experience, and the scholar's knowledge of the past as well as of current events. No one person can be expected to possess this entire combination.

But June 4, 1989, is a watershed not just for the political observer of China. It will mark the turning point for many others: for the larger public in the West, whose initial curiosity has changed to compassion for the Chinese people and revulsion for the state, and for the China trader who has decided that we no longer have "business as usual." More importantly, it has become a watershed for the overseas Chinese community, which had previously preferred to project an apolitical image (while maintaining certain group differences) but now has arisen, with one voice, to support the student demonstrators and to condemn the bloody crackdown. We now witness the irony of a united ethnic front, an enhanced awareness of "being Chinese" among the overseas population, supporting the calls for freedom and democratization in China, which are basically also calls for the recognition of human rights and human values.

June 4, 1989, is also a watershed for China scholars—both those who interpret the past and those who explain the present—who have to demonstrate that they are keeping their feet on the ground rather than working in an ivory tower, that they are not eulogizing a monolithic state, whether that be of today or of long ago, and that they are not romanticizing a cultural heritage that some claim has ill served the people.

Writing This Book

This is where I come in as a human being and a scholar. As an expatriate and a specialist on China's so-called traditional wisdom, I feel the need to probe my own soul as well as China's. I need to answer especially one set of questions: Is today's despotism the result of the old philosophical and religious legacy, or is it strictly communism, or does it combine elements of both? Indeed, I feel that I would be unable to do my own "business as usual," which is that of teaching and writing about China, especially about its past cultural legacy, unless I have first confronted the problem.

I therefore write the book first as an observer of events, both current and not so current, embracing the political history of Communist China viewed in the light of the Tian'anmen Incident of 1989. I will pay special attention to the role of students and intellectuals, since many of them have been especially active in protesting against the abuses of power. I will also attempt to identify the past in the present, by pointing out Confucian or Taoist overtones and residues in China's political life, even when Marxist slogans are at the forefront. In addition, I seek to discuss the situation of China's religions, which I have surveyed recently in a book written jointly with Hans Küng (*Christianity and Chinese Religions*, Doubleday, 1989), and shall not repeat explanations and interpretations concerning Confucianism, Taoism, and Buddhism. In the present context, I focus on the question, How are we to explain the dehumanization of the past forty years, in light of the so-called humane wisdom of the past millennia?

I cannot adequately answer the questions I am posing here, because they are big questions, and need a lot of reflection. I wish, however, to start answering them, to invite others to join in the discussion, so that together, we may be able to make more sense of the past and the present, and perhaps, offer a beacon for the future.

Of course, I am also writing this book as a cathartic exercise, as I ponder with deep sadness the events that led to the Beijing massacre of June 3–4, 1989. Dimly aware of certain repetitions of the past, I feel that the best way for me to understand the recent events more fully is to place them in some historical perspective. In doing so, I have become persuaded of the historical repetitions (especially those occurring during the forty years of Communist rule) that I call the "dictatorship syndrome." I am not saying that this cycle of recurrences, the periodicity in loosening and tightening the reins of power and control, is a *necessary* law of history. But I do think it offers a predictable pattern, so long as the government remains dictatorial. Will democratization or "people power" ever break this cycle? This is another question to which I hope future events will indicate a positive answer.

I was not an eyewitness to the Tian'anmen demonstrations or the crackdown that followed. But then, I am not trying to write an eyewitness account. I was throughout an avid observer of the events, reading every bit of newsprint and poring over news analyses. I have written this book without the help of anyone on the mainland—since I was not there myself. My objective is to understand and interpret what has happened, in light of the recent past—the last forty years—while reflecting as well upon a possible future. I hope that the historical account I present will be useful to others, and that there are also a few insights, coming from an attempt to examine the very recent past in light of a longer past, even in the context of so-called ancient Chinese wisdom.

On account of the Communist government's strict control of the sources as well as of the dissemination of information, the best information has always come from Chinese sources outside China—especially the Hong Kong press. This is what China-watchers have traditionally relied upon (though to a lesser extent during the years immediately prior to the crackdown, when the government had relaxed some controls). It has been joined recently by the Taiwan press, which also sent reporters to mainland China to cover the events of the Asian Development Bank meeting (May 4–6), followed by the Gorbachev visit. I am speaking not just of newspapers and televised reports, but also of periodical literature with its analyses of events. For some years, dissident students from the mainland have also been producing their own periodicals. Their reports have usually been based on solid information sources from within the country.

True, this Chinese-language press has printed fiction as well as fact. Recently, its reports included rumors about Deng's death and an impending civil war. My account here in this book represents a synthesis of information from both East (including Japan and Korea) and West. It may not appear fair to base our information about a regime on what we hear from those it calls its foes. However, recent events have confirmed another suspicion: that the regime has alienated itself from its own people. There is no other way one can understand its handling of the student protesters and their sympathizers—who were far from being "a minority," as the party line would call them. The changes in Poland and Hungary, the popular demonstrations in East Germany and Czechoslovakia (August–December 1989), and the general unrest in the U.S.S.R. reinforce the impression that disenchantment with communist regimes is indeed widespread.

The book begins with the seven-week-long "event" that shocked the world, from April 17 to June 4 (chapter 1). The historical reporting follows from this as a sort of extended flashback. Western perceptions and the now obsolete stereotypes they represent are then analyzed (chapter 2). As I have sought to explain, these stereotypes are not found just among Westerners, but are, to a degree, shared by other China-watchers, such as the Japanese, as well as by expatriates. This has been due mainly to the long-time lack of adequate information. But it can also be explained in part by psychological factors: the desire to see the best in a wretched situation, and to relieve one's own feelings of guilt—whether that be on account of the Japanese War with China, or of the expatriate's own departure from China, or of the Westerner's subconscious guilt about the evils of imperialism. There is, besides, the outsider's inability to comprehend just what makes China so different from the rest of the world.

The book proceeds to explain the manifold drama of the Tian'anmen Square events by going into a bit of modern Chinese history, taking in turn such issues as power struggles under Mao Zedong and Deng Xiaoping and their systematic elimination of would-be heirs to power (chapter 3), the distinction between what is "traditional Chinese," whether Confucian or Taoist, and what is "Marxist" in these power struggles and in recent history in general (chapter 4), student protests of the remote and recent past (chapter 5), a comparison of the two "Tian'anmen Incidents," 1976 and 1989 (chapter 6); and the religious situation in China and its unknown future (chapter 7). The question of "moral legitimacy" follows, placed especially in the context of the traditional Chinese understanding of this question, as well as of the regime's credibility record (chapter 8). The question of what China wants from democracy and whether she is ready for it follows (chapter 9), before the book concludes with a discussion of Chinese self-deprecation and self-hatred among intellectuals, contrasted with the courage demonstrated in 1989, which gives us reasons to look forward to a better future.

Indeed, I have sought, in this book, to give a voice to the "silenced" intellectuals of mainland China, especially those who are under arrest. I have tried hard to include in my references their publications, whether as articles in journals or as books. In the latter case, many of these books that I have consulted are now "prohibited" books.

Once again, the big questions behind all these chapters remain: Is being Chinese more important than being human, or is it the other way around? Can one not be both at the same time? Will China remain a world apart, and for how long?

We have seen country after country in Eastern Europe replacing the old-guard communist leadership with reform-minded persons who are not always members of the party. We know that the news of these events is strictly censored in China. But we cannot help but ask, How much longer do the people there have to wait for their turn to assert their dignity and their rights as human beings?

Let us together ask these questions and seek some answers.

J. C.

CHAPTER 1

■

The Event

It was impressive to watch students and other demonstrators in Prague, Czechoslovakia (December 1989), carry banners with Chinese characters, mourning the martyrs of Tian'anmen and asking for the same freedoms as six months earlier in Beijing. As a Chinese, I cannot but wish the East Europeans well, while envying them a little and wondering when the events in China of April–June 1989 will reap their fruits.

University students are an elite in every country. They have a status that is envied, and yet they are quite powerless. They have the time and the luxury to think, but often little opportunity to implement their thoughts: every year, the institutions empty many of them into the real world and its job market. This is as true in China as it is everywhere.

There are special circumstances in China. There is a tradition of student activism, dating back at least to 1919; many leading Communists were student activists in their own youth. And university students are particularly an elite in China, a land where the illiteracy rate is still roughly 30 percent of a total population of more than a billion.

This helps to explain why student unrest is such a headache to China's party government. In the late spring of 1989, student unrest almost paralyzed the regime, splitting the ranks of the top leaders. It was finally put down in a most brutal fashion.

Fang Lizhi, the best-known dissident in China, once quoted a vice-minister of education to illustrate how much the government fears student unrest:

Comrade Huang said something very forthright. He said: "students must not make trouble. . . . Should they make trouble, the central [authorities] would not be able to do anything else. They would be spinning around [the students]."[1]

For a whole month, from mid-May to mid-June 1989, the news media of the entire Western world were reporting on the students' confrontation with the Chinese authorities. Night after night, this was the top story on television; time and again interviews took place on "Nightline," eclipsing everything else, whether that be the discomfiture of U.S. House majority leader James Wright or even the death and funeral of Iran's Ayatollah Khomeini. Millions of people found themselves riveted by the news from China, as they watched the story unfold on their television screens, gripped by the twists and turns of human as well as political drama, until suspense turned into tragedy.

The news reporting was even more intense in East Asia, especially Hong Kong and Taiwan, but also in Japan and South Korea. The coverage started a month earlier in Asia, and was much fuller. Many readers may be familiar with these events, in which case they may wish to skip this chapter and proceed immediately to the analysis beginning in chapter 2. I offer this review of the basic narrative for the benefit of readers who may not remember some of the important details.

The Background: Student Life in China

As a visiting scholar for a semester in Beijing in 1981, and as someone who has traveled extensively in mainland China, returned there virtually every year, and visited both Xinjiang (Chinese Central Asia) and Tibet, getting acquainted with dozens of universities in the course of the last decade, I was able to meet many people and to have fairly intimate conversations with some students and teachers. But student dormitories were off limits to outsiders, so I cannot speak of them with authority. However, I had to give lectures in unheated halls, wearing a ski jacket to keep warm, facing hundreds of students wrapped up in their nondescript Mao suits, and I presume their private space was much less attractive than their public classrooms.

A more recent visiting scholar from the West who taught for some time in a teachers' college in Shandong (northern China) has been able to give a realistic account of student life in his college. He writes about the student residence, with its "cracked concrete blackened by coal smoke," and with "rusted frames of broken windows" swinging loose in gusts of wind, as "light splinters in from a smashed window at the end of the hallway." He could smell "the stench of urine," and found his students, eight in a room, living and working "in an inch of muddy water."

> With just the faintest note of complaint in their voices they answer my questions. They tell me that there is no heat in the dormitory—even

though the temperature often drops well below freezing for weeks on end. The electricity is often out at night. . . . The latrines on each floor do not have water and the toilets are blocked.[2]

Moving to the description of meal services, the writer continues:

About 1,000 young people crowded around two huge bowls, from which the cooks dished out a ladle of soggy vegetables and *tofu* (bean curd) stewed in pork fat. To round out the meal they were given a piece of *mantou* (steamed, crustless white bread).

I am not saying that all university life in China is as bad as described here. According to former students, Beijing dormitories do get heat for limited periods, and have four or five to a room. But even foreign students, placed two in a room, are known to have to use their electric hair dryers to keep their hands warm in times of no heat. For the local students, it has been reported, the quality of food is so base that hungry students often spit out big mouthfuls after finding sand, stones, or some other unidentified substances inside. Nutritionists hardly exist on university campuses, although they were known to be employed by overseas-funded institutions like Yenching University in Beijing before 1949.

All this might have been endurable, had there not been the widening gap between the higher government officials and their circles and the ordinary citizens without access to privilege. The demonstrating students belong to an elite especially in the sense that they have passed through stringent examinations to gain admittance to the universities. Only the top 1 percent or so can get into universities in China. Most of them put up with a hard existence on campus, while awaiting job assignments that will further separate those with connections from those without. Interestingly, the younger undergraduates are the most activist, since they are least threatened by job assignments that may very well mean banishment to a remote area.

Student demonstrations occur much more often in China than is known in the West. In 1988, we had reports of the Nanjing demonstrations against alleged abuses of privileges enjoyed by African students in China on fellowships. The above account of harsh living conditions and often unattractive employment prospects may help us understand that these demonstrations were not just motivated by racist sentiments. What had not been reported in the West were the "anti-hunger" strikes in Beijing in 1988 and before. This might help us realize what a hunger strike meant to the often emaciated university students in China during the Tian'anmen Square events. No wonder they thought themselves patriotic in doing so, and wore headbands saying, "Mom and Dad, please forgive me. . . . "

I sometimes feel that the best thing authorities can do to prevent further student unrest is to improve student living conditions. Student dormitories have to be the hotbed of revolution, with so many to a room in double bunks, and plenty to complain about. Were the students to occupy only double or single rooms in residence halls, as do their counterparts in the West, and were they given better nourishment and brighter career prospects, half the battle would be won. Instead, Chinese authorities boast about a system that "nourishes and supports" students almost free of charge—but to what good? No wonder student apathy is rampant; instead of the old "Long Live Karl Marx" or "Long Live Chairman Mao" slogans, they have been crying "Long Live 60 Marks [that is, a passing grade]."

Our description of student life in China should be helpful against the background of claims of a growing prosperity. According to Premier Li Peng's report to the People's Congress (1988), China's gross national product in 1987 had gone beyond a trillion RMB (renminbi), which is nearly double what it was nine years before, while the average peasant's annual income in 1987 was over four times what it used to be in 1978, and the average urban worker's was nearly three times that of nine years earlier. However, it did not mention that the gap between rich and poor was widening at an amazing pace, so that the term "average" no longer referred to the typical person; moreover, inflation had been approaching 40 percent, and many people, in cities as well as villages, could not always afford enough to eat.

I remember a Chinese visiting professor in the United States who gave me a piece of his mind about Li Peng. That man, he said, was the person in the State Council responsible for education, and things went from bad to worse—so they made him premier.

Undoubtedly, university life is linked to politics, and politics is what ignited the student demonstrations in the spring of 1989.

The Place: Tian'anmen Square, Beijing

Tian'anmen Square, named after the Palace Gate of Heavenly Peace, was built in 1417 and rebuilt in 1651 at the main gate in the south wall of the Imperial Palace complex, the "Forbidden" City. Here, the emperors of the Ming and Qing dynasties from the fifteenth through the nineteenth centuries published their edicts and decrees. They passed through this gate for the important rituals of their reigns, like annual sacrifices to

Heaven and to Earth, imperial weddings, and the like. Behind this gate are the huge grounds with nine thousand rooms that make up the former imperial palace. The Square itself measures approximately twice the length of a football field in each direction. At the south of the Square is Mao Zedong's Mausoleum, on the west side is the Great Hall of the People, and on the east are two museums: the Museum of the Chinese Revolution and the Chinese Historical Museum. It was in this square in 1919 that the historic May Fourth Movement erupted; it was here that over 50,000 people marched and demonstrated in response to the May Thirtieth Incident in 1925, to condemn Japanese brutality in China; it was here that warlords suppressed a demonstration on March 18, 1926, causing about two hundred casualties. Some of these events are represented in relief at the base of the Monument to the People's Heroes, built between 1952 and 1958, which stands today in the very middle of the Square.

Tian'anmen is more than just a huge gathering place in Beijing. It was here that the People's Republic of China was declared on October 1, 1949. It serves as China's equivalent of Red Square in Moscow, and is considered by some to be the world's largest urban square. The official emblem of the People's Republic has five yellow stars placed over this Gate of Heavenly Peace against a red background. The five stars stand also on the national flag, representing the Communist party and the four social classes. At Tian'anmen, the annual festivities commemorating the Communist victory of October 1949 are always held in the presence of the country's top leaders.

Since Communist rule, Tian'anmen Square has witnessed many changes and upheavals. Mao's first review of a million Red Guards (August 1966) during the Cultural Revolution was especially stirring. Tian'anmen Square has also been the particular location for two large-scale protests, in spring 1976 and again in spring 1989. Each incident occurred in the background of tragedy and mourning; each developed along dramatic lines, and each was followed by a bloody crackdown.

Demonstrations: The First Stage
(April 16–May 4, 1989)

As reported by the *Far Eastern Economic Review* (May 4, 1989), Chinese authorities had been "tightening surveillance of campuses and filling academic calendars with official programmes and exams" to forestall unrest. They knew that China's students would have taken to the streets in any case that year, for the seventieth anniversary of the May Fourth Movement, remembered as an inspiration to the Communist party as well as to students' participation in politics. But things happened earlier than expected, because of the death of the former party general secretary Hu Yaobang on April 15, 1989. A man of little formal education but an avid reader, a political liberal, and a leader of personal integrity, Hu became the darling of the people after he was made a scapegoat as a result of student demonstrations in December 1986 and January 1987. He had refused to crack down on the students, and that was counted against him, just as Zhao Ziyang's refusal to suppress the students in 1989 would lead to his loss of power. Of the two men, Hu was more popular than Zhao and was regarded as more sincere and selfless.

It was an unusual April. Students could not forget April 5, the anniversary date of the Tian'anmen Incident of 1976, which had been triggered by the death of Premier Zhou Enlai. In 1989, they had to deal with Hu Yaobang's death, which served to unleash pent-up frustrations, just as a crack in the Yellow River's dikes could permit the waters to overflow, after which no one would be able to put a stop to the flood. At Beijing University, to the northwest of the edge of the city, the "Triangle Place," the site of weekly informal lectures, is known as Beijing University's "Democracy Place." After news broke of Hu's death, slogans and limericks were at once hung from trees and branches, mourning the loss of a leader in whom many had placed their hopes. One set of verses said:

> Good scores against bad scores,
> Bad scores against good scores.
> More good than bad.
> Dying against living,
> Living against dying.
> Dying surpasses living.

The implicit judgment is that the dead Hu Yaobang is superior to many living officials.

It was thus that the death of a political leader became the occasion for the biggest student movement in recent history, not only for China, but also for the world. And this also led to the worst government repression of students yet known in the annals of humankind.

The following morning, April 16, students from People's University were the first to arrive at Tian'anmen Square. People's University is nicknamed "The Second Theological School" because, like the party's own Central Institute, it specializes in the training of future party bureaucrats, custodians of the established ideology. These students came to offer white flowers, white being the color of mourning by Chinese custom. The time was just after 10:30 A.M. At 11:30 A.M., they were joined by student representatives from the Northern University of Communications, who left a banner on the Monument to the People's Heroes: "In Memory of Yaobang, Friend of the Young." At 3 P.M., three students from Beijing University arrived with their wreath. By 11 P.M., several hundred were assembled there.

Strictly speaking, student demonstrations did not start until April 17. These would reach a first climax on April 27, and a second on May 4. Little did the students know when they began demonstrating that their action would be supported by overseas Chinese students all over the globe, and that they would meet with such a tragedy in the end. They were powerless young people, but they came from the best universities; many of them were party members; some of them had influential family connections. They were, after all, an elite. They felt that they were acting altruistically for the good of the country, to awaken the soul of the nation. They were determined that their action should remain peaceful, for the sake of their cause and for their own safety as well. In this spirit, a large group of students from the University of Government and Law chanted slogans in honor of Hu and against official corruption, as well as in favor of freedom and democracy. They placed their wreath in Hu Yaobang's honor at Tian'anmen Square, and were joined there by Beijing University students. Their action attracted several thousand onlookers that first day, but the students returned to their campuses, as peacefully as they had left them, around 5 P.M.

That same day and late that night, thousands of students from several universities who had come from Shanghai, the site of major demonstrations in December 1986, were also in the streets, chanting slogans of freedom and democracy. By that time already, an anxious government was instructing the news media in the country not to print anything about these demonstrations and their political slogans. As usual, the Communist leaders were afraid, both of what student demonstrations might lead to and of the very words "freedom" and "democracy."

Every day from then on, students would be in the streets, and their numbers kept growing. On April 18, the second day, several thousand from Beijing University and People's University marched to Tian'anmen Square where, after a memorial service of their own in Hu's honor, they started a sit-in outside the Great Hall of the People, presenting seven demands to the People's Congress:

1. to make a fair reevaluation of Hu Yaobang's life and work;
2. to abolish the Campaign against Liberalization which had been conducted since the 1986–87 demonstrations;

3. to publish the incomes of high officials;
4. to augment funding for education;
5. to abolish municipal regulations forbidding demonstrations in Beijing (which were placing "unconstitutional" limits on their rights);
6. to introduce freedom of the press; and
7. to permit a fair and accurate reporting of their own demonstrations.

The sit-in lasted all day, from dawn to dusk. At about 8 P.M., roughly sixteen hours later, three members of the People's Congress finally emerged, and accepted the written petition. That evening, tens of thousands of onlookers were already at Tian'anmen Square, where they listened to improvised speeches, from students and other people.

Beginning that night, a large group also approached the Xinhua Gate, just outside Zhongnanhai, the former palace compound two kilometers west of Tian'anmen that is now the seat of the government as well as the residence of its highest echelon. The unprecedented protests there unnerved the authorities even more than that at the Square, as thousands and then tens of thousands of students asked, two days in a row, for a dialogue with Premier Li Peng. They were dispersed every time by several thousand police, who did not hesitate to use blows and kicks, causing injuries and making arrests especially on the dawn of April 20. Cameras and films were seized from Hong Kong reporters. This first bloodshed aroused concern on the part of many teachers, as a group of 143 professors addressed an open letter to the People's Congress and the Political Consultative Conference that very day, asking the authorities to grant the students a dialogue.

Under government inspiration, newspaper reports appeared, twisting the facts and reproaching Beijing students for beating the police and attacking Zhongnanhai! It was, we may say, a foretaste of what was yet to be expected from the officially controlled media. Angered and disturbed by the news reports, nearly the whole student body—about a hundred or so—from the Institute of Journalism were the first to march to the Square on April 21, carrying banners asking for freedom of the press.

By that time, students from Beijing's universities had started their own organization to give some direction to a movement that was escalating. To prevent any disorder as well as outside infiltration, students organized their own disciplinary and supervisory groups for their demonstrations, marching each time with hands joined. Besides, the unrest was continuing and growing in strength—in Shanghai, Nanjing, and elsewhere—with criticisms of government dictatorship and corruption, and petitions asking for freedom and democracy.

The official memorial service in honor of Hu Yaobang was scheduled for April 22, to take place in the Great Hall of the People. Students, of course, had no place there, and were even warned not to go to the Square, which was adjacent to the Great Hall. But the students were determined to hold their own memorial service at the Square, to take place simultaneously with the service inside the Great Hall.

On the 22nd, nearly 200,000 students from over thirty institutions in Beijing as well as some from Shanghai and Tianjin were gathered at dawn at the Square, most of them having passed the night there, and resisted government orders to stay away that morning. This was about a hundred times the number of those at the sit-in two days earlier. The authorities were ready with thirty truckloads of soldiers, making up a human wall to defend the Great Hall of the People against any attacks, though that was not necessary, as the student demonstration remained peaceful and disciplined. But many of the four thousand officials at the memorial service that morning inside the Hall could see from a distance the demonstrators shouting their political slogans. After avoiding a clash with the authorities and the soldiers that day, a group of students knelt outside the Great Hall of the People with their petition for over forty minutes, in the spirit of the student petitioners of old imperial China, but without getting any hearing. Also that day, students from over thirty institutions in Beijing joined with students from Tianjin, Nanjing, Shanghai, and Guangzhou to make up a nationwide Students' Federation, to be based at Beijing University. This also was illegal, but they felt the need to differentiate themselves from the government-sponsored Alliance, which they did not trust.

Beijing had remained nervous but peaceful. According to the official media, however, riots took place on April 22 in Xi'an (Shaanxi) and in Changsha (Hunan), where tens of thousands of people burned cars and set fire to government offices, crying slogans against the Communist party and its dictatorship, and hundreds were arrested.

On failing to receive any response to their call for a dialogue, the Beijing students announced a strike, beginning April 24, to continue at least until May 4, and sent hundreds of representatives to fifteen cities to spread the news and ask for support, since the official media could not be trusted. An exception was the *Science and Technology Daily* in Beijing, which on April 23 published an accurate account of the students' activities commemorating Hu's death, and was lucky at that point not to meet any official reprisal. A Shanghai paper, the *World Economic Herald*, known for its avant-garde reporting, had also prepared an article honoring Hu Yaobang and criticizing implicitly those in power. Its 300,000 printed copies were seized by the government and its chief editor, Qin Benli, was fired. This first blow of official repression came on April 26.

Rumor says that Deng Xiaoping had already authorized Li Peng on April 25 not to refrain from harsh measures to suppress the students and assure stability to the country. He allegedly said then that even if students were to get the support of workers and peasants, "we can still count on three million soldiers to maintain law and order." An ominous article appeared in the official *People's Daily* on April 26, calling the demonstrations a conspiracy and a "riot" directed against the Communist party and the socialist system. It was the regime's first counterattack, but the authorities were probably prevented from cracking down right then and there because half a million people took to the streets to show their sympathy for the students the following day. Instead, the regime made another half-hearted attempt to satisfy the students' demand by organizing meetings between some officials from the State Council and student groups—except that the student group participating in this dialogue was nominated by the officials rather than the students! The authorities used those occasions to warn against any reenactment of the chaos of the Cultural Revolution.

The students demonstrated again on April 27, a high point of their movement. They had been listening to campus broadcasts that the authorities were prohibiting further protests and predicting dire consequences should students disobey. They had understood as well the warning issued by the *People's Daily* and realized that it represented the voice of Deng Xiaoping himself. But the will to demonstrate was strong despite the danger; many started writing their own last wills and testaments. That day, thousands of students from over fifty institutions in Beijing marched around the city for sixteen hours, cheered on by half a million residents lining the streets and helping to make way for them across police lines. The masses offered them food and drink, while a dozen or so Buddhist monks collected donations for the students. This marked a climax to the movement so far, as students discovered the support they were getting from the people of Beijing. Their slogans were moderate, and they carried quotations from the Constitution regarding the freedoms of demonstration and association. They returned at midnight to their various campuses to a heroes' welcome from their teachers. This widespread support encouraged student leaders to continue to push for a dialogue with high officials. Students threatened to demonstrate on

May 4 unless their request was met. The government's reply was received on May 3; it was *no*.

After the tensions of April 27, the May 4 demonstrations appeared relaxed. Official broadcasts urging students not to go to the streets again went unheeded. The occasion was, after all, the seventieth anniversary of the most important modern student movement in China, a movement in which many senior Communists had participated when they were young. Everywhere, students poured out of their campus gates, easily crossing police lines to celebrate May Fourth and to continue with their political demands. At Tian'anmen Square, the 100,000 students were encouraged by the sight of five hundred newspaper workers who marched around the Square, making their own demands for freedom of the press. Their banner carried the complaint: "Our pens cannot write what we want to write; our mouths cannot say what we want to say." Many journalists remarked that there had been more freedom of the press under the warlords and the Nationalist authorities than at present under the Communists.

But May 4 this year was more than an anniversary for the student movement of modern China. It also marked the opening meeting in Beijing of the Asian Development Bank. And this time, a delegation from Taiwan (Republic of China), was also present, under the leadership of its finance minister Shirley Kuo. That was how a number of Taiwan reporters became witnesses to the demonstrations and to the final crackdown. The estimated number of people at the Square that day was about 100,000.

Demonstrations: The Second Stage
(May 13–June 3, 1989)

After May 4, students went back to classes. According to eyewitness accounts, their enthusiasm had abated, and was only restored by the thought of Gorbachev's visit on May 15. The Soviet leader was much admired for his introduction of *glasnost* as well as *perestroika*. He represented the kind of leader they wanted: vigorous, courageous, taking the initiative in democratizing a fossilized system of government. So the students organized a "dialogue group" and renewed their demand to speak with the government, hoping that this could be done before Gorbachev's arrival. Interestingly, the authorities had ordered removed from the Square some time before May Day (May 1) the huge portraits of Marx, Engels, Lenin, and Stalin—all foreigners—that had been displayed for four decades. Instead, they placed at the Monument to the People's Heroes, a portrait of Sun Yat-sen (the revolutionary leader recognized by both Communists and their Nationalist rivals who now rule Taiwan), facing the huge portrait of Mao Zedong above the Tian'anmen Gate.

Not having received an answer from the authorities, the students decided to make a new move: a mass hunger strike. This began on May 13, initially with a thousand people, but eventually with three thousand. The Canadian professor Ruth Hayhoe went to Tian'anmen that evening and wrote down what she saw:

> For two hours we stood on the steps of the monument to the revolutionary heroes watching contingents of students on bikes arriving from all the major universities, each with their banners of protest. The students who had undertaken to fast sat in rows in the centre surounded by supporters. Cheers rose as new groups were seen approaching, and as each arrived, they carried their banners around the circle so all could identify them.[3]

Tian'anmen became the stage for a demonstration that resembled in part a carnival with colorful banners, and in part a tragic stage for fasting students who won the sympathy of the world but became branded as rioters by their own government. By May 15, Western and Japanese journalists started to arrive to cover the Gorbachev visit, joining with Hong Kong and Taiwan reporters already there. For the Western world especially, the spotlight was on Gorbachev, and the students started to receive more attention only after his departure from Beijing on May 18.

From the government's viewpoint, the Sino-Soviet rapprochement was to end an era of hostilities that had stretched over three decades, and to mark the beginning of what was hopefully an era of collaboration between the two greatest communist powers, each of whom was now engaged in economic reforms. News had been circulating that Deng Xiaoping planned to retire soon after this summit, at the latest by October, so the summit was to serve as a crown to all his other achievements. But the students' desire to exploit the situation by their peaceful occupation of Tian'anmen Square obstructed the official plans. The proud regime was probably enraged that the Square, which "rightfully" belongs to them, had been occupied by "the people." It could not permit the distinguished visitor to see those protesting against its regime, even though the students had reportedly left enough space for Gorbachev to enter the Great Hall of the People by the front door. Instead of a large welcome for Gorbachev at the Square itself, a smaller ceremony took place at the airport. And instead of using the front door, the Soviet leader had to enter the Great Hall of the People through a side door, without sighting the amassed protesters, their sympathizers, and onlookers.

On May 17, over a million people rallied at Tian'anmen. Many of the hunger strikers were refraining from liquids as well as solids, and quickly collapsed in the early summer heat as volunteer rescuers were busily transporting them to hospitals or distributing salt packages to others at the Square. More than four hundred hunger strikers fainted on May 16; by May 17, more than two thousand students had to be sent to emergency hospital care.

That day, May 17, three million people took to the streets in Beijing. They included soldiers, workers, peasants, and Buddhist monks, as well as government employees from over a dozen ministries and agencies, teachers and students of all ages. All were in support of the hunger strikers and their demands. Mass demonstrations and sit-ins also took place in over twenty other cities, with a hundred thousand in Shanghai, where over four hundred people were also on hunger strike. The following day, May 18, witnessed another, even bigger mass demonstration in Beijing despite rainfall. This time, tens of thousands of cars joined the parades, and participants included judges, police, and students from military academies. At the same time, a million people were on the streets in both Shanghai and Shenyang, as students were on hunger strike in at least six large cities. Twelve members of the standing committee of the National People's Congress and other public figures, including certain Liberation Army officers and the provincial governor and party secretary in Zhejiang, joined in asking the government to hold a dialogue with the students.

The students had asked for a meeting with Gorbachev himself; many had carried his portrait and marched with the sign saying "Democracy" in the Russian language together with the comment "our common desire." The Soviet example assisted their claim that they were seeking not to overthrow the Communist rule, but only to reform it. Gorbachev himself had shown some interest in meeting with his young Chinese admirers, but this was not to be. He left Beijing on May 18 for Shanghai, where another hunger strike was taking place in front of the city government, and students there had erected a larger-than-life likeness of the Statue of Liberty even before this was done in Beijing. Indeed, student protests were spreading like wildfire all across the country, affecting dozens of cities, representing several hundred institutions, and nearly paralyzing rail traffic at many points. In several provinces, they had the support and permission of their university administrators as well as local authorities.

For a while, the outside world wondered. Could this prove to be a genuine spring for China as it was for Moscow, Budapest, and Warsaw? The demonstrators "had brought China to the edge of anarchy—and the farewell to Communism," wrote the German-language *Der Spiegel* (May 22, 1989). As an ideology, communism is clearly finished, but can there be a peaceful transition to a more responsible and humane government?

According to Hong Kong reports, the five-man standing committee of the Politburo met several times on May 17 and May 18, as Premier Li Peng urged a crackdown on the students and Party General Secretary Zhao Ziyang resisted. Allegedly, there were several votes, and while Zhao represented the lone voice at first, Hu Qili later crossed over to his side and Qiao Shi abstained. (The fifth member was Yao Yilin, a conservative.) If those reports are correct, the vote would have been 2:2:1, an impasse. In any case, it is very difficult for the outside world to understand how Zhao had been pushed aside for advising reason and moderation rather than brutality in handling the demonstrators.

Early in the morning of the day Gorbachev left Beijing, Zhao Ziyang, together with Li Peng, propaganda chief Hu Qili, and security chief Qiao Shi, visited the ailing hunger strikers at the hospital. That afternoon (May 18) a strange attempt at dialogue took place when Premier Li Peng received a small group of student representatives, including Wu'er Kaixi, who was called out from his hospital bed. At this nationally televised event, the premier was obviously more interested in lecturing to the students than in listening to their petitions.

At a Politburo meeting the following day (May 19), Deng is reported to have been furious with Zhao for seeking to use the students to enhance his own popularity, and warned, "I have the army behind me." Allegedly, Zhao replied, "But I have the hearts of the people," to which Deng answered, "You have nothing." That evening, presumably after Zhao realized that the battle was lost, he went to the Square to speak to the students. Li Peng followed suit but stayed only a few minutes. Zhao made a tearful speech to the students, affirming that their action was patriotic and urging them to return home. It was his last public appearance to date, and it was considered another sin: the premier would later say that the party chief did so without party authorization. That evening, Li Peng announced to a full meeting of the party, army, and municipal government convened in the Great Hall of the People that firm measures were called for against the turmoil taking place outside, as President Yang Shangkun declared that troops had been called in to deal with the situation. This meant martial law, which could constitutionally be declared only by action of the standing committee of the National People's Congress. However, the regime had for some time feared that inflation and price rises would bring about riots, and had put through "emergency legislation" in 1988 authorizing the suspension of the Constitution at a time of crisis. This fact is not well known, and, of course, the judgment regarding the "crisis" was left to a few people making up the ruling group. In this way, China's power clique considered itself above the Constitution and the law. Their accusation was that "a small handful of people" were exploiting the situation to overthrow the government and put in jeopardy the results of the economic reforms.

Students and others had expected military action on the night of May 20, right after the declaration of martial law. Helicopters had been dropping leaflets on the Square, telling the crowds to leave. Nothing, however, happened. In the days that followed, as the government failed to act quickly, rumors spread that the military had come in through the subway at night, and had entered the Forbidden City and the Great Hall of the People.

The world watched in horror, as tanks and armored vehicles started arriving in Beijing suburbs along five major roads, some bringing along surface-to-air missiles. The authorities also cut off the water supply to Tian'anmen Square, but Beijing residents started transporting water by motorcycles to the students. People were bringing in daily portions of food as well to feed the multitudes that had stopped their week-long fast. Sanitation workers had also taken the initiative to add temporary toilets to the Square, to take the pressure off the small number of available public toilets.

The declaration of martial law and the approach of the military pushed students and sympathizers further over the political precipice. Already, they had been comparing Deng Xiaoping unfavorably with Mao Zedong; more and more, they would demand his resignation. A group of workers who were party members had been on strike, carrying a banner that read: "The behavior of the party's central committee is causing great grief to party members." A band of workers on motorcycles even dared to circle Deng's residence in a lane behind the Ministry of Defense, honking their horns and shouting slogans calling for "the emperor" to retire.

Western viewers also saw Beijing students and residents trying to block the progress of an estimated 150,000 troops in army vehicles stretched nose to tail, between Chengde and Beijing. Everybody seemed to be on the roads, putting up roadblocks, talking to the soldiers, even sleeping in front of the tanks to prevent them from reaching Tian'anmen Square. Tension was building once more, and this time it was much more intense than even April 27. The demonstrators were saying, "No government can survive by using the army against its own citizens." As for an explanation of why so many troops were summoned against unarmed students, "They are worried about a mutiny" was the conclusion of the crowd.

In reflecting upon what might be forthcoming, people realized too late that a power struggle had already occurred at the highest level, and the loser was the moderate leader Zhao Ziyang. From reports that circulated afterward, this had already taken place on May 8, at a meeting of the "seven octogenarians," all allegedly retired leaders except for Deng himself.[4] According to a party circular released later, Deng had been furious at Zhao for his "soft" handling of the student turmoil, and decided to strike back at the second of his two designated heirs, the other being Hu Yaobang. Be that as it may, Zhao was still on hand as party chief to greet his counterpart, Gorbachev, although he would be faulted later for disclosing to the Soviet visitor the open secret that the man in charge was still Deng himself. With regard to the "Return of the Dinosaur," as the rule of the elderly has been dubbed, the comment went, "The eighty-year-olds are calling meetings of seventy-year-olds to decide which sixty-year-olds should retire." .

May 20 and May 21 went by without any military action. Students were then calling for Li Peng and Deng Xiaoping to resign, while demonstrations took place in China and abroad to stop the government from cracking down. A million people marched in Hong Kong on May 21, and thousands of overseas Chinese students were demonstrating outside embassies and consulates in Western countries. Indeed, this became a sort of joke, as journalists teased about how a relatively unknown premier of China was "unifying" the Chinese across the country and beyond, all of whom appeared to want his scalp. *Asiaweek* even quipped, "Maybe someone should build a monument to Mr. Li: engineer of the Eighth Wonder of the World."[5]

For a while, reports started circulating even in Hong Kong and Tokyo that Li Peng at least would have to resign to "appease the outcry." This would have been in keeping with the age-old Chinese despotic tradition, when emperors used to reproach themselves for what went wrong with the nation. "If I, the one man, have sinned, blame it not on the myriad directions. If the myriad directions have sinned, blame it on myself" are the words of a sage king over four thousand years ago.

But the Communists are different from the old despots. They do not march to the tune of the people. It was more important that Li Peng was popular with the elders in the party than that he was disliked by millions. Their calls and petitions would all be to no avail, as, unknown to them, the hard-liners and reformers of the top echelon were still debating, but with the reformers losing steadily and Deng Xiaoping calling Zhao Ziyang a counterrevolutionary and a traitor (May 23). Hit lists of intellectuals and dissidents were already being drawn up.

As for the demonstrators at Tian'anmen Square, they had stopped their hunger strike effective May 20, at the news of the imposition of martial law. Tired and weary, many students from Beijing universities were going back to their campuses. Meanwhile, students from all over the country arrived to camp at the Square, starting especially around May 19. On May 23 a million people took to the streets of Beijing as the demonstrators (including students, teachers, writers, journalists, factory workers, and even party cadres from government ministries) initiated another "march around the city." Angered at the declaration of martial law, people were calling for the resignation of both Li Peng and Deng Xiaoping. Ruth Hayhoe offers this account of what was happening that day:

> I watched for two hours as people from all walks of life went by with their banners and flags: truckloads of workers from factories, fleets of buses . . . , a delegation of handicapped people in wheelchairs, seniors and young parents pushing baby carriages, infants on the front of bicycles, etc., etc.[6]

Students from the provinces were arriving every day, replacing others who were returning home to spread the news. Demonstrations were taking place everywhere: in Hohhot (Inner Mongolia), Xi'an, Zhengzhou, Wuhan, Chengdu, Guangzhou, Shenzhen, and many other cities—and they were being supported by demonstrations overseas, by students from mainland China as well as expatriates. Conscious of constitutional procedures, the demonstrating crowds all over the world were calling for the return of Wan Li, head of the standing committee of the People's Congress then visiting Canada and the United States, who had authority to convene an emergency meeting of that committee to deal with the crisis. The seventy-three-year-old Wan had sounded sympathetic to the student cause during his travels, and returned to China on May 24. He remained for a time in Shanghai, allegedly resting at a hospital. After three days he pronounced himself in favor of martial law.

Students in Beijing once more called a mass protest "all over the world where the Chinese live" for May 28, but the local turnout was getting smaller: about 50,000 in Beijing, 100,000 in Shanghai, although a million or more assembled once more in Hong Kong, and thousands overseas, both in the Americas (thousands in San Francisco, Los Angeles,

New York, Washington, D.C., Toronto, and elsewhere) and in every major European capital.

On May 30, students in Beijing unveiled their own thirty-foot model of the Statue of Liberty, made of plaster-covered Styrofoam, which they christened the "Goddess of Democracy" and placed across from Mao's portrait at the Square. With this action, their numbers began to swell again. The government tried to strike back by organizing "anti-liberal" demonstrations of workers wearing uniform straw hats. When asked on television by an outside reporter whether he was paid to join, one member laughed and said, "Better not ask me such a question." Meanwhile, authorities also ordered the cutting of satellite ties and sought to block Western journalists from reporting on the events at Tian'anmen. The news blackout became near-total by June 1, although reporters were still able to use video cameras and cellular phones.

Student demonstrators had postponed several times the date for their withdrawal from the Square. First set for May 30, the withdrawal was not carried out since the new arrivals from the provinces, now constituting up to 90 percent of the group, voted otherwise. Noises were being made about continuing the sit-in till June 20, the date scheduled for the meeting of the standing committee of the People's Congress. Little did they know, after the long impasse, that troops would move in during the dead of night on that fateful June 3. Actually, the crackdown was preceded by government-organized demonstrations in the suburbs on May 31. Meanwhile the popular singer from Taiwan, Hou Dejian, who had been living in the mainland for the past six years, the literary critic Liu Xiaobo, the planning head of Stone Computers (a successful private company) Zhou Hang, and the editor Gao Xin—the "four intellectuals"— went on hunger strike on June 2 at Tian'anmen Square.

What Happened on June 3–4?

What happened on June 3–4 is difficult to piece together, even though there were many eyewitnesses and scenes of bloodshed splashed across our own television screens. No one eyewitness saw everything, even though some reporters went across the city of Beijing that night and witnessed the massacre from several vantage points. The Chinese government knows this, and offered its own official version, which is too farfetched to be acceptable. As with past incidents under Communist rule, many things may never come to full light. The account I offer is based on both published and unpublished reports, including those of reporters at the scene and individuals recently arriving in the West from

Beijing. The *Wen Wei Po* in Hong Kong, although a Communist-funded newspaper, openly defied the authorities for a time and published a special illustrated brochure in Chinese to support its report of the atrocities.

The final crackdown itself was full of puzzling and dramatic twists. On Friday, June 2, unarmed, very young-looking soldiers in shirtsleeves tried to disperse the crowds, but quickly turned back. Was that part of a conspiracy to unnerve students, or were these the troops that the government was not sure it could count on and therefore had not provided with ammunition? Answers are not available. That same day, other truckloads of soldiers were abandoning their guns and uniforms, again for reasons unknown to the public. But students, wary of a possible trap, gathered these up only to hand them over to the police. Another story, little told, is that tens of thousands of people in the streets to block the soldiers that day actually forced hundreds of soldiers into the compound belonging to the Central Ballet in southern Beijing, and then locked them up for the rest of the day!

On Saturday afternoon, June 3, other troops popped tear gas shells and beat up people trying to stop them from moving into central Beijing, especially near the Xinhua Gate (Zhongnanhai). An hour later, just behind the Great Hall of the People, on the west side of the Square, helmeted soldiers lashed out at students and bystanders, whipping them with belts and beating them with truncheons; still the students did not disperse and held together for another five hours. As these troops disappeared, twelve hundred others appeared on the southern end of the Square, only to retreat when surrounded by civilians.

According to the student leader Chai Ling's testimony on June 8, she was receiving news of casualties from all over and held a news conference at the Square between 8 P.M. and 10 P.M., mostly to reporters from Hong Kong and Taiwan. At 9 P.M., students rose and swore to dedicate themselves to the modernization of the country and to defend Tian'anmen peacefully. At 10 P.M., students announced that their "University of Democracy" would start classes near the statue of the Goddess of Democracy. But nearby, Chang'an Street, both to the east and to the west of the Square, was already a battlefield, with dead bodies piling up. After 10 P.M., the students at the Square held hands and sang the "Internationale," and then remained seated at the Monument to the People's Heroes awaiting the final moment. Shortly after midnight, gunshots could be heard from the Square. Student broadcasts were announcing the news of troop movements and the number of casualties, and urged all present to refrain from violence. Official broadcasts could also be heard, telling the crowds to leave at once, or face the consequences. At 2 A.M., a convoy of fifty trucks emptied soldiers into the Square as advance troops torched buses and trucks set up as barricades. And then, suddenly, to the unarmed crowds assembled, troops seemed to be everywhere: on the rooftops of the Great Hall of the People and of Mao's Mausoleum, on the side streets on the south, west and east.

With the students determined to stay to their deaths, the "four intellectuals," on hunger strike since June 2, decided to take things in hand to prevent unnecessary bloodshed. Hou Dejian went personally to an officer, who, in turn, obtained permission from a higher command to permit all those present to leave the Square in peace. At 4 A.M. the lights on the Square went dead, while sporadic gunfire continued. At 4:25 A.M., most of the students were gathering at the Monument to the People's Heroes, while a large group of workers and other citizens were coming toward the Monument from the southern end. At that time, Hou Dejian reported to the assembly his unauthorized negotiation with the troops, and begged everyone to leave the Square. By 4:39 A.M., the lights returned, as helmeted troops were pouring in. The soldiers first aimed their shots at the public address system on the monument, then their bullets ripped through all the banners on display, and battered the tents on the ground. According to a Canadian correspondent present, the shooting triggered a minor stampede, "but amazingly, some people called out to others to stop running and not to panic, even when danger was near."[7] At 4:55 A.M., students finally started leaving, moving in a southerly direction from the monument. Within five minutes, the tanks entered the Square, rolling over the tents without regard for whether anybody was still there, and pushing over the Goddess of Democracy. The retreating students, hand in hand and singing the "Internationale," were chased by the troops, who continued to fire at them and beat them with sticks and truncheons. A survivor mentioned seeing about a thousand people lying on the ground at the Square, still being shot at by soldiers and struck by bayonets. At 5 A.M., an ambulance tried to enter the Square along Chang'an Street but was waved away by the soldiers, as the crowd was yelling "Fascists!" By 5:30 A.M., soldiers had completely seized the site of the monument, now emptied of the demonstrators, while tanks were smashing over a small bulldozer and other obstructions, followed by armored personnel carriers and military trucks. At 5:43 A.M., the firing reached a climax. Soldiers were also piling up corpses and burning them, making it difficult to get a final count of the dead. One reporter said:

It was getting light, and some of the carnage became visible. People in tattered blue tunics or bare from the waist up began carrying the wounded down the alleyway to nearby Capital Hospital. . . .

Later, at the Beijing Hotel, a waiter served a breakfast of coffee and neatly cut papaya slices. "I am very surprised," he said as ambulance sirens wailed outside and rifle fire crackled a few blocks away. "I always thought the People's Liberation Army loved the people."[8]

But Tian'anmen Square was only one of the sites of the massacre. Other areas of the city were also affected, and perhaps suffered worse. The military convoy passed through the Muxidi area and the Chang'an Streets, especially West Chang'an, to reach the Square. An eyewitness counted within one hour, over twenty armored vehicles, 450 military trucks, and over one hundred jeeps along part of this route. According to Chai Ling's testimony on June 8, 1989, "blood was flowing like river in the streets."[9] Panic-stricken people fell to the pavement or hid behind trees and frail roadblocks, but the troops were burning trees, and tanks were rolling over obstructions. The merciless guns were aiming at young infants as well as grandmothers, shooting upward at houses from where people were looking out or throwing objects from windows. The masses started to fight back with what they could: sticks and stones and Molotov cocktails, as the fighting spread into many Beijing neighborhoods. Another Hong Kong reporter present at Xidan on Chang'an Street said, "The Beijing residents were trying to stop the soldiers from killing. But the troops were shooting at fifteen-minute intervals, every time a small crowd gathered."[10]

Newsweek quotes one survivor, Huang Jing:

We expected tear gas and rubber bullets. But they used machine guns and drove over people with tanks. . . . It was like a dream. From where I was, the sound of crying was louder than the gunfire. . . . One line of students would stand up and then get shot down and then another line of students would stand and the same thing would happen.[11]

The same report quotes an anonymous eyewitness:

I saw two tanks coming at high speed. They went around the square and right over tents with students still inside. I saw completely smashed, paper-thin bodies of those students with my own eyes.[12]

This man helped take the wounded to a hospital, where a nurse coming out to ask citizens to donate blood was shot by soldiers on the spot.

Indeed, "it was the massacre on the square, not the demonstration that had preceded it, that seemed like an unnatural act."[13]

If the soldiers were throwing "people off the tips of their bayonets like bales of hay,"[14] it appears that they had been drugged before doing so. A nurse tending to wounded soldiers found levels of the amphetamine "speed" in blood and urine tests. Besides, there were also reprisals. People were also surrounding individual soldiers and killing them. The worst case was a soldier, burned alive in a tank, whose body was then disemboweled and hung onto a burned-out bus.

Shortly before 6 A.M., the game was over. Tian'anmen Square was emptied of protesters, but full of smoldering vehicles and debris, while sporadic skirmishes continued elsewhere in the city. At sunrise the sky was still enveloped in smoke, as angry residents continued taunting soldiers with cries of "Beasts! Beasts!" The response was more gunfire and thousands once more fled for their lives. That day, June 4, the army paper, the *Liberation Daily*, proclaimed a great victory over "a counter-revolutionary insurrection." But an independent eyewitness summary commented: "This is worse than the Cultural Revolution. Chairman Mao mobilized the people against the bureaucracy and it turned violent. Deng Xiaoping has simply murdered his own people."[15]

How many people died in the June 3–4 debacle? There are various estimates. Calculation is made difficult because hospital personnel were forbidden to speak to reporters, and because the official report was obviously unreliable: 300 dead among soldiers and civilians, 23 students dead, but no casualties at the Square. Just after the bloody crackdown, the Beijing Red Cross gave the figure of over 2,700 dead, not counting casualties at Tian'anmen itself; students claim that over 3,000 died at Tian'anmen on June 3–4, and over 7,000 were wounded; another report gave 1,433 as the figure provided by hospitals, but added that 2,000 others died in the streets, making up over 3,433 dead, with nearly 40,000 wounded and another 30,000 missing. U.S. diplomats also surmised at the time that at least 3,000 died. Since then the Hong Kong newsmagazine *Cheng-ming*, well known for its mainland exposés, claims to have confidential information obtained from hospitals and government offices. It published in late June the following figures: some 8,720 dead between 1 A.M. and 7 A.M. at Tian'anmen Square, along Chang'an Street, East and West, and at Qianmen; some 1,720 dead, between June 3 and June 9, among those who sought to block military vehicles and other bystanders; the total number of deaths is, then, over 10,400; the number of wounded is over 28,790; but, by contrast, the number of dead soldiers is 17, the number of wounded soldiers 2,043.

We may never find out the real figures. But we do know that many of the dead were workers and other Beijing residents, either seeking to help students or just watching. For expatriates in the West, there are friends and acquaintances missing, some known to have helped the demonstrators, or to have blocked army advances, who have not since appeared at work. Presumably, the families of these unfortunate people are aware of their losses, although even the nearest and dearest may just wish to believe otherwise, that the person may be in hiding somewhere. The Beijing universities must also have a list of students missing since the crackdown. But students from outlying provinces who came to the capital were also among those killed; in fact, more of them were demonstrating during the last days than local students. Western English teachers even from remote Longjing, in Jilin province not far from Vladivostok, reported that two of their students from an agricultural college went to Beijing and had not returned. But with the institutions announcing an early summer vacation and sending all students home, it is difficult to ascertain the number of victims. Families missing sons and daughters often do not know for weeks or months after the fact whether their children are still at school, or in hiding, or dead.

The Aftermath

"They are worse than the Japanese," many enraged Chinese have been saying, whose memories stretch back to the days of the war with Japan and to the "rape of Nanjing," in which Japanese soldiers had killed tens of thousands of unarmed civilians after their surrender. But such a massacre of the people by their own government is unprecedented. The Japanese occupation itself never took such action against students' or workers' demonstrations; neither did the warlords in charge of China in the 1920s or the Nationalist government after them. The massacre surpasses understanding: the students represent the elite of the country; their demonstrations were dwindling, and could have been allowed to die a natural death. As a Hong Kong editorial put it, a search for historical precedents for the Beijing massacre would take us rather to the Soviet intervention—with tanks and armored vehicles—in Hungary (1956), when they entered Budapest to suppress the anti-communist freedom fighters, and again in Czechoslovakia (1968) to put an end to the Prague Spring. But those were "outside interventions," and they ruined the Soviet image in the world without actually ending the demand for freedom and democratization in these countries. The damage to Communist China's image is now well-nigh irreparable.

As an outside observer, what I found most surprising was not so much the admirable courage displayed by Beijing residents in resisting soldiers and tanks and transporting wounded to hospitals. Rather, I was especially astonished to find Beijing residents continuing their protest afterward, putting out public posters in honor of the dead, while students who returned to their campuses also posted such notices as "Down with the Fascist Regime!" I was also astonished to read about the thousands of students and other people who took to the streets the day after the massacre, in Shanghai, Nanjing, Chengdu, and elsewhere, in some cases carrying banners saying "Blood for Blood!" Obviously, the news had spread in the immediate aftermath of the bloodbath, and a stunned population could hardly care about consequences to themselves as they protested the worst single atrocity in modern Chinese history.

Rage has also been palpable outside China. Thousands took to the streets again in North American and European cities, and even more in Hong Kong and Taiwan. For a while, it looked as if there were no more "leftists" in Hong Kong; the Communists' own Bank of China skyscraper building hung a drape to commemorate the dead right after the massacre. In Taiwan, reaction had been relatively low-key—until after the crackdown. Taiwan campuses turned into "funeral chapels," with black letters on white streamers flying everywhere, whether asking blood for blood, or offering condolences to the families of the dead. Mourning the departed students whose loss will certainly be felt in a land where millions remain illiterate, a Taiwan student remarked, "They are better students than we are; these mainland students are selected one out of a thousand for admission into universities."[16]

According to *ex post facto* laws, it has become a crime to have been on hunger strike, to have tried to block the onslaught of the military, to have cried slogans against the rulers proved tyrants. In fact, the government has announced nineteen categories of people considered as having been themselves counterrevolutionary or having assisted the counterrevolutionaries, including those who had offered food and drink to demonstrators. Even if demonstrators resisted calling themselves anti-Communist, the regime itself has affixed that label to them nevertheless. A few student leaders have escaped the mainland, but most will have no place to hide in today's China. Talk of an "underground" is basically illusory in a country where neighborhood gossips wittingly or unwittingly serve the authorities to maintain near-total control.

Ironically, the authorities complained that the protesters were reverting to the chaos of the Cultural Revolution, whereas they themselves are once more falling back on the methods of reprisal of those days. All this serves as a reminder that there never had been a total break with the regime of old. A story I heard in September is of a family with three sons, one of whom was studying in Beijing. Some time in May, the parents, living in a small town in Zhejiang, had sent the other two north to fetch their brother home, to forestall any trouble for him. None of the three ever came back. Instead, the ashes of three dead persons were sent to their house in August, draped in white, with the label "counter-revolutionaries." There was no explanation of what had happened, where or how.

But China can no longer wash her dirty linen completely unobserved by the rest of the world. No one takes the government seriously anymore when it warns others against "interfering" in its internal politics by publicizing the atrocities and the continuing terror. According to reports from Hong Kong as of July 21, 1989, as many as 10,000 or more have so far been arrested in Beijing alone, and the total number for the country is 120,000. Organizers of "illegal unions" among workers and students are the worst hit everywhere. Obviously, Deng Xiaoping and his cohorts are afraid of their China becoming another Poland, where Solidarity has become a partner of the ruling coalition. They are also uneasy with Hungary's democratization, and the rehabilitation of Nagy's memory, not to mention Gorbachev's *glasnost*.

Conclusion

The world knows of the economic effects of China's brutal action against its own people. This has been dubbed "Deng's Great Leap Back-ward." For the outsider, it has been difficult, if not impossible, to compre-hend how Deng could still talk about "business as usual," reassuring that China's open economic policy is there to stay. As a Western firm got ready for evacuation from Beijing, an employee described his sentiments: "Only a few days ago, we thought everything looked fine. . . . Then wham! You have to wonder about the stability of the whole regime."[17] He was speaking of the army crackdown, not of the student protests.

> In just a few violent days last week, Deng Xiaoping may have crippled the courtship of foreign investors he had patiently conducted for the past decade. In that time, foreign corporations had committed $25 bil-lion to nearly 16,000 enterprises. . . . But business as usual is no longer possible.[18]

"The fruits of ten years of reform have been annulled in one stroke," many papers are saying. Economic consequences follow swiftly. In Washington, $200 million in World Bank development loans effectively went on hold. In Tokyo, a group of about a hundred firms—including Toshiba, Mitsui, and Mitsubishi—indefinitely postponed a project to promote Japanese investment in China. The European Community hastily suspended high-level contacts with Chinese leaders, and voted to impose more sanctions. In the London-based Euromarkets, the price of a $1 billion issue of Chinese bonds plunged overnight. On other fronts, the Hong Kong stock market plummeted, and the Tokyo stock market also suffered. Eager investors from Taiwan and Hong Kong are now transferring their capital to Southeast Asia, another area of instability, but where they hope they can find more protection for their money as well as for themselves.

To quote here from Harrison Salisbury, who was in China June 2–13, 1989:

> I don't know what to think except that Deng [Xiaoping] has blown it, really blown it—himself, his great reputation, China present, China future. A big price for a night of bloodshed.[19]

Even communist Eastern Europe made its disapproval known to China—with the exception, intially, of East Germany, where the 1953 military crackdown on an East Berlin uprising (with eight dead) is still remembered. (And even in this case, Egon Krenz's support of the Chinese crackdown only contributed later to his own downfall as new party chief in December 1989, following successful popular protests in his own country.) Trying their best to preserve the fruits of a recent détente, the Congress of Soviet delegates expressed the hope that China would continue to advance on the road of "economic and political changes." In Vietnam, the crackdown was reported, but without comment. Communist parties in Western Europe, especially Italy and France, have been particularly swift and vehement in their denunciations of the massacre. In Paris, the leftist paper *L'Humanité* asked: "Why this innocent blood in the streets? They were singing the 'Internationale' while waving the Red Flag!" France has shown itself most sympathetic to the Chinese people's cause.

There is, besides, this new twist in Chinese politics: the growing importance of one powerful clique. It includes Yang Shangkun, president of the People's Republic and vice-chairman of the central military commission; his brother, Yang Baibing, chief political commissar in the armed forces; his son-in-law, Chi Haotian, chief of staff; and his nephew, allegedly commanding officer of the 27th Army, nicknamed the "Yang Family Troops," who were also the butchers of Beijing. (One report says that Yang had tried to summon the army once before in December 1987 against students protesting lack of campus security and police atrocities, but was stopped at that time by Deng Xiaoping.) Rumors of civil war had not proved correct. But the rest of the military may not continue to take orders from the Yang clique after Deng's death. (Reports in August 1989 indicated that both the 38th Army and the 15th Army had also participated in the massacre of Beijing, and that some of the worst atrocities were committed by the 38th Army as it moved west to east on Chang'an Street.)

The crackdown has also united all Chinese overseas, be these from the mainland, Taiwan, or earlier immigrants, as well as the entire populations of Hong Kong and Macao. Among overseas protesters were many party members who marched with others in front of embassies and consulates, crying for vengeance against the perpetrators. "Communism is over!" one of them cried, as three hundred publicly renounced their party membership.

In Taiwan, despite the fairly responsible administration and democratization of the Nationalist government, the "February 28" Incident of 1947, a brutally crushed uprising allegedly claiming thousands of victims, has not been forgotten. (Ironically, it was carried out by Chen Yi, a military governor who later defected to the Communist side.) And how can we expect the people of the mainland ever to forget June 4? Even with the news blackout and the government's disinformation campaign (or sometimes because of this campaign), many people know what happened. In fact, the people of Beijing are said to be concerned that the outside world may not be informed of the facts. Little do they know that some of the atrocities have already flashed across television screens all around the globe.

Obviously, the regime made a serious mistake in calculation. It thought that cutting off the satellites would result in a total news blackout, but had not realized that journalists with cellular phones could continue to make immediate and direct contact with the outside. Still, it is difficult to understand why the regime had not expelled all outside journalists from China before committing such a crime, if it did not wish the world to know. Presumably, it was in too much of a rush to clean up the Square, in order to be able to get on with its inner-party political struggles.

The present regime has lost the good will it had carefully cultivated in the outside world, and whatever faith still left among its own people. More than half its overseas students may not be returning home, and will continue to serve as a source of irritation to the Communist government by keeping memories alive. Hong Kong has become a hotbed of resentment, perhaps a base for a future revolution, even if its reunification with the mainland turns out to be be a peaceful one in 1997. Virtually the entire population of 5.5 million there supported the student movement, decried the crackdown, and now wishes to emigrate! As for Taiwan, who will believe any longer the Communist overtures for "peaceful reunification" and "one country, two systems"—as offered to Hong Kong and extended as well to Taiwan? The few well-known people from Taiwan who had returned to live in the mainland had all sided with the students. The singer Hou Dejian, missing for some time afer having negotiated with the troops for a peaceful withdrawal of the protesters from Tian'anmen Square, has since resurfaced (August 1989) and claims that he saw "no bloodshed at Tian'anmen." Journalists and eyewitnesses argue to the contrary. In any case, it makes no sense to deny the massacre, since the world clearly witnessed how much blood was shed elsewhere in Beijing.

In hindsight, it should be said that the students' movement was not intended to turn into a mass rebellion against the government. It could easily have been contained during an early phase. It could have been left to die on its own during the final week. Instead, it was considered to be a test of strength for a regime that feared any and all threats to its power.

It is appropriate here, if ironic, to quote from Communist China's own national anthem, so often repeated by the student protesters during their long struggle and final ordeal. Composed during the Sino-Japanese War (1937–45), even the song's stirring words could yet be banned after June 1989:

> Arise, all you who refuse to be slaves!
> Build a New Great Wall with our flesh and blood.
> People of China, arise, this is the hour of danger:
> Every one of us is forced to make this Final Call.
> Arise, Arise, Arise!
> We are millions, but with one heart
> Facing the firing power of our foes,
> Advance!

CHAPTER 2

■

Through Western Eyes

China occupies a special place in a great many American minds. It
is remote, strange, dim, little known. But it is also in many ways
and for many people oddly familiar, full of sharp images and
associations, and uniquely capable of arousing intense emotion.
— HAROLD ISAACS, 1958

A recorder as well as a shaper of public opinion, Harold R. Isaacs
characterized American attitudes toward China well. His books, although
published three decades ago, still have something to say to us today. In
them, he talks about the "ebb and flow" of American images of the Chinese, moving from the impressions of wisdom and civilization, loyalty
and perseverance attached to the reports from Marco Polo and Pearl Buck
to the cruelty and savagery and the "teeming masses" or "human sea"
associated with the "Mongol hordes" and the Mao Zedong of the fifties.

What is interesting is not that there has been ebb and flow, but that
there have been such swift turnabouts, from admiration and affection to
fear and hatred. When this is reconsidered in light of the events of April
through June 1989, the effect is even more fearsome. Are the Chinese
people to be associated in our minds with the freedom-and-democracy-
loving student demonstrators and their brave sympathizers in Beijing, or
with the regime that cut them down with soldiers and tanks in front of a
shocked world?

At this point, I trust that the choice is still open: that people are not
yet sure exactly which way to turn. What happened from April through
June 1989 was an event of the greatest magnitude, and its two faces
continue to return to haunt us. As millions of television viewers had first
been amazed and aroused by the students' activities, so too were they
shocked, to tears in many cases, by the callous cruelty displayed by the
Communist regime. The shock was all the greater as many had not
clearly distinguished between the regime and the people it controls.

China had always appeared monolithic: totalitarian control only made it more so. People remember the Red Guards waving their Little Red Books some years ago, and the crowds bicycling to work in the teeming cities seeking to modernize a world that had been left behind by time and the party line. And later they read about economic reforms and a prospering countryside, and some of them became engaged in the joint ventures that have been transforming China's skylines and hemlines. And then this.

The China-Watchers' Self-Reproach

The circle of people who apparently felt the most shock were the professional "China-watchers": men and women who used to spend much of their time reading meaning into which of the top party bosses appeared or disappeared in newspaper reports of China's October First (National Day) celebrations. Following upon the footsteps of Kissinger (1971) and Nixon (1972), they too were permitted to enter the long-forbidden People's Republic and started talking to the multitudes gathered at the Xidan Democracy Wall during the days of *dazibao* (literally, big-character posters) and their political messages (1978), or participating in official news conferences. (For more on *dazibao*, see chapter 9.) For a while, China seemed to be getting so "normalized," as far as the outside world was concerned, that she was also losing in newsworthiness. And then this . . .

China-watchers, it has been said, love China, whereas Soviet-watchers generally hate the Soviet Union. This assertion has been verified by the uphill battle Gorbachev had to wage to gain international acceptance for his policy of *glasnost*. On the other hand, Deng Xiaoping, on gaining power, became an instant public figure in the outside world, was twice named "Man of the Year" by *Time* magazine, and was received during a visit to America (February 1979) with an enthusiasm that would incite envy in the pope himself. This is understandable, when we realize that many of the pundits specializing in Soviet studies are of Eastern European origin, coming from countries that have been forcibly incorporated into the Soviet empire. In the case of China studies, we have a group of Americans and Europeans with different kinds of ties to the country: as former missionaries or their progeny, sometimes born in that country, as former State Department experts, or as former students of the language and culture. Many of these people are genuinely devoted to the land of their past and the subject of their studies; some have guilt complexes regarding the "colonialist-imperialist" past and prefer to believe that the Communists have done well to rid China of the vestiges of that era. They have tended to dismiss strong criticisms of the regime as "refugee talk" or as Taiwan-inspired propaganda. Even after the country was opened, the initial discovery of its shocking poverty was quickly replaced with an optimism about its present and future.

So we turn now to a surprising chorus of breast-beating among China-watchers, reacting to the news of 1989 that shocked the world and disturbed its former images of China:

> I am a chastened China-watcher, as are many of my colleagues. . . .
>   Appearances have proven deceptive. China seemed to be thriving. Its economy was booming. A cultural renaissance was underway. . . . Deng Xiaoping's economic reforms were well ahead of Gorbachev's in the Soviet Union. . . . But no China specialist—in or out of government —foresaw the massive setback that occurred.[1]

Rightly or wrongly in recent years, the world has grown used to this *normalized* China, with its problems of inflation and corruption, but otherwise developing quite rapidly along lines akin to our own. Indeed, the world has found the country's economic growth quite phenomenal, especially in the countryside, and has compared it favorably with the even more recent but apparently less successful efforts of the Soviet Union's *perestroika*. True, the world was taken aback by the bloody suppression of dissent in Tibet, but rationalized that as a conflict between the Han Chinese authorities and the local Tibetan population, rather than as the result of tension between a Communist government and a restless people. The world was at times mildly interested in the statements on human rights made by the Chinese physicist and dissident Fang Lizhi. But it considered his very forthrightness to be the result of much more tolerance of dissent within China itself, as it wondered how long this lone voice would continue to be listened to in the seeming wilderness of quiet apathy in a vast country more intent upon making money.

By and large, China-watchers were being forgotten, almost passed over, by the rapid developments within China. And indeed, the term "China-watching" was no longer "in." Instead of peeking through a bamboo curtain, scholars, journalists, and the general public from outside were all able to visit almost every corner of the country, even if fewer people were interested in what they had to report. China seemed on the verge of becoming eventually another Asia-Pacific economic power, perhaps eventually to overshadow the four small dragons—South Korea, Taiwan, Hong Kong, and Singapore. The world was interested in doing business with China. And if certain Western companies experienced losses, other Asian businesses—more recently from Taiwan and South

Korea—were nonetheless ready to try their hand. The same was happening on the tourist scene. Perhaps the U.S. and European markets were becoming saturated with China tours. But the Chinese compatriots in Taiwan had grown eager to visit the land of their ancestors, a land so very near but yet till recently so very far. They, in turn, were filming and showing it to an insatiable public either nostalgic about the past connections or just romantically attracted to a land they had only heard about but never before seen.

But then, all of a sudden, China became once more top news in the Western press for many weeks—even during the near-blackout of information following the exodus of outside journalists from the country and the official control of the news media within. And what news! The world saw unrolled before its eyes a drama of surprise and suspense, a top mystery story, with its twists and turns, with its high points and low points.

All this while, the whole Western world—as well as much of the Eastern—had its eyes glued to the television set. Early on, the focus was Gorbachev's historic visit to China, and, following his departure, the spotlight was squarely on the students themselves. Meanwhile, the palace intrigue went on within the Zhongnanhai compound, the nerve center of the Chinese Communist power structure and itself a former Manchu palace. Then the military arrived: the soldiers, the tanks, and a long and suspenseful impasse. The world marveled at the students' discipline, indeed fell in love with their youthful seriousness as well as exuberance. It watched the sprawling tent city set up at Tian'anmen Square, witnessing the statue of the Goddess of Democracy rise up, with its back to Mao's gigantic portrait, and sighting the soldiers and the tanks approaching ominously. The length of the confrontation between the students and the Communist authorities, as well as its full exposure to the world's news media, gave news-watchers false hope: that something positive might come out of it, somewhat like the "people power" in Manila that had thrust Cory Aquino into the saddle of government as it sent Ferdinand Marcos scurrying away to Hawaii—another drama that was rendered possible and made vivid by television news coverage.

And then came the debacle—also fully covered, if only miraculously, by television as well as print journalists. And what a different debacle from that in the Philippines! Grown soft in the last ten years of relative and increasing openness, China-watchers started to wonder what had gone wrong, not only with China but also with themselves, in their inability to foretell the news, be that the student unrest, the power struggle, or the final, ruthless crackdown. It has become routine for many of them, now writing articles of analysis or making oral expositions of the social and political background that led to the Tian'anmen events, to begin their task, as did Michel Oksenberg, with self-reproach.

The Circumstances of Timing

The summit meeting between the Chinese and Soviet leaders followed closely in time another newsworthy event: the meeting in Beijing of the Asian Development Bank (May 4-6, 1989). And this seemed to be just another piece of evidence that the Chinese Communist leaders were finally entering the ranks of the Establishment—the civilized and polished elite that was ruling Asia and the world. Meanwhile, China itself remains a developing nation. That meeting was all the more interesting because of the presence of such erstwhile foes as delegations from South Korea (whose representative publicly lauded the People's Republic of China for its economic accomplishments of the past ten years), and even from the Republic of China on Taiwan, a regime with a rival claim to legitimate control of the territory. The Taiwan delegation, ably led by Shirley Kuo, minister of finance, marked the first time that a person holding a high government position in Taiwan had taken part officially in a meeting at the capital of the People's Republic, albeit as leader of a member delegation of the Asian Development Bank rather than as a direct representative of the Republic of China. While South Korea was ready to invest in various projects within mainland China, Taiwan seemed also prepared to funnel funds to Communist China through the Asian Development Bank. The world could foresee a period of active collaboration, of common efforts involving both communist and capitalist governments, which would draw out the potential energy, economic and otherwise, of the vast population of mainland China.

During the Gorbachev visit that took place subsequently, there was no public viewing of the event within China, as the authorities refused to air the student protests, even though the students of Beijing were occupying only the sidelines of the show. True, the students had been restless since the death of Hu Yaobang on April 15. And they could hardly be expected to stay quiet on May 4, 1989, a date marking the seventieth anniversary of the original May Fourth Movement. But it would appear that the Communist leaders themselves did not anticipate that the university students would launch such massive demonstrations in April and May 1989, and were for a considerable time themselves deeply divided over the methods of responding to these demonstrations—so much so that the confrontation lasted over a month and misled many, including many students, into thinking that the imminent suppression (which martial law was supposedly about) might never materialize.

We have no intention of joining the chorus of reproach or of self-reproach. Rather, we want to understand better what happened and why it happened the way it did. We attempt this at a time when the events in China are still at the forefront of many people's minds and tongues, and give rise to conversations everywhere—at hair salons, at wedding receptions, in government offices, in business towers, and on university campuses. Indeed, everyone has become, quite suddenly, a China-watcher, whether he or she has toured the country, as did 300,000 Americans in the first half of 1989, or has become fascinated by the haunting televised images of the once hopeful but eventually doomed students, as well as with the brave citizens of Beijing who risked their own lives to help save the students.

Indeed, the sympathy for the students, the identification with their cause, was so strong both within and outside China that, before the crackdown, a million people or more twice marched peacefully in Hong Kong to support their cause, while Chinese students all over the world responded with their own demonstrations. Blood donations and fund drives in Hong Kong and Taiwan attracted thousands of responses, on the assumption that the government that cracked down so brutally might just allow money and blood supplies to reach the victims and their families, which was *not* the case. Indeed, overseas Chinese continued for some time to collect funds for the support of victims of the crackdown even though the government refused all blood donations and confiscated the first millions that went into the mainland from Hong Kong. This follow-up is itself evidence of the outside world's disbelief that the Chinese Communist government could consider as its own enemy the thousands of students who petitioned for political and social reforms and won the hearts of millions of television viewers all over the world.

The Elements of Surprise

The events in China have taken everybody by surprise. I am referring not just to the power struggle and the military crackdown, but also to the student demonstrations and to other events before these. The West had been used to the image of a billion Chinese blindly following Mao Zedong and waving the Little Red Book of quotations from him during the aberration that was the Cultural Revolution (1966–76). The West was taken by surprise in the late seventies, when Deng Xiaoping opened

China's doors. Westerners hastened to enter, inviting Deng to respond by visiting Western capitals, where they showered glamorous attention on him. By contrast, Gorbachev's *glasnost* met initially with American suspicion under Ronald Reagan, and the Soviet leader had to wait much longer for media acceptance.

The Western press reported with stunned interest the student demonstrations of December 1986, which led to the downfall of then party general secretary Hu Yaobang. That occurrence catapulted to world attention the excommunicated party member Fang Lizhi. At the time, the West had been astonished at the size of the demonstrations (especially in Shanghai, but also elsewhere). But it had not followed with any intensity the issues and the personalities, as it would in May of 1989.

This time, therefore, the surprise was at the size of the turnouts in so many cities, as well as at the students' self-discipline and organizational skills, which seemed to surpass all expectations. There was surprise also at their youthful exuberance and their attraction to Western ideals, as shown in the making of the Goddess of Democracy. In comparing the students with their counterparts, be these American, French, or Japanese student demonstrators of the late 1960s, or more recent Korean students (armed) in Seoul's streets, one is struck by the peaceful character of the Chinese groups—all the more so when their gigantic numbers and the arrival of the military suggested the possibility of violence. How charming it was to witness the students defending themselves peacefully, by attempting to befriend the troops, and how moving it was to see them and fellow Beijing citizens initially blocking the army tanks with their own bodies.

The "Monolithic" Stereotype

The West was surprised by the student demonstrations, and shocked by the final crackdown, because the West tends to think of China in monolithic terms. Earlier, it had seemed Maoist; more recently, "reformist." Lately it has seemed somehow reasonable, although mysterious because of its ancient civilization (which many Westerners have never been able to entirely disengage from the Communist reality). Even at the height of the student demonstrations, a Western cartoon made fun of the fact that *all* Chinese were united against one presumed enemy, as they sang in unison the slogan: "Down with Li Peng!" But China is no simple monolith, at least not in the Western sense of that term.

By the "monolithic" approach I am referring to the tendency—a stereotype, of course—to think of all Chinese as more or less the same.

This tendency is more characteristic of the general public than the specialist, the China-watcher, although the latter is not always exempt. It probably proceeds from the perceived principle that all Chinese *look* more or less the same, at least to the outsider, especially when clothed, for a long time during the recent past, in their unisex Mao jackets and grayish-green baggy pants. And it is reinforced by past propaganda in China that made every Chinese a Maoist, happily different from the rest of mankind, allegedly content in his or her poverty, his or her acceptance (and even glorification) of the status quo that was Communist China.

Nearly twenty years ago the Australian Ross Terrill had this to say about the image of China in the West:

> Shimmering mirage, a China is conjured in our minds by scraps of news and speculation. Devilishly well organized; neat and regimented; striding ahead to overtake Russia and America; clean, abstemious; an army of sexless puppets, their daily life an incarnation of the Thought of Mao Tse-tung. Absence from China feeds the mirage. Fear, buttressed by ignorance, hints that China is formidable, or awful, or awfully formidable. How cunning those Chinese are! Do they not constantly surprise us?[2]

This first and grossly simplistic stereotype gradually gave way, with the opening of China to the inspection of the outside world.

The "Exotic" Stereotype

But there were other stereotypes. I am thinking, in the second place, of the Western stereotype of the East as *different* from the West—the East, that is, with the exception of the phenomenal economic achievement of Japan. According to this view, the Chinese people are not expected to desire human rights, freedom and democracy, which are *Western* ideals. And of course, this stereotype has been strengthened by the Chinese people's apparent acquiescence without dissent under Mao Zedong to innumerable official harassments and virtual enslavement. Has it not been said that unlike the Soviet Union, China had no Sakharov—at least until the emergence of Fang Lizhi in 1987? Hence a certain double standard prevailed in Western society until the Tian'anmen events, where the travesty of human rights in China was condoned while it was condemned in the Soviet Union and elsewhere. Hence the astonishment that arose this time when the world witnessed the students' willingness to risk their lives for their beliefs in just these "Western" ideals. Included in this approach is the failure to distinguish in China between the ruler and the ruled, to treat the two as a continuum.

China-watchers, of course, are a mixed lot. Of the Westerners among them, some specialize in Chinese language and history while others happen to be appointed to correspondent posts in China but do not read the language. And there are the Japanese scholars of contemporary China who watch from much closer, as well as the Chinese themselves, based especially in Hong Kong and Taiwan. Under the pen name Simon Leys, the Belgian Sinologist Pierre Ryckmans commented on the general attitude regarding human rights in China:

> On the question of human rights in China, an odd coalition has formed among "Old China hands" (left over from the colonial-imperialist era, starry-eyed Maoist adolescents, bright, ambitious technocrats, timid sinologists ever wary of being denied their visas for China, and even some overseas Chinese who like to partake from afar in the People's Republic's prestige without having to share any of their compatriots' sacrifices or sufferings). The basic position of this strange lobby can be summarized in two propositions:
>   1. Whether or not there is a human-rights problem in China remains uncertain—"we simply do not know"; and
>   2. Even if such a problem should exist, it is none of our concern.[3]

Pierre Ryckmans was trained as an art historian, and speaks and writes impeccable Chinese. In China-watching circles, he has been treated as somewhat of a loner, more ready to criticize the country than to find anything good in it. The events of 1989 have proved him right on most things. The Canadian John Fraser is of a somewhat different background. The erstwhile theater critic has never claimed a scholar's expertise about the country or its culture. As the China correspondent for the Toronto-based *Globe and Mail* soon after Deng Xiaoping had opened up the country, Fraser had this to say about his journalist colleagues in Beijing at the time when big-character wall posters in the part of the city called Xidan were making noises about human rights, freedom, and democracy:

> Conditioned to the seeming docility of the Chinese people, quite a number of foreign observers—certainly some of those stationed in Peking—were genuinely shocked to discover that citizens were able and eager to voice the most diverse kinds of thoughts, criticisms and aspirations. To travel from the absurd paeans of praise for "the wise leader Chairman Hua," pouring forth from the official media in 1977, to the eloquent manifestations of the Xidan Democracy Wall was to travel from duplicity and surreal fantasy to the very conscience of a generation that had lost its innocence at an early age.[4]

The "Benign Revolution" Stereotype

There is yet a another kind of stereotype that is much subtler and affects both the casual observer and the professional China-watcher, whether Westerner, Japanese, or expatriate Chinese. Presumably, it was motivated by the liberal urge (in many cases, the socialist critic's preference) to believe the best possible about the Communist Revolution, and to compare it always favorably with the Nationalist or Kuomintang regime that preceded it, and even with the same regime that moved to Taiwan in 1949. Many of these Communist sympathizers were motivated by their discontent with their own governments, and wanted very much another model elsewhere with which they could identify. But this stereotype also conditioned many old "China hands" as well as former missionaries and fervent Christians, probably because of their own guilt complex regarding the involvement of their government or the missionaries in what has been called "cultural imperialism." Besides, the term "liberation" has created quite a fashion in theological circles during recent decades, and certain believers in liberation theology had regarded Chairman Mao in symbolic terms as the new Moses, and even as the new Messiah (a second Jesus Christ!) leading his people out of slavery.

Even if such people had been disappointed with the disclosures of excesses committed in Mao's name during the Cultural Revolution, they persisted in thinking that the Communist Revolution was itself basically good. In the case of the Japanese, who usually knew the language and history well, this same stereotype could be accompanied by an underlying guilt complex about the Japanese invasion of China (1937), which merged with the Second World War (1942–45) and contributed directly to the eventual Communist triumph (1949). Indeed, nearly all the Japanese scholars of and commentators on contemporary China have tended to represent the Communist regime as more benevolent than despotic. According to this view, Communists remain forever superior to the Nationalists, the rulers now in Taiwan and the eternal villains of history.

For a long time (until after the opening of China permitted family visits and family briefings on sufferings endured before and during the Cultural Revolution), this stereotype had also influenced many expatriate Chinese, China-watchers or not. They wanted desperately to believe that the Communists had at least brought about some improvement in their ancestral land. I refer here to their feeling that the Chinese Communists were, after all, "liberators" of the country from both foreign imperialist powers and a corrupt Kuomintang.

To this last stereotype, one can perhaps add another feeling, or rather another self-deception—perhaps one more deserving of self-reproach among specialists. It is that Communist China is changing very rapidly, not only in the economic realm, but also in the political, and in the arena of human rights. After all, visitors have noticed the constant complaints on the lips of the Chinese, about inflation and government corruption, about the inadequacies of life and living. Are not these voices of discontent—as well as the expressions of protest on the part of intellectuals like Fang Lizhi, Liu Binyan, and Wang Ruowang—living evidence of the growth of freedom of speech? Had not Fang Lizhi, together with thirty-three other intellectuals, petitioned for amnesty for the political prisoners in China, in anticipation of the coming fortieth anniversary of the founding of the People's Republic (October 1, 1989)?

> For some years, this view of China has been emerging: that it was becoming a pro-Western semi-democracy, a place that almost inevitably would, with the passage of time, increase in contacts and greater prosperity, become ever more relaxed, open and even free. The country had improved so much since the Maoist years.[5]

How did such a view gain acceptance? Certainly, there was much wishful thinking on the part of people *wanting* to believe in China's getting better and better. There had been a different kind of wishful thinking under Mao Zedong, when Western Maoists wanted very much to believe that all was well, that China could not have done better than she was doing under the "beloved Chairman." So many times, I heard it said that although China *looked* poor, its people were really doing better than they ever had, indeed for thousands of years. China's standard of living, after all, had not changed that much, even if that of the rest of the world had.

To this, one should answer: China's visage of poverty today should be compared with the archaeological wealth that has been unearthed in the recent decades. It is ironic that archaeology alone has shone as a cultural field that has grown since 1949, whereas a great population has been unable to produce a great literature, great art, or great scientific accomplishment. Indeed, the archaeological digs, frequently an accidental by-product of construction or some other activity, have brought to light the material culture of a long past, a comparison with which is sufficient to shame the present. With all their exaggerations, Marco Polo in the thirteenth century and the Jesuit missionaries in the seventeenth century depicted a country that was much more interesting and impressive than Mao's or Deng's China. Change had been enormous, with sharp rises and falls in prosperity and cultural achievements during the millennia. In our own times, what the Communists achieved before Deng Xiaoping was to reduce the whole country to poverty, rather than to raise the people's living standards. Politically speaking, the Oriental despotism of past centuries pales in comparison with the Communist despotism of the present, as will be discussed further in chapter 4. Scholars have observed that China's long history has witnessed a dishearteningly *increasing* centralization of power, rather than the opposite.

China-watchers had also made wrong prognoses. In the fifties, when the Communists first gained control, the feeling was that their regime lacked stability, and therefore (among other reasons) diplomatic relations should be withheld. In the recent past, recognition was made on the assumption that the regime had become stabilized. In actual fact, Communist China was much more stable in the first decade of its existence, at the time when it enjoyed wide support of the population, than in the more recent decades, whether during the Cultural Revolution, when lawlessness was rampant, or during recent years, with the growth of popular dissatisfaction. The fact that even Deng Xiaoping acknowledged, on June 9, 1989, that "this storm was coming sooner or later"[6] indicates how insecure the regime had been feeling. The Western press had reported the problems of inflation and rising prices in China, but had not taken their implications seriously enough.

People who know the system, however, did sound the alarm. In an article published in July 1988 in the dissident journal *China Spring*, Yang Nung and Lai Shi predicted a crisis:

> In the next few years, Chinese Communist power struggle and the social movements of workers and students will all enter another cycle. What is unfortunate is that the Chinese strongman Deng Xiaoping will very possibly die during that period. This will increase the mutual provocation between politics and the economy [on the one side] and the social crisis [on the other side] and lead possibly to a total collapse of stability.[7]

The "Romantic" Stereotype

The "romantic" stereotype refers more to China scholars working on the country's traditional legacy than to China-watchers. It affects many Western scholars in love with China's culture; it also affects many expatriates (including scholars) who glorify China's ancient civilization, its humanistic wisdom, and its religious values. We have been hearing of the Confucian work ethic and its role in quickening the pace of economic development in the Asia-Pacific regions. We are also told of the Taoist attitude of harmony with nature and its potential role in safeguarding the ecology, as well as the Buddhist compassion for all life. There is truth in these statements; in fact, I have made such assertions myself. But there has not been as much eagerness among certain scholars to critically evaluate China's traditional cultural legacy in terms of its relevance to the present.

I am not saying that all China scholars are romantics. Far from it. There are those who have been quite critical, sometimes overcritical, of the past. The "China field" is divided in many respects, between humanists and social scientists, between those who study antiquity and tradition, and those who concentrate on the more recent past, between those who glorify the philosophical and religious legacies and those who reject them. Speaking generally, they mirror the division between the Chinese in Taiwan and Hong Kong (and also overseas), who are proud of their traditional heritage, and the intellectuals within China, many of whom express a profound dislike for the whole of traditional history and culture, and hold it responsible for all the ills of today's society. There is an inherent irony: that the people in the freer and more developed Asia-Pacific areas show much more attachment to their traditional culture than those in the "old country" itself, a country that claims to be the "new China."

Why has traditional China always maintained a despotic form of government? Why is it that Confucian humanism can ask for only a "benevolent" despotism, and not a government by the people? Why is it that ideals of equality between the sexes came to China only from the West? These very important questions have not been seriously asked by the scholars. Instead, those of us who are expatriates living in the West have been generally happy with putting "the best foot forward." In contrast, mainland scholars have been searching history as well as their own souls, seeking to explain why China has been a closed world to itself for so much of its existence. And the most outspoken among them have offered a practical solution to perceived problems; they have been saying: the Chinese tradition is responsible for the corruptions and despotism of today; let us embark on a course of *total* Westernization. Even before the events of 1989, I had been uncomfortable with such a call. I did not, and do not, believe that China as a country has always been poor and miserable in her existence. I also do not believe that Westernization alone can solve all her present problems. After all, is not Marxism itself a Western import?

But the tanks and gunfire of June 3–4, 1989, have awakened us all. China scholars in the past have been divided over political issues (loyalty to mainland or Taiwan) or over ideological questions (approval of, or opposition to, traditional values). Today, those based outside the country have all rallied (figuratively speaking) behind the student demonstrators, and against repression. A few people have slept through the gunfire noise of June 3–4, and ignored the demonstrations at Tian'anmen, but they too have to wake up unless they wish to become Rip van Winkles.

A stock-taking is due, not only about the presuppositions and methods of China-watching, but also about the orientation of the whole China field. I, for one, think that the question of the intrinsic values of traditional wisdom and culture (for example, the Confucian "amateur" ideal of a classics-educated scholar-official) should be reexamined much more critically, not only in terms of how they might serve the West—for example, that the ideas of harmony with nature could contribute to ecological balance—but also in terms of how and whether they have served and will serve China ill or well. I am not necessarily saying that my own attitude has changed radically, from that of appreciating the cultural legacy to that of rejecting it. But rather, I believe that many questions have been reopened. On the last point, there have been debates and discussions ensuing from Joseph R. Levenson, in *Confucian China and Its Modern Fate: A Trilogy* (1968), who sees the Confucian ideology mainly as a thing of the past: W. T. de Bary defends the relevance of Confucianism as a "liberal" tradition, Thomas Metzger compares the Confucian ethic favorably with the Puritan ideal, and Tu Wei-ming asserts that Confucianism can generate the seeds of democracy. These debates and discussions need to be undertaken once more, in a new light. Is not Hegel correct, for example, in asserting that Chinese history has never known the ideal of freedom, but that it has known only the rule of one man, the emperor, at any given time? Have not Mao Zedong in the past, and Deng Xiaoping in the present, proved this correct? On the other hand, is not the despotism of the present worse than that of the past? Has not political power become more and more concentrated in the hands of the few, even of the one man, rather than less and less?

To what extent is the system in China Marxist, and to what extent is it feudal? This is a question often asked, but little answered.

Picking Up the Pieces

China-watchers are not to be rebuked for not having foretold the many events surrounding and concluding the student protests. They could not have foretold these events. Nor, indeed, could any of the Communist leaders themselves have done so until, of course, they sat in closed sessions conspiring to put an end to what must have been for them a huge embarrassment and especially a perceived imminent threat. On the other hand, China-watching will not be the same again. Here, I am not merely talking about the reversion to past methods, learned during the thirty years when China was largely closed to the world, of watching the leaders' public appearances and ranking precedences, of reading between the lines in the Chinese newspapers, of interviewing refugees in Hong Kong.

China-watching and even China-interpreting have to change because certain basic concepts about Communist China have changed. During the relatively open atmosphere of the last ten years, the earlier stereotype—of the happy Chinese population under the guidance of Chairman Mao Zedong—was seriously disturbed by the outpouring of tales of trials and tribulations endured under the Cultural Revolution. Now, during the space of roughly six weeks, the remaining stereotype has also gone out the window—the stereotype of the Chinese people as not really understanding or wanting human rights, freedom, and democracy, whether because they have already been sufficiently "liberated" by the Communist Revolution, or because these are strictly "Western" concepts.

In one sense, China-watching will become infinitely more difficult, since one can no longer expect the Chinese population to continue to be passive, even if they may look impassive and repeat what is expected of them by the powers that be. In another sense, however, China-watching will become infinitely easier, because the outsider should now know that the Chinese people are not *that* different from the Westerner used to the conveniences of human rights, freedom, and democracy. One swallows one's pride and acknowledges that the Communist leaders have acted brutally, even bestially, in suppressing a peaceful student movement. No matter how many strategic mistakes the students themselves might have made in persisting to occupy Tian'anmen Square after having been told repeatedly to withdraw and go home, the actions of the Communist regime are reprehensible. One may be tempted to conclude simplistically that all Communists are brutes, and therefore turn to "Communist-bashing," this time not at the Soviet Union but at China. One might then proceed to link the age-old Chinese history and civilization with the Communist brutality one has witnessed, and to conclude, again all too simplistically, that this last event is also nothing new to China.

While it may seem that I am speaking especially about Western (and Japanese) China-watchers, I do not mean to leave out the expatriates. Many of them subscribe to this last stereotype about Communist China: that it is not that bad, that it cannot be that bad, that it is better than its precedents, be these the imperial rulers or the Japanese occupation or the Nationalist government, and even better than its counterpart Kuomintang government in Taiwan.

In the last analysis, this is wishful thinking. Indeed, such ideas are more characteristic of those with ethnic pride and also a more comfortable life-style than those others left behind on the mainland. The stereotype is especially espoused by the people in Taiwan, so used to Kuomintang control and Kuomintang propaganda that they are no longer sure of what their now open news media are telling them. Such people include members of the Kuomintang party themselves, who have been only too willing to give up some of the excesses of the past *Fangong dalu* ("Recover the Mainland") slogans and have wanted very much to find something good to say about their erstwhile enemies, the Communists, with whom they sense they will eventually have to reunite politically.

In summing up how we watch and interpret today's China, we can take to heart the words of two individuals: a veteran American scholar of modern and contemporary China, and a recent academic visitor from Canada. John K. Fairbank, for years the best-known U.S. "China hand," knows only too well the snags and snares created by our own images of China:

> A residual ambivalence underlies our post-cold-war view of China. How come these same Chinese could be such bad guys in the 1950s and such good guys today? This shift of view springs partly from our own capacity to spring from one to another interpretation of foreign reality. Our grip on reality in distant places beyond direct observation is of course weakened by the way we feel. At any given time the "truth" about China is in our heads, a notoriously unsafe repository for so valuable a commodity.[8]

John MacDonald, a Canadian educator and eyewitness to student protests in several cities had this to say after making his first-time visit (May 2–June 2) to seven Chinese campuses during the recent events:

> For most of us in Canada, China defies comprehension. The unfailing cheerfulness and generosity of its ordinary people is difficult to square with the sickening atrocities now being visited on thousands of university students, intellectuals and workers by the secret police. For them there is no place to hide. . . . I do not know how to embrace such a mass of beleaguered humanity, but I can mourn for all those individuals whom I am proud to remember as friends. Mourn for them, and pray for their safety.[9]

Clearly, the time for a double standard is over. No one can continue to point the finger at the Soviet Union for its *gulags* while condoning the Chinese Communists for their purges and crackdowns. This is all the truer as we watch the rapid pace of political change in Eastern Europe and the Soviet Union, and contrast it with the ongoing repressions in China in the fall and winter of 1989. But our current view of China is also at a crossroad. Should we think of the Chinese as being "good" and brave, as we remember the images of the peaceful and ill-fated student demonstrators—different, though not that different, from our own youngsters—and of the citizens of Beijing, who gave their lives to defend the innocent? Or should we think of the Chinese as being "bad" and hateful and repulsive, as we turn to the images of the soldiers, the tanks, and the brutal leaders who were commanding them?

Many people are awaiting answers to such questions, since millions have joined in watching the events taking place in China. Hopefully, they will not replace one old stereotype with a new one. As John Fraser once commented:

> In the West, Chinese people under Communist rule are often thought of as brain-washed blue ants. In reality, the diversity and individuality of Chinese people is one of the wonders of the world.[10]

CHAPTER 3

■

The Dictator and
His *Tabula Rasa*

Apart from their other characteristics, China's 600 million people have two remarkable peculiarities; they are, first of all, poor, and secondly blank. That may seem like a bad thing, but it is really a good thing. Poor people want change, want to do things, want revolution. A clean sheet of paper has no blotches, and so the newest and most beautiful words can be written on it, the newest and most beautiful pictures can be painted on it.

—MAO ZEDONG, 1958

There is no question that the Communists have made solid contributions to China. They unified the mainland, kept the country independent of foreign control, instilled self-respect in the population at large, and made the country a world power of sorts. These achievements are often attributed to Mao Zedong personally. He bears responsibility as the paramount leader for several decades, although he was aided by the party as a whole. The achievements of the past decade include opening the country to the West, accepting investments and joint ventures, changing the face of China with the building of skyscrapers, permitting private plots in the countryside and enabling peasants to develop initiative. These have often been attributed to Deng Xiaoping alone. He was of course *the* crucial leader in question, although he, too, was helped by capable persons like Hu Yaobang and Zhao Ziyang.

Nevertheless, all these contributions, which have been recognized by China-watchers and historians, become ambiguous when we take account of other factors. I am speaking here of balancing costs and benefits. Could China have done better? Have the costs been too high against the people's welfare and happiness? Is the country's unification worth the loss of freedom, and should it be maintained by methods of repression? To answer such questions, I find myself especially preoccupied with two more specific questions:

1. Why has China remained so poor after forty years of Communist rule?
2. Why is there such suspicion between the Chinese people and the Chinese government, as well as vice versa?

Why Has China Remained So Poor?

A research team was sent in 1988 to investigate the financial conditions in Xinguo, Jiangxi, a prefecture where Mao Zedong had personally conducted an investigation into the lives of the poor peasants (October 1930, during the days when he was directing Communist activities there). The researchers found that little had changed in the families concerned after the passage of fifty-eight years, whether in terms of income, mode of production, food supply, or educational level. All eight families investigated still struggle under the poverty line, living in debt after yielding their crop allotment to the government. In 1930, the six persons questioned by Mao had gone to school for an average of 5.25 years. In 1988, the nine individuals questioned had gone to school for an average of 5.1 years.[1]

Why has China remained so poor after forty years of Communist rule? This question has been frequently asked by people both inside and outside China, and especially by those impressed with the achievements of other Asia Pacific nations: South Korea, Taiwan, Hong Kong, and Singapore. With one exception, these are regions populated by Chinese, and the Chinese worldwide are known for their work ethic and resourcefulness. Put simplistically, why is it that the Chinese do so well once they leave the country, and so poorly in the country itself?

True, China had been very poor and underdeveloped before the Communist takeover. And Communist propaganda has always compared the best of life today with the worst of life before 1949 to make the point that the Chinese people owe their collective improvement to the forces of liberation. Is that, however, a fair assumption? From my own meditation on history as well as conversations with many Chinese intellectuals, I can safely say that this answer is no longer acceptable. China forty or more years ago had been subject to foreign invasions and dominance (Western powers, Japanese war) as well as domestic disunity (warlords, civil war). The Communists' big claim is that they have liberated China from its two worst enemies: foreign imperialism and the age-old feudal system. They have, in other words, given China a new start; they have created a "new China." Speaking historically, they appear to be right: for the past forty years, this new China has enjoyed unprecedented peace and independence. But why has it not also had prosperity? Has the main mistake been poor management?

The question raised here has also been posed by the Chinese dissident Wei Jingsheng, who offered his own answer in 1978:

> Without the personal despotism of Mao Zedong, would China have fallen to the point where we see her today? Or must we believe the Chinese are so stupid, or lazy, or deprived of all desire to improve their lot? On the contrary. What has then happened? The response is evident: the Chinese have taken a path on which they should never have engaged themselves, and they followed it on account of a clever despot. . . . There is hardly any choice left to them besides. . . . The people, held in ignorance of any alternative, has been persuaded that this was the only way possible.[2]

Wei was arrested and sentenced to fifteen years, but his views were basically confirmed by the government itself under Deng Xiaoping. Deng and his supporters repudiated the Mao Zedong era, even if the Chairman's memory was spared total condemnation. Mao's mistakes were acknowledged: together with the Gang of Four (Mao's wife Jiang Qing, Zhang Chunqiao, Yao Wenyuan, Wang Hongwen), he was responsible for the chaos of the "ten years of turmoil," a term that came to describe the Cultural Revolution. This grave error was made under the years of Mao's alleged senility. But his earlier mistakes, going back to the Great Leap Forward (1958–62) and the expanded Anti-rightist campaign (1957), were also highlighted upon Deng's comeback.

When we consider the severity of these mistakes and their consequences, we might further wonder: Why was Mao permitted to make these mistakes, and is there any redeeming quality to his rule, once the mistakes have been pointed out? Of course, Mao's successors have had to face these questions. They have agonized over the mistakes made during Mao's thirty-year dictatorship, which had entailed so much suffering, not only for the nation but also for themselves as individuals. They have acknowledged a shared responsibility, to the extent that they had not prevented him from plunging the country into chaos and catastrophe time and again. They could not totally condemn Mao Zedong, because they owe the legitimacy of their government to his leadership. So they enshrined him in history with a distribution of merits (70 percent) and demerits (30 percent). Basically, this meant that Mao has done more good than bad. But the line of demarcation between the good and the bad was drawn at the years 1957 and 1958—not quite ten years after the Communists had seized power. The distribution of 70:30 does not therefore conform to facts. To forestall the mistakes of another one-man rule, however, Mao's successors established a new regime under Deng where responsibility was shared more collectively.

The Dictator as Visionary: Mao's Mistakes

The words of Mao quoted at the head of this chapter refer, of course, to his concept of a "permanent revolution," a concept that had brought China the endless instability that preceded the Deng Xiaoping era beginning in 1978. A better guerrilla leader than an administrator, Mao represented a curious combination of visionary and crafty politician. As a visionary, he had two contradictory desires: to modernize the country, and to keep the revolution going. He shifted from one to another, first trying to modernize—in a naive way—and then, on failing to achieve that goal, trying to perpetuate the revolution and manipulate it against his own political foes. Pondering Mao's enormous mistakes, we cannot help feeling that it was Mao who actually kept the Chinese people "poor" and "blank"—not because he necessarily wanted them so, but because *he* had been an erratic and inept ruler.

An enigmatic character, Mao wanted a permanent revolution, provided there could also be enough stability for him to remain the dictator. Mao's greatest achievement had been the Communist triumph of 1949, which drove the Nationalists to the island of Taiwan and laid the foundation for the People's Republic of China. That this happened was not just the triumph of good over evil, of clean government over corruption; it was the result of many historical circumstances, especially the devastations of the war with Japan (1937–45). This historical event debilitated the Kuomintang or Nationalist regime and diverted it from its earlier attempts to suppress the Communists. Mao Zedong and his men got from the war the breathing space they needed and the opportunity to organize the countryside in preparation for the eventual struggle against the Nationalists for supremacy in the country. During a visit with some Japanese guests, who sought to apologize for the wrongs that the Japanese invasion had caused China, Mao, a man known for his bluntness, once replied that apologies were basically out of place, since without the war the Communists might not have won the mainland.

But the Communists began their rule over the entire country with a people eager to cooperate, to bring about the stated goals of achieving a modern, socialist nation. Many among the young volunteered to fight in Korea against the Americans from 1950 to 1953, while others showed their loyalty to the regime in other ways back home. Already in those early years, the population was mobilized with unparalleled intensity and on an unprecedented scale to build new cities, roads, factories, dams, and dikes, while the Communist party expanded its membership rapidly. True, the Communist regime was accompanied by its advocacy of class struggles with all their injustices and inhumanity. But the country was content with peace and stability and the hope of steady economic growth.

A Dead End: "The Great Leap Forward"

In 1957, when the country seemed secure against foreign aggression as well as domestic unrest, came the Anti-rightist campaign, a wide-ranging purge of those suspected of anti-government sentiments. This will be further discussed in chapter 5.

The Great Leap Forward, which followed in 1958, has also been criticized by the present leadership under Deng, even though Deng himself was personally involved in its implementation. And indeed, when one looks back to this first of many big mistakes, one cannot but wonder: Why? Why not leave well enough alone?

The answer is Mao's impatient and naive modernization urge. He literally regarded the country as a laboratory for his experiments. The term "Great Leap" was extended to mean everything from increases in productivity to the transformation of social consciousness as well as social organization. Ever a guerrilla fighter, Mao made use of militaristic slogans to mobilize the masses to "fight battles against the natural world," to carry out "three years of struggle" in order to bring about "a thousand years of Communist happiness." In the countryside as well as in the cities, one short-lived experiment involved "backyard furnaces," set up for the smelting of iron and steel; whatever these produced was wrapped in silk and submitted to the authorities. In general, workers had to work longer hours, often for lower wages, to meet higher and unrealistic production quotas, both in small-scale, labor-intensive cottage industries as well as in modern factories. Peasants first saw their private plots reduced, while they were made to work on irrigation and water conservation projects. Then, as if all this were not enough, villages were further transformed in mid-1958 into "people's communes," as peasants were organized into "production brigades" and all property became communal. One can easily imagine the ensuing organizational chaos of such rapid changes. To appease a dismayed party, Mao yielded his position as head of state to Liu Shaoqi, but rejected the sharp criticisms of Peng Dehuai, minister of defense. The latter was purged and replaced by Lin Biao (1959).

Besides an unusual share of floods and droughts, the year 1959 proved critical in another way. China had not approved of Khrushchev's efforts to denounce Stalin posthumously and resisted doing so within its own borders. As Sino-Soviet relations deteriorated, the Soviet Union decided on the abrupt withdrawal of fourteen hundred Soviet scientists and other advisors from China, leaving behind many projects that would never see completion. Food shortages and a mismanaged countryside led to a nationwide famine (1959–61) resulting in an estimated ten or twenty million deaths. The policies of the Great Leap Forward had proved to be a national disaster, although the regime blamed it especially on the Soviet Union.

Thus, one man's mistakes in policy had marked the plunging of a whole country into a wrong direction, resulting not only in economic losses, but even in the worst famine of modern Chinese history. Because of the even longer-lasting period of the Cultural Revolution, the Great Leap Forward has often been overlooked. But it stands as a landmark of Mao's mistakes as a dictator, mistakes for which the people and the country had to pay a high price. Of this, Deng Xiaoping admitted to an American journalist in 1986, "We have made some mistakes, such as at the Great Leap Forward. . . . Of course I was not its chief advocate, but neither did I oppose it, which means I shared in the mistake made."[3]

With Mao sulking over his own mistakes, Liu Shaoqi and others (including Deng Xiaoping) reassembled the pieces as best they could, reestablishing Leninist control through party bureaucracy. As the party chairman, Mao found himself little consulted, and began speaking about elements in the party who might turn reactionary or bourgeois. He ordered a massive ideological campaign, called the "Socialist Education Movement" (1962–66), which was met by both apathy and resistance.

The Ten Lost Years: The Cultural Revolution

We come now to the year 1966. Complaining of being treated as a "dead ancestor," Mao directed his fury in the beginning at his presumed successors in the party bureaucracy. The bureaucracy had permitted his purge of Peng Dehuai, but only reluctantly. Liu Shaoqi and his followers were then undoing the work of Mao's "permanent revolution," and they were presumably waiting for Mao's demise, after which they could complete the task of building their own bureaucratic empire.

In a totalitarian regime like that of China, political criticisms are usually veiled, frequently with the use of historical parables. Under the Communist rule, this became a standard practice, as Mao was recognized as a parallel to the third-century-B.C. emperor of the Qin dynasty notorious for his despotic rule and for "burning books and burying scholars." In the course of the Cultural Revolution, his wife Jiang Qing also grew in notoriety, with her persecutions of Liu Shaoqi's wife and her role in the suppression of other "enemies of the state." She would be called "empress dowager," after the hated Manchu woman who presided over the disintegration of the last imperial dynasty. We could almost say that a new literary genre was developing, that of "using the past to criticize the present." But then, the powers that be were not easily fooled; they could frequently recognize themselves under these veiled attacks.

Indeed, the first act of the Cultural Revolution was the attack on a play written by the historian Wu Han, which satirized Mao's earlier dismissal of Peng Dehuai. Wu used a historical theme that pointed to political reality. He dramatized the life of a sixteenth-century official, Hai Rui, who had been dismissed from office for criticizing the emperor's penchant for experimenting with Taoist elixirs of immortality. Mao recognized the reference instantly. The emperor was none other than himself, now in his dotage and wishing to live forever. And Hai Rui stood for the disgraced Peng Dehuai, who had dared to criticize the chairman. Ironically, Wu Han's work was written according to orders from the party, on cues received from Mao himself, who had praised Hai Rui's boldness and forthrightness at a time when he found that party cadres were afraid of telling the truth, since they feared becoming victimized as "rightists."

A critical review of this play bringing out its political agenda became the focus of the country's attention. It was written in November 1965 by Yao Wenyuan, a member of the eventual Gang of Four. The subsequent purge extended from writers and scholars to party stalwarts, and took place with the help of the mass movement called the Red Guards— mostly young students fired with zeal for implementing Mao Zedong's orders. After insults and tortures, Wu Han and his wife both died in prison; their young daughter eventually committed suicide.

To destroy his hated bureaucracy, Mao would eventually decide to unleash once more the energies of the masses. "Bombard the Headquarters!" he wrote on August 5, 1966, on a big-character poster of his own. He was fortunate to have the help of Lin Biao and the People's Liberation Army. Lin proceeded to build up an exaggerated cult of the Great Helmsman, especially making a fetish of the Little Red Book.

While the Great Leap Forward had represented a gigantic effort, and led to party struggles in which Mao was a loser of sorts, the Cultural Revolution was to be Mao's revenge over his comrades turned rivals: Liu, Deng, and others. It was also to bring to fulfillment his dreams as a revolutionary. Power struggle was at the core of this man's dreams, and in the course of this struggle, Mao turned the country upside down but emerged personally victorious, even deified. It should be remembered that he was already seventy-two years old in 1966, and very worried that the Revolution, his life work, would be destroyed by those party bureaucrats bent more on normalizing the country than on continuing change.

Mao's behavior during the Cultural Revolution seems to fit neatly into a quest for what the American psychologist Robert Jay Lifton has called "revolutionary immortality."

> By revolutionary immortality I mean a shared sense of participating in permanent revolutionary fermentation, and of transcending individual death by "living on" indefinitely within this continuing revolution. Some such vision has been present in all revolutions and was directly expressed in Trotsky's ideological principle of "permanent revolution" . . . ; but it has taken on unprecedented intensity in present-day Chinese Communist experience. . . . [4]

Lifton does not dispose of the theory that the Cultural Revolution was the playing out of a power struggle that began with the Great Leap Forward; he proposes a psycho-historical framework that explains such struggle:

> During a visit to Hongkong in February 1967 I found many Western and Chinese observers, rivaling in agitation the participants in the Cultural Revolution itself, putting forth endless—and endlessly elaborate—speculations on how Liu Shao-ch'i or Lin Piao or Chou En-lai really felt about Mao Tse-tung, or, when these were exhausted, how their wives really felt about one another. Such speculations, when offered as a *total* explanation for the Cultural Revolution, were consistent with certain cultural tendencies affecting the observers: the Chinese inclination to see the world as no more than a network of human relationships and rivalries. [5]

As the Communist gerontocracy perpetuated itself from Mao to Deng, we can perceive how each, in turn, was motivated by this "revolutionary immortality"! However, the Chinese-language press has pointed out precisely that one of the mistakes made by Western China-watchers is the neglect of the family networks and interpersonal rivalries among the Communist leaders. In any dictatorship, the survival of one leader or faction usually means the destruction of another. Called *Ni-si wo-huo* (You must die so that I can live), this dictatorship syndrome was delineated even by student leaders in May 1989. In a country governed by a dictatorship, suspicion reigns, not only between the rulers and the ruled, but also within the ruling clique itself, and on every level.

Many Western intellectuals perhaps have found it difficult to accept the power struggle theory as the best heuristic key to the understanding of Chinese politics because it represents such ugly realities, so unbecoming of any people, especially one that prides itself on the achievements of five thousand years of civilization. But they should remember that the Communists have not claimed to be heirs to this civilization. On the contrary, they regard themselves as rebels and revolutionaries who have turned their backs on the ancient civilization.

The first victims of the Cultural Revolution were the "capitalist roaders," who included many party stalwarts, such as Mao's presumed heir and the head of state. Liu Shaoqi found himself branded a counter-revolutionary, expelled from the party in 1968; he died of sickness and neglect in 1969, in Kaifeng.

Deng Xiaoping, party general secretary, and many others were also removed from office, and the entire party as well as government apparatus were paralyzed. In their stead, Mao and his wife Jiang Qing (who came more and more into prominence) favored the grass-roots movement of the young Red Guards and looked to them as potential revolutionary successors. Many of these were ultra-leftist, and ran rampant in the country, ransacking homes, arresting suspected enemies of the state—all in the name of Chairman Mao. Finally, concerned about the chaos being created all over China, Mao disbanded the Red Guards in 1968, sending most of them into the countryside "to learn from the peasants." But the Cultural Revolution was by no means over. Everywhere, "revolutionary committees" took over the functions of running the day-to-day affairs of the country.

For a time, Lin Biao was acknowledged as Mao's closest comrade and chosen successor. As the nation's Number Two, he promulgated a nation-wide movement of loyalty to the Number One, the "reddest sun in people's hearts." In those days, every family had a picture of Mao. Three times a day, people would read from the Little Red Book in front of this picture, as though reciting morning, noon, and evening prayers. Every public action, even that of stepping on and off a bus, was accompanied by the recitation of a verse from the chairman's writings. During weddings, couples congratulated themselves in public for the good fortune of having Mao as leader, rather than having each other. Indeed, the cult of the chairman meant that even his pictures were sacrosanct, and individuals were executed on the *suspicion* of having defiled these.

After the Cultural Revolution came to an end, many accounts were written about those days of terror. Visitors to China in the late seventies were also treated to many stories by their hosts. Professors and even university presidents were literally dragged in the mud and made to wash latrines; clergymen, even those who had collaborated with the regime, were paraded on all fours in the streets, in the role of "running dogs" of the imperialists. But I was most impressed with the stories of children who got themselves and their parents into trouble for just play-ing with the chairman's pictures—which were omnipresent—or for say-ing careless things with political implications. Even kindergarteners were imprisoned for doing and saying the wrong things, interrogated at night under strong lights, and made to denounce their parents and friends.

All this time, what was the great chairman doing? It appears that he was suspecting everyone around him. He turned successively on his longtime personal secretary, Chen Boda, and on his "close comrade" Lin Biao, ally in the struggle against Liu Shaoqi and designated heir. Lin's sudden and precipitous fall from grace was especially mysterious, as he had been so closely associated with Mao in the country's propaganda. The political campaign against him would only begin after his death, since Lin just suddenly vanished from public view in September 1971. It was about two months after Henry Kissinger's China visit. Many months later, it was explained that Lin had plotted to assassinate Mao, and when this was discovered, had attempted to flee to the Soviet Union with his family, but perished in an air crash.

The Revolution was devouring its own children while its deified Chairman was presiding over the demise of law and order in the People's Republic. The sole survivor among Mao's comrades was Premier Zhou Enlai, ever trying to keep together whatever pieces he could. As person-alities, Mao and Zhou are a study in contrasts. Zhou had early yielded the party leadership to Mao, and seemed content to serve his bidding, while also keeping the country together. Even the state council had to put up with retrenchment, mob accusations, and army intrusion. For a while, it had virtually ceased functioning (1968–70), as each of its ministers of state was paraded in turn in the streets with dunce cap on and the humiliating charges of alleged crimes.

The country also appeared belligerent toward virtually the entire out-side world, with the possible exception of communist Albania and the Viet Cong. China had been preaching its own doctrines of world com-munism, and calling the Soviet communists "revisionists." Until 1964, there were more states that recognized the Nationalist government in Tai-wan than the Communists in the mainland. And China's isolation was all the more defined when it skirmished with the Soviet Union over a dis-puted island on the northern borders in 1969. The United States, of course, was considered as imperialist enemy number one, whom the Chinese had fought against in Korea during the fifties, and who had always recognized the Nationalist government in Taiwan as the sole legitimate government of China. So it was a great surprise to the nation when Henry Kissinger and Richard Nixon came successively to visit China in 1971 and 1972. A complete about-face in China's foreign policy was on its way.

About-face it was, for the United States as well. Literature about Mao Zedong and Communist China mushroomed, as American reporters planned to penetrate the forbidden land. I have been told by a mainland Chinese that Mao Zedong's reputation was at its lowest ebb in China, because of the Cultural Revolution, when it reached its peak in the United States during the early seventies. Americans were fascinated with him, because he was so unlike them. And they reasoned that his regime could not be so bad, after all. Gradually, the opinion spread that the Chinese people were probably doing better under Mao than they ever had before in their long history. After all, had he not liberated them from the evils and inequities of the past? Scholars wrote about the "new man" that Mao had fashioned in China, a new breed, indeed unselfish, dedicated to the service of the people—as was himself, their great model.

It was Zhou Enlai's finest hour. The work of shaping a new diplomacy was basically his, although undertaken with Chairman Mao's blessing. The People's Republic entered the United Nations in February 1971 and a rapprochement was finally made in February 1972 with the United States, previously the country's presumed worst enemy. Follow-ing two decades of turbulence and six years of chaos, the Communist government suddenly ceased to be the world's pariah. It had become legitimate.

But the Cultural Revolution was not quite over. In 1973, a new and bizarre campaign soon got under way, called the "Criticize Confucius, criticize Lin Biao" campaign, which vilified the historical figure of Con-fucius and attacked Lin Biao posthumously. It appeared directed (by Mao's wife and friends) against the living premier, Zhou Enlai. Borrow-ing from those who use the past to criticize the present, Jiang Qing's cam-paign identified the sophisticated Zhou with the ancient sage. It is harder to understand what Lin Biao had in common with Confucius, but he was the more obvious political target, even two years after his death. Despite these odds, the bureaucracy was encouraged to reemerge, and a new constitution was enacted in 1975. Already ailing, Zhou died in January

1976. Mao followed in September, not long after a massive earthquake in July in Tangshan, east of Beijing, claimed at least 200,000 victims.

In the old days, Chinese emperors entered their eternal repose accompanied by many "burial companions," whether concubines, old retainers, or war captives. The seven-thousand-strong terracotta army discovered outside Xi'an in 1974 recalls this convention, since the figures were buried to augment the living victims who followed the First Emperor (Qin Shihuang) to his death (210 B.C.). True to the style of the ancient Chinese emperors, Mao Zedong was entering his eternal abode preceded by his faithful retainer and thousands of reluctant companions.

To recapitulate, Mao's victims included Liu Shaoqi, head of state, right arm and appointed heir of Chairman Mao, who was suddenly persecuted for being a traitor working for the restoration of capitalism; Chen Boda, the Chairman's confidential secretary and the master ideologist of the Cultural Revolution, who was made out to be a crook; Lin Biao, Chairman Mao's closest comrade in arms and his second heir-designate, who was unmasked as an abominable plotter, assassin, and potential usurper.

All the time, the people had to put up with the resultant struggles, turmoils, and change of rhetoric; they had to stomach the dogfights of their leaders and alter their slogans of political support. All that remained was for the Chairman to die, for his wife and accomplices to be declared the ultimate villains—and all this would happen, after the Tian'anmen Incident of April 1976, to be related in chapter 7. We have been watching the unfolding of the many acts of the ugly drama that is recent Chinese history. Its subsequent acts will continue to shock their viewers.

The Dictator as Enforcer of Law and Order: Deng's Mistakes

The systematic elimination of designated heirs left unresolved the problem of revolutionary succession. At Mao's death, the potential heirs included his widow, Jiang Qing, a former actress, whose attempts to foment chaos during the Cultural Revolution had made her immensely unpopular both with the party and with the nation. The party struck back successfully, in a *coup d'état* directed against Mao's widow and three of her accomplices (the Gang of Four), with the help of the head of the secret police, Hua Guofeng (October 1976). He was given Mao's mantle, at least temporarily. But he proved to lack the needed party support to remain in charge. Deng Xiaoping reemerged. Deng had thrice been purged (the first time was from 1933 to 1934, just before the "Long March"; the second time was from 1965 to 1973 as a "capitalist roader"; the third time was from 1976 to 1977, after the Tian'anmen Incident of 1976). But he had always maintained a certain hold over both the party and the People's Liberation Army. He was to preside over the post-Mao decade, without the title of chairman, while always keeping military power. But the banner of change would no longer be that of "permanent revolution." It was, instead, the "Four Modernizations": the modernization of industry, agriculture, defense, and science and technology—in other words, economic development in an environment of stability. This policy was nominally set in place before the deaths of both Zhou Enlai and Mao Zedong in 1976, while Deng was vice-premier working with Zhou, and its implementation would be on his agenda for the following decade.

Deng projected himself as a man for law and order. Together with such comrades as Peng Zhen, Chen Yun and Wan Li, Deng had suffered the injustices of a political purge during the Cultural Revolution, and had learned the risks involved in a dictatorship that did not have clear laws of succession. He was to redress these problems by encouraging and instituting a rule of law, and by appointing younger qualified persons to responsible positions. He chose Hu Yaobang and Zhao Ziyang in 1981, the former as party general secretary and the latter as premier. They were to implement his vision of economic recovery and development. To restore faith in government, Deng declared that truth should be found in the examination of facts, and not in political slogans. Recognizing initially the abuses of "class struggles," Deng's government also declared that the country had lost the old class structures and could rest, free from further struggles.

To demonstrate good faith in a rule of law, the new government held open trials of its political enemies: the Gang of Four and their associates followed these up with open trials of provincial and lower levels of the Gang's followers. The crimes listed included plots to overthrow the government, assassination attempts against Mao, illegal arrests, torture, and the persecution of 700,000 people, resulting in 34,000 deaths. The Gang itself escaped execution, which was meted out to some of their associates in the military, and to lower-level cohorts.

The new regime had inherited a population now numbering a billion, and an economy near bankruptcy. It put in a strict family control policy, and dismantled the commune system by reverting to private plots. Normalization of relations with the United States under Jimmy Carter (January 1979) brought in an era of joint ventures with foreign businesses and even investments overseas. China's urban and rural landscape became rapidly transformed by skyscrapers, highways, and new peasant housing, and by the "special economic zones" given exemptions from administrative and economic controls. These five zones (three cities in Guangdong and one in Fujian, plus the island of Hainan) have been dubbed the "Golden Coast" because of their growing entrepreneurial prosperity. Looking toward the return of Hong Kong to the mainland in 1997, the People's Republic also directed its attention to courting Taiwan to "peaceful reunification." Under Chiang Ching-kuo, an increasingly wealthy Taiwan also lifted its thirty-year martial law and permitted visits to the mainland in 1987. Taiwan business interests were already rushing in to do trade with the mainland.

But all was not well in the People's Republic. The government had to deal with deficits, inflation, and unemployment, as well as increasing corruption in its bureaucracy and rising expectations from the governed. Meanwhile wage increases were kept too low to enable the people to enjoy a better standard of living. "To get rich is glorious" was the new and shocking government slogan, but the new rich were also those with the best ties to the bureaucracy, while most of the urban population were deprived of incentives for greater productivity. Moreover, the central government was split on the question of economic directions, with the older comrades from an earlier period preferring central planning, and Deng's own protégés opting for more diversification.

The most visible protests to the regime came in the form of the student demonstrations, first in December 1986, and then in April and May of 1989. The students wanted more recognition of human rights and wider political participation, but they also complained of government corruption, the low level of spending for education, and economic hardships. And then came the military crackdown on the students and their sympathizers, to the horror of a world already closely watching the development of the student demonstrations.

Each time (in 1987 as well as 1989), the casualties included the political demise of one of Deng's chosen heirs. Deng Xiaoping was going down the road of Mao Zedong. Each time, the party turned against its own secretary general. It has indeed been reported that Deng has called Zhao Ziyang a counterrevolutionary. The logic is once more puzzling: Why should the party head and designated heir to Deng himself oppose the Revolution in China? The succession to follow his own demise would not likely be a peaceful one, even as Deng promised his new heir-designate Jiang Zemin (June 29, 1989) that he would no longer oversee things, but would remain "ready to help out when needed."

The question is once more: Why? Why did Deng Xiaoping choose to suppress the peaceful student demonstrations (even though these were spreading to other sectors of society as well as to many cities and towns in the whole country) with such brutal callousness? Why did he twice clip his own wings?

My theories are:

1. Deng did it in the name of preserving law and order, even though the crackdown and its accompanying power struggle were a travesty of the Chinese constitution and its promise of due process. In one single night, after weeks of anxiety and of hopes for a compromise between the students and the government, Deng's troops and tanks were undoing years of careful cultivation of respect for popular opinion and for the *spirit* of law.
2. Like Mao before him, Deng wanted "revolutionary immortality." He was unable to trust his own best assistants, even his chosen heirs. Trust, indeed, is a rare commodity among old revolutionary comrades.

But then what about another question: Was he not also aware that the crackdown might worsen the situation, rather than patch it over, and so actually hinder further economic reforms?

The Chinese-language news reports from Hong Kong and Taiwan have offered an answer to this question. They have described Deng and the hard-liners sitting together in consultation. They are represented as feeling gravely threatened by the disturbances everywhere, and saying: What's the use to us, if the country is to change leadership? What good is it to have continued economic openness, joint ventures, and the rest, if we are no longer in control?

We have reached here the *gut* reason for the bloody suppression. The elderly comrades, united behind Deng Xiaoping, opted to crack down on the student protests out of fear that their own days as leaders were numbered. Sad to say, this group was all octogenarian—besides Deng Xiaoping and Yang Shangkun, it included Chen Yun, Peng Zhen, Bo Yibo, Li Xiannian, and Wang Zhen. Hong Kong's *Sunday Morning Post* dubs this event the "return of the dinosaur," and describes the "night of the long knives":

> To his senior colleagues around the table, according to a party circular released . . . on Thursday night [May 25], Mr. Deng had only one question. . . . "If we step back from our judgment, where do we draw the line?" he asked rhetorically. The plans to purge began.[6]

To the further question as to why these octogenarians cling so to power, we may once more proffer the answer of their desire for "revolutionary immortality." These old men are afraid of dying without power. They are afraid that their vision for China will fail. It was a vision different from that of Mao's, different, in detail, even one from another's. In Deng's case, it was especially a desire for "stability" as he sees it—a stability without opposition. When he saw opposition, he decided to will it away.

There may yet be another answer: their desire to protect their own progeny. After Deng's return to power in 1978, Chinese-language publications reported on how the old comrades (then only in their seventies) had reunited and exchanged their stories of pain suffered under Mao's Cultural Revolution. Never again, they said. Let us at least protect the gains of the liberation, for ourselves and our children.

Nicknamed the "princes," these children of the top leaders have benefited most from the economic reforms. They include Deng's crippled son Pufang, head of the Fund for the Disabled, which has collected much overseas money, and for a long time head of the Kanghua Development Corporation, which bought raw materials at government prices to sell them high on the free market; his other son Zhifang, now working at China International Trust and Investment Corporation (CITIC); his son-in-law, He Ping, head of Poly Technologies, a subsidiary of CITIC, which deals in arms trade, including the sale of missiles to Iran; a daughter (Mrs. He), deputy head of a bureau in the State Science and Technology Commission; another son-in-law, mayor of Wuhan; Yang Shangkun's younger brother Baibing, director of the People's Liberation Army's political department; his son-in-law, Chi Haotian, its chief of staff; and his nephew, head of the 27th Army that butchered Beijing; Chen Yun's son, a member of the standing committee of the city of Beijing; Bo Yibo's two sons, one in charge of tourism in Beijing, the other, a mayor in Dalian (Liaoning); and Wang Zhen's son, a high military official in the Chengdu military region.

Nepotism has been one of the students' complaints about the post-Mao era, and this information comes partly from one of their big-character posters. Things might not be so bad were some of these princes better behaved. The opposite is more frequently the fact. And so, "Under Deng, Running China Has Become a Family Affair" (the front-page headline of the *New York Times* on July 2, 1989), with many members frequently abusing their powers and privileges for material gain. To the information given there, one may add that such nepotism is found on every level of government—central, provincial, municipal, and local. Whereas, in the old days, under the empire, there was a civil examination system to screen candidates for the bureaucracy, this no longer exists, and connections count more than diplomas. Whereas, in the old days, a successful candidate entering the bureaucracy was never permitted to serve as official in his own native place, such checks and controls also no longer exist. The country is being served up like a piece of meat, and the people around the table have the protection of their connections. The problem is that the scraps left behind are not enough to feed the population.

It is interesting that the people in Eastern Europe, especially East Germany, also protested in December 1989 against special privileges and government corruption. It is another sign of how the Communist system has functioned to serve the leaders, not the masses.

More and more, mainland critics have been saying that China is no longer Communist, even if it is not yet fully capitalist. The adjective they use to describe the present government is "feudal." Strictly speaking, Western historians see the term feudal mainly as descriptive of the period of European history in the Middle Ages, and the period of Chinese history around the time of Confucius and Mencius; and classical Marxist scholars use it technically to refer to the pre-bourgeois period in European history. However, in general usage in Chinese at present, the term simply implies looking out for the interests of oneself and one's clan.

The dual-control system of China's economy invites corruption. Compromises have been the order of the day, rather than real structural reform. There are two prices for things in China, the official price and the market price, just as there are two kinds of currency, the official RMB, and the so-called Foreign Currency Exchange Certificate. The country also possesses a market economy in the "special economic zones" but a controlled economy elsewhere in the country. It enforces a dual system of internal trade barriers. By circumventing currency controls, diverting products from the controlled to the free market, and avoiding tariffs and quotas, the politically privileged have been taking advantage of an anomalous situation to create their own financial empires.

In the events of June 1989, the octogenarian leaders acted to protect their own interests and the interests of their children. And what about the people?

A Balance Sheet

In the past forty years, the people have lived under a government making arbitrary and capricious decisions. We have outlined the major policy changes, especially under Mao Zedong. We know of the reluctance of the hard-liners to replace the planned economy with a market economy. A major abuse, perpetrated especially by the children of the high officials, has been to buy commodities at the official price and to resell at the market price, thus making a profit margin several times that of their capital outlay. Besides, the Chinese government has always complained of a lack of foreign currency reserves. Yet it has allowed its own bureaucracy to make overseas investments, to own shares in commercial real estate and in multinational corporations. The talk is that private persons stand to profit in these ventures. I have heard this said myself by mainland scholars. This was also the accusation made by Fang Lizhi that most enraged Deng Xiaoping.

There have also been thousands of minor decisions, under both Mao and Deng, decisions that unsettle the people whose lives they govern. There was a time in Sichuan, for example, when all food coupons were declared void. How were people to get food? In recent years, peasants in certain regions granted permission to plant cash crops were told arbitrarily to revert to growing grain—against the stated contracts issued by the government. In more recent days, peasants have been issued I.O.U. chits instead of cash for the grain they sell the government. Can they live on these? And can they trust the government to redeem them? There was the comical situation of the resale of the Red Flag cars. Once considered a status symbol for high officials, these cars were being replaced by Mercedes, and were resold to private citizens. Reports have said that private citizens such as the wealthier peasants or would-be taxi drivers who purchased them had not been permitted registration licenses—because they were considered to lack the "status" for driving such vehicles. As a result, minor bureaucrats took advantage of the cars, and drove them without any registration. After June 1989 the government changed its policy and reinstated the use of Red Flags by high officials.

Despite widespread outcries about the growing global environmental crises, the government has nonetheless sought to profit from the outside world's need for nuclear waste dump sites. It has especially offered land in Xinjiang to West Germany for that purpose. At a time when African countries are refusing to accept the dangerous chemicals on their shores, the People's Republic is saying: it is safe, we are digging deep holes.

We have here a government that does not heed its own people. Time and again, the government under Mao faced a crisis of confidence. But the political consciousness of the population was low, until it was heightened by the Cultural Revolution. The country was ready to explode, and did explode in the Tian'anmen Incident of 1976. The common people were overjoyed when Deng Xiaoping reemerged and directed the country on an entirely new course. In the intervening years, this new course has proved beneficial in many, but not all, rural regions. And some of the gains are being offset by new policies for the countryside. In any case, it has hardly helped the working people in the cities. According to unofficial figures (who can believe the official statistics?), inflation is supposed to be reaching 30 or 40 percent while wages have hardly gone up. There are the self-employed, those eking out a living by peddling goods, by repairing bicycles and the like, and others opening small restaurants and stores, who appear to be doing better than the factory workers. But the scope in which they operate is small, the taxes high, and the risks heavy. In many ways, the new economic prosperity is only a façade, hiding the deep resentment of the large bulk of the population.

For a time, during the heady days of the student protests, demonstrators within and without China cried the slogan: "Down with Li Peng!" Some people in the West thought that Li's political fate was sealed, for how can any political leader survive such an outpouring of resentment? On the contrary, Li has remained in power, serving the dictates of Deng Xiaoping and cracking down on those who had wanted his downfall. Obviously, Li was concerned, not with any popularity contest or people's mandate, but with the support of the party elders. By contrast, the Japanese prime minister Noboru Takeshita did not survive the Recruit scandal and popular demonstrations on a scale much smaller than those in China. Neither did his successor Sousuke Uno survive the 1989 sex scandals.

Mao Zedong regarded governing the country as though he were painting on a *tabula rasa* that is the people, covering up old blotches by new strokes. Deng Xiaoping was doing the same, while changing the entire style. But then, at the time of crisis created by student unrest, Deng was ready to destroy his own handiwork, to apply blood rather than paint on a much-abused canvas. For the Communist old guard, the country is their own private fiefdom. They governed with the people's support only when it suited them. They will also govern despite the people's opposition.

And the people's verdict? Chinese-language newspapers say that Mao sacrificed the country for the party, and then the party for his own power. Deng is obviously doing the same. Mao is known to kill people slowly, but he sometimes permits them a way out, through so-called repentance and reform. Deng appears impatient to kill. He is already being judged worse than Mao, but not because Mao was any good.

And should we be that surprised? China has never de-Stalinized itself as did the Soviet Union under Khrushchev. Until today, many party elders who never knew Lenin are still devoted to Stalin's memory, while

Khrushchev is considered a villain for having withdrawn the Soviet experts from China. Mao turned against the Leninist party structure; Deng rebuilt it. But both Mao and Deng can be said to be ruling in Stalin's model, especially now that the Deng "cult" is being built up. "That means he is going to die soon," said an irreverent young man who spent his childhood under Mao. That same young man, while in junior high school in the West, had great difficulty grasping the principle of the separation of powers inherent in our political structure. "What is all this business about the executive, the legislative, and the judiciary?" he used to ask. "I thought there was only one leader to each country!"

The German philosopher G. W. F. Hegel had commented that China was a civilization in which basically only one man, the sovereign ruler, was free, while all others were his slaves. Traditional Chinese history was a history of despotism, to be sure. But scholars have remarked, correctly, that the modern period has seen the worst concentration of power in the hands of the few—the Communist party. "The victors are the kings," was the traditional adage, explaining the rise and fall of dynasties. The Communists have not left this feudal attitude behind. The survivors of the Long March (1934–35) continue to believe that the country belongs to them by right of conquest, even after their own circle has been depleted by infighting. Did not Mao Zedong once say that where there is no tiger, the strongest ape becomes the ruler?[7]

In the period between 1916 and 1919, just before the May Fourth Movement, when China was being ruled by warlords, Li Dazhao, one of the future founders of the Communist party, had already much to say about the polarization of the people and the political rulers of his days: that people and rulers cannot co-exist, just as freedom and dictatorship cannot co-exist. A romantic and a revolutionary, he wanted to replace dictatorship with a more humane government.[8] His indictment of dictatorship has been proved right in the case of the Communist rule in China. After years of political struggles, hundreds of campaigns, and years of famine—all of them, in part or in whole, the results of human mismanagement—the people have become tired of their rulers and are now showing a willingness to take things into their own hands. After decades of peace, during which South Korea, Taiwan, Hong Kong, and Singapore have joined Japan in achieving prosperity, mainland China remains behind, kept backward, many would now say, by her own politics and policies. How much longer will this last?

The words of Nien Cheng, author of *Life and Death in Shanghai* (1984), ring in my ears as I try to answer the other question: Why is there so much suspicion between the government and its people?

Constant change is an integral part of the Communist philosophy. The Chinese leaders expect the people to rush headlong into whatever experiment they wish to carry out, whether it be liberalization or collectivization. For the whole thirty-six years of Communist rule, the Party's policy has swung like a pendulum from left to right and back again without stopping.[9]

Can a people trust a government that does not know what it is doing, and worse still, has no regard for the people's welfare? Although I started the chapter acknowledging certain contributions made by the party and its leaders, I cannot help feeling that the human costs have been enormous, and the results have benefited the leaders much more than the populace, who have been deprived of their basic rights.

And what of the stability Deng so wanted for his economic miracle? Forget about it. The *instability* reserved for the days following his death has already arrived. Only the world now knows that the Chinese, like the people in communist Eastern Europe, are no longer willing "to be blank slates on which the state shall scribble its blueprints for the future."[10]

Interestingly, Chinese students published a list of mistakes made by Mao Zedong and Deng Xiaoping that echo the contents of this chapter. It came from a flyer from Beijing University under the title "Who caused instability during the past forty years?" I shall quote a few sentences:

> Practice proves that the many turmoils that have taken place since the founding of the Republic are not caused by students, or by democratic parties, or by the masses of people, or by Taiwan, or by America, or by the Soviet Union. . . . These were caused by a very small minority. . . . The source of turmoil: the very, very small minority inside the central politburo which has usurped the powers of the party, the government, and the military.[11]

Indeed, the "blank slate," the *tabula rasa*, bears too many errors, too much pain and suffering. Wang Ruowang, a literary critic, has repeatedly pointed out the abuses of being made to "report" on one another, of purges and false accusations that have characterized Communist rule— not only at the top, but also on every level of society. Expelled from the party in 1987, he is reported to have later used this same metaphor:

> Chairman Mao had said that one can paint a very beautiful picture on a blank piece of paper. China was like a blank piece of paper. But after decades of work, the painting has gotten quite messy. It isn't the modernists' [fault]. It is [the fault of] learning from the Soviet Union, and then adding to it some feudal colors. It will be hard now to change things back. One must first erase all the messy oil colors.[12]

■

Chinese Communism: Old Wine in New Bottles?

There is no such thing as abstract Marxism, but only concrete Marxism. What we call concrete Marxism is Marxism that has taken on a national form, that is, Marxism applied to the concrete struggle in the concrete conditions prevailing in China, and not Marxism abstractly used.

—MAO ZEDONG, 1938

As a "hybrid," Chinese Communism is not always well understood. Even people who have lived in Eastern Europe say: Yes, we know communism, but we don't know China. China is different. So what is this difference? What are the theories and accomplishments of the ideology called Chinese Communism? After the account given in the last chapter, there is need to discuss this question. There is also need to distinguish between what is Chinese and what is communist in Chinese Communism, to see whether it is nothing but an import from the Soviet Union, or whether, to modify a biblical image, it is "old wine in new bottles."

Actually there have been two points of view on this subject that are very much at variance with each other. The first is that there is little that is "Chinese," meaning traditionally Chinese, in the communism that country has produced: in other words, communism in China is a Soviet import. The second is that there is little that is communist in Chinese Communism: that the phenomenon that goes by that name is basically *un*-communist, but purely a Chinese product that goes by the *name* of communism.

To examine the question carefully, we should first distinguish between Marxism and communism. In our understanding, Marxism refers to the original communist theory, as this was taught by Karl Marx and Friedrich Engels. The term "Communism," however, connotes not only this theory but also the political practice developed by Lenin and Stalin. They stand as the architects of Soviet Communism, which became the yardstick of communism everywhere. The Chinese are aware of this situation, and refer to the ruling ideology as "Marxist-Leninism," which they even differentiate somewhat from "Mao Zedong Thought."

How Marxist-Leninist Is China?

The People's Republic calls itself a state founded on the principles of Marxist-Leninism and of Mao Thought. But just how Marxist and Leninist is Communist China? And what is Mao Thought? How does it differ from Marxism and Leninism? To answer these questions properly, it is best to take Marx, Lenin, Stalin, and Mao separately and examine how the ideology represented by the Chinese state relates to each of these figures.

Karl Marx and Chinese Communism

There is a difference between Marx and Marxism that is greater than that between the philosopher and his philosophy. It is that there exist many versions of Marxism. Speaking of political options today, there is the Marxism of social democracies (as in Sweden) and the Marxist-Leninism (with its own various versions) of the Soviet Union or of China. The former insists on achieving a total democracy, starting with political life; the latter justifies the seizure and control of power by a communist party that regards itself as the watchdog of orthodoxy. The attraction of Marxism is the hope it offers for liberation from social and economic oppression. The anomaly in communist countries is that the government in power usually controls all aspects of life and claims to act always in the interests of the people.

A German Jew familiar with the immediate aftermath of the Industrial Revolution in England and Western Europe, Marx disapproved of the exploitation of the workers by the capitalists and predicted a proletarian revolution for that part of the world. According to his theory of historical materialism, socialism should follow bourgeois capitalism. Of course, as a country, Russia had known little of bourgeois capitalism before it was overtaken by the October Revolution in 1917. The "success of Marxism" in the Soviet Union would have surprised Marx greatly. But Marx would have been even more surprised, we should say shocked, had he seen China turn communist. As far as he was concerned, "Asiatic society" did not have the "self-transforming" forces found in the societies of the West and conducive to class struggle and revolution. Like Hegel before him,

Marx did not have a high opinion of the "Oriental peoples." He thought them too passive and "submissive," even "slave-like" in their attitude to institutional authority. He inherited the Hegelian belief that Oriental empires demonstrate a historical immobility. This means that he acknowledged the recurrence of change on the leadership level, that is, where the "political superstructure" is concerned—for example, palace coups and power struggles—but he saw no real change where the "social infrastructure" was concerned. In other words, throughout the rise and fall of the dynastic cycle, changes in China had been in the "political skies" or on the leadership level only, leaving the peasant population apathetic and unchanged. Interpreting history economically, Marx observes that the "Asiatic mode of production" is dependent on the combination of "small agriculture and domestic industry" with its lack of impetus for social change. Against this perspective, we can understand why Marx regarded favorably the changes set in motion by the British in India as "the only *social* revolution ever heard of in Asia," that is, one started by the forces of colonialism or imperialism.[1]

In China itself, a serious effort to reevaluate the whole of history came from Jin Guantao, who together with his wife wrote the book *Xing-sheng yu weiji* (Prosperity and crisis) (1984). Jin and Liu seek a broader explanation for what they see as an "ultrastable system" in Chinese history despite periodic manifestations of instability—a kind of "changeless China" with Hegelian overtones. This is manifest in the rise and fall of dynastic cycles as well as of prosperity and decline throughout many millennia. Going beyond mere economic determinism, they explain this system as the result of mutual interactions and adjustments between political, cultural, and economic structures. They stimulate looking at and thinking over the entirety of history, even if some have objected to the suggestion that there are "scientific laws" for cycles of progress and decline. At various times, because of social conflicts and lack of balance between the structures, this basically fragile "ultrastability"—which has overtones of stagnation—is shaken. "Ultrastability" also suggests a monolithic order, with its danger of fossilization as well as mass alienation. For these reasons, dynasties have come and gone every so many centuries, but new ideas and life-styles usually have difficulty taking root.

We are all familiar with Chinese Communist propaganda against imperialist encroachments in the Third World, especially in China itself. I remember how surprised I was in 1981 when a professor from Beijing University, now deceased, told me that the reason why Japan had become democratic and China had not is that the American occupation had *taught* the Japanese democracy. At the time, he did not link it up with any of Marx's theories. But it did make me think that Chinese intellectuals might know classical Marxism better than many people outside realize.

Karl A. Wittfogel, who spent many years studying Chinese history, asserts that Karl Marx had been ignorant of the peasant movements seeking economic and political changes. Wittfogel considers that these *were* revolutionary mass movements, even if they involved little class struggle in Marx's sense. Indeed, Chinese Communists had always looked back to peasant uprisings throughout history as historical role models.

Indeed, the Chinese Communist Party under Mao's leadership was not the party of the industrial proletariat that one would expect an orthodox party to be. By winning the revolution through the mobilization of the peasants, Mao and his followers rewrote Marxism, as it were. (Adulation follows success and victory, rather than orthodoxy.) A closer scrutiny would reveal that the party he organized was not even a party of the peasantry in the Marxist-Leninist sense. Rather, it was an "elite corps" organized along Leninist lines but drawn — on its top levels — from various strata of Chinese society.[2] In the face of Marxist-Leninist dogma, this elite group had come to realize that the peasantry could itself provide the mass basis for a revolutionary transformation. If Mao won China in 1949, it was due especially to two factors: the Sino-Japanese war, which had broken the backbone of the Nationalist government; and Mao's own Draft Agrarian Law, which proclaimed the redistribution of the land to the tillers and the cancellation of all earlier agrarian debts. This second measure inspired peasant unrest everywhere in the country and gave impetus to student and worker demonstrations in urban centers.

Lenin and Chinese Communism

We are using the term "Marxist-Leninism," as do the Chinese Communists themselves. Lenin had much to do with the victory of communism in China. Theoretically, he inspired many intellectuals with his theory that imperialism is the "highest stage of capitalism" and inevitably spells its doom. Practically, the example of his success in overthrowing Czarist Russia encouraged the Chinese to do the same with their imperial regime. The Chinese students and intellectuals were also grateful for the Soviet announcement in 1917 that all "unequal treaties"— treaties granting territorial or legal concessions to foreigners — imposed by Czarist Russia upon imperial China were abolished. When the Communist party organized itself in China, it followed the Leninist model of the Soviet Union. Mao and his supporters did the rest.

We might therefore say that Chinese Communism is more Leninist

than Marxist, as is also the Soviet communist party. But there are problems here too, as our account in chapter 3 has revealed. If in the Soviet
Union the party had usually been more important than the leader, in
China the emphasis had been the reverse. Interestingly, Lenin, the
architect of Soviet power, had also warned in the case of Russia that the
failure of the socialist revolution could mean an "Asiatic restoration"—the
return of what has been called Oriental despotism (which in Russia is
especially associated with the Tartar rule in the Middle Ages).

However, in China as in Russia, once it had achieved power, the aspirations or intentions of the party's leaders were not necessarily determined by their peasant background or by the interests of the peasants.
Mao's own utopian ideas in favor of communes certainly spelled havoc
for the livelihood of the peasants. Rather, what did happen represented
the continued oppression of the peasants and workers by the all-
powerful state, now the only landlord as well as the only factory owner.
In this sense, Marx and Lenin have both been proven correct: with all the
political changes (and even the social changes), the people's livelihood
has not seen much, if any, fundamental improvement.

From this perspective, we may better understand the assertion of the
Chinese students and intellectuals themselves that the government no
longer represents Communism as an ideology, but is rather the reincar-
nation of the forces of "feudalism" (fengjian). For Marxist-Leninists as
well as others (although the reasons differ), the use of this term is controversial, as is the periodization of Chinese history, which resists the fac-
ile Marxist categories. After all, when compared to feudal Europe, China
was unified very early, in 221 B.C. However, in today's Chinese, fengjian or
"feudalism" basically indicates the continuance of Oriental despotism—
of the worst kind. The new leaders are also the new emperors, but
stripped of any veneer of benevolence, and much of the traditional
checks and balances (including the critical advice of Confucian scholars),
as the old tradition would have had it.

Stalin and Chinese Communism

Joseph Stalin (1879–1953), for a quarter of a century ruler of the Soviet
Union, was the supreme political manipulator, the model dictator, who
governed through the use of terror. He has been compared in the West to
Russia's Ivan the Terrible, just as Mao has been compared to China's First
Emperor. In his relations with the Chinese Communist Party, Stalin con-
sistently sought to impose his own will, but seldom succeeded. Despite
his well-known purges, Stalin was succeeded by others in the Soviet
Union (including Khrushchev) who started to dismantle much of his

mystique and some of his policies. Interestingly, the Chinese Communists disapproved of these efforts and continued officially to laud him. Among other things, they had learned from him how to apply the Marxist-Leninist ideology creatively, with the lesson especially that "socialism can triumph first in one nation" before proceeding to conquer the rest of the world. One of his faithful admirers was Mao Zedong, who eulogized him as "the greatest genius of the present age, the great teacher of the world communist movement, the comrade-in-arms of the immortal Lenin."[3] After Stalin's death, Mao Zedong also probably felt more comfortable in cultivating a cult of his own, not only as the paramount leader and savior of the Chinese people, but also as the ultimate "wise man" of the communist world.

China never ceased to be Stalinist, even as Deng Xiaoping launched the policy of openness and reform. Stalin's portrait was only removed from Tian'anmen in May 1989, together with those of Marx, Engels, and Lenin. Many of the present leaders, including Li Peng and Jiang Zemin, had studied in the Soviet Union at a time when Stalin was all-powerful, and must have learned much from Stalin's methods of government.

Mao Zedong and Chinese Communism

For Karl Marx, the central drama of social revolution was to be enacted in capitalism's original home rather than in the less developed areas. He was proven wrong, to the extent that this revolution did not really happen in Western Europe. But the fact that the Soviet Union and China both turned communist is another case. One could always question whether the revolutions that did succeed in these countries *were* Marxist, or were they something else? In the case of the Chinese Revolution, those intellectuals who turned to the Soviet Union for inspiration and leadership did so less because they were searching for philosophical truth, and more because they were preoccupied with the fastest way of "saving China" from the twin evils of imperialist threats and a fossilized, "feudal" system. To quote from Li Dazhao, who accepted the messianic message of the Russian revolution (1918) and founded the party in China:

> Our nation has gone through an extremely long history and the accumulated dust of the past is heavily weighing it down. By fettering its life it has brought our nation to a state of extreme decay. . . . What we must prove to the world is not that the old China is not dead, but that a youthful China is in the process of being born.[4]

Whereas Li was an intellectual with a penchant for theories, Mao Zedong, his self-styled disciple, appreciated the merits of Leninism as an organizational technique rather than as simply another doctrine. His experiences in organizing peasants in Hunan made him realize that "only mass political power secured through mass action could guarantee the realization of dynamic reforms." Having seized leadership of the party, he proceeded to seize power in the country. After that, he was capricious in the choice of policy directions, acting sometimes as a utopian visionary, sometimes as a realist politician, and always as a paramount dictator. He and his comrades had also learned much from Lenin as well as the great dictator Stalin, who could tolerate no dissent and whose stature had never been officially questioned in China.

There is, indeed, little doubt that Mao Zedong and others of China's leaders rose to power by addressing themselves to the immediate needs of the peasant masses. This does not mean that they thereby became the embodiment of the people's aspirations or that they would automatically press for the fulfillment of the needs of the masses. Such is, of course, party propaganda: a myth designed to sanction all their activities, including those of the repression of all potential rivals.

But the party in China did assimilate a basic faith underlying Marxist-Leninism. I refer here to the Hegelian and Marxist faith in the redemptive character of the historical process, and the Leninist faith in the party as the sole agent of such redemption. Therefore, despite the doubt regarding the party's credentials as a party representing the proletariat, its leaders — both Mao and Deng — saw themselves as instruments of history, destined to lead China on the road to modernization and socialism.[5]

Added to this is their long-term revolutionary experience — as guerrillas in a remote corner of the country. They had settled in mountainous Yenan after the formidable Long March (1934–35). They lived there in cave dwellings, using mobile guerrilla tactics in their struggles against both the Nationalists and the Japanese. For over two decades, their concern had been for survival, and for overcoming the enemy. All this meant shrouding themselves in secrecy, a practice that is still carried out, even forty years after they gained power. They were also preoccupied with military tactics, rather than with constructing a modern economy. They have been known more for their military tactics and battle exploits than for economic management. The following is a poetic rendition of a strategy popular among Chinese Communists:

> When the enemy advances, we retreat.
> When the enemy halts and encamps, we advance.

When the enemy tires, we attack.
When the enemy retreats, we pursue.[6]

Unfortunately for today's China, it was an experience that the leaders have not yet gone beyond. When I first revisited China in 1978, at a time when the People's Republic still perceived itself as somewhat opposed to both superpowers, I was struck by the slogans still visible everywhere:

Dig deep trenches
Keep big grain storages
But never claim hegemony!

The digging of air-raid shelters and the storing of grain in mountain caves were then being done ostensibly against a perceived Soviet threat. The rejection of any hegemony was aimed at both the Soviet Union and the United States. But the methods invoked were those of guerrilla fighters. China had become a militarized nation, I thought to myself, and a *guerrilla* nation. I was just as impressed by the military overtones of a proletarianized language. Everywhere, the communes were subdivided, along military lines, into "production brigades" with peasant leaders called "brigade leaders." Life had been turned literally into warfare, with "class struggle" as its cornerstone. The problem with that was that there were no more real landlords. So the leader (whether of the country or of the locality or of the work unit) is free to supply "class enemies" depending on the political climate of the moment.

Mao's tragedy was that he was unable and unwilling to go beyond his achievements as a guerrilla leader and become a statesman. This became the tragedy of the nation under him as well. When Deng Xiaoping and his comrades opted for openness and reform, it was thought that they would give the country a government of law. Instead, on perceiving any real or imaginary threat to their power, they turned not to constitutional procedures but to the army, and gave a military solution to what could easily have been settled through dialogue or discussion.

How Chinese Is Communist China?

To the assertion that Chinese Communism is not orthodox Marxist-Leninist, one may offer the explanation that Communist China is only "old China" in new disguises. I am referring here to the China of the old days, under the dominance of an "activist" Confucian philosophy allied to a "contemplative" Taoist philosophy. Our task here is to answer the question of whether that really is so. To what extent, then, is Communist

China Confucian or Taoist? To what extent is it therefore different from the East European countries that have also been ruled by communist parties?

Chinese Communism and Confucianism

At first sight, there may seem little in common between traditional Confucianism and Chinese Communism. The older philosophy teaches a humanism based on the moral dimension of human relationships. Its core is the virtue of humanity or human-heartedness (*ren*), sometimes defined as "loving others." It teaches people "not to do to others what you would not have them do to you" (*Analects* 15:23), which is diametrically opposed to the practice of class struggle. It also envisages a humane government under a benevolent ruler who puts the interests of the people before his own. Of course, any regime, including the present, might seek to portray itself in this light. But there is still a fundamental contradiction between a doctrine of humaneness and social harmony and that of class hatred and historical determinism.

All the same, it has often been assumed that Chinese Communism as an ideology is only Confucianism in a different dress. Those who make this assumption have in mind the highly authoritarian emphasis of both ideologies, and the patriarchal character of the Communist state, which reflects that same character in the traditional, imperial state. In other words, the two ideologies share a common denominator: respect for authority.

This is, of course, a gross simplification of both ideologies that does not take into consideration any of the important differences between the two. After all, the Leninist party organization, and all the Marxist-Leninist states belonging to the Soviet bloc exhibit this emphasis on absolute political authority. At least, this was so until very recently, that is, with Gorbachev in the Soviet Union and with "cracks" in the system appearing especially in Poland and Hungary. What may still be argued is whether in China the Leninist emphasis has been reinforced by a traditional Chinese (or Confucian) respect for authority, making the state structure or the mentality of the leadership even more impervious to ideas of democratic reform.

During the last forty years, Communist China had witnessed critical reevaluations of, as well as diatribes against, Confucius and Confucianism. The worst came in 1973 and 1974, when the ancient philosopher was depicted as a political reactionary, a counterrevolutionary, a hypocrite and a murderer. His teachings were considered class-biased, with no universal meaning, his scholarship was said to be mediocre, and his temple and tomb in his native town, Qufu, were ordered desecrated. Ironically, this anti-Confucius campaign was associated with the campaign against Lin Biao, the former defense minister and Mao's designated heir.

The anti-Confucius campaign came toward the end of the Cultural Revolution and has since been officially repudiated as an effort to besmear Zhou Enlai, then premier and a man with genteel qualities. At its peak, it made world headlines, and there were journalists and others who judged that the campaign was directed against the authoritarianism symbolized by Confucius. Actually, the campaign raged in a country that no longer knew Confucius's own words, since these were no longer studied. In the end, Confucius's reputation appears to have survived the Cultural Revolution much better than Mao's.

Will there be a reversion to the pre-communist model of a Confucian state, or is there any future to a synthesis of Confucian and Communist values? These are questions that arise, especially for those attached to Confucianism and familiar with its merits in the Asia-Pacific region. Among the Chinese leaders, Liu Shaoqi was known for openly favoring Confucian values. In his address "How to Be a Good Communist" (1939), he quotes *Analects* 2:4, which gives Confucius's description of his own spiritual evolution:

> At thirty I became firm.
> At forty I had no more doubts.
> At fifty I understood Heaven's Will.
> At sixty my ears were attuned [to this Will].
> At seventy I could follow my heart's desires, without overstepping the line.[7]

Referring also to Mencius's admonition that anyone with a mission need first be toughened by suffering and toil, Liu offers the following counsel:

> As Communist Party members have to shoulder the unprecedentedly "great office" of changing the world, it is all the more necessary for them to go through such steeling and self-cultivation.[8]

In supplementing Communist ideology with Confucian spiritual teachings, Liu even exhorted emulating the Confucian quest for self-cultivation:

> The Chinese scholars of the Confucian school had a number of methods for the cultivation of their body and mind. Every religion has various methods and forms of cultivation of its own. The "investigation of things, the extension of knowledge, sincerity of thought, the rectification of the heart, the cultivation of the person, the regulation of the fam-

ily, the ordering well of the state and the making tranquil of the whole kingdom" as set forth in the *Great Learning* also means the same. All this shows that in achieving one's progress one must make serious and energetic efforts to carry on self-cultivation and study.[9]

In unleashing a vicious attack on Liu Shaoqi, the Cultural Revolution also criticized his Confucian leanings and banned his writings. Indeed, Liu's defeat by Mao Zedong may be regarded in some ways as the defeat of a "Confucian" faction within the party by a Legalist one. However, my own surmise is that the present regime, which is quite unscrupulous in its search for ideological allies as well as in its attacks on rival theories, may very well seek to make use of Confucianism to strengthen its own authority. To this end, they recruited the support of a lineal descendant of Confucius who was made to echo the official line in the wake of the military crackdown. But I doubt that this will give rise to a revival of the old tradition. The tradition itself is, however, still alive, in the hearts and minds of many. Its humane legacy still has a tempering function on human relations in general, even while it confronts the legacy of "class struggle," which has long deteriorated into power struggle or personal vengeance.

The writer Lu Xun, still very much venerated in the People's Republic, made a vehement attack on the Confucian ritual order in his first short story, "The Diary of a Madman" (1918), which was followed by many others. He called Confucianism a "cannibalistic religion" that stifled human freedom and individual initiative in the name of passive, conformist virtues. He was speaking of a fossilized ideology, embedded in a hierarchical social order, in which the individual had to defer to the family in what concerns him- or herself most: education, career, marriage.

This metaphor, the "cannibalistic religion," can be better applied today to Chinese Communism, since the state has replaced the family as the primary object of people's loyalty. It has been alleged that any soldier who refused to shoot at the people in Beijing risked being shot by his officers, and that this did happen on June 3-4, 1989. This is corroborated by the official statistics regarding army casualties. Although several dozen soldiers were reportedly killed, according to the government spokesman Yuan Mu, only ten were acclaimed "martyrs" by the state, for having been killed by unruly mobs. Who then killed the others? During China's skirmishes with Vietnam in 1979, the remains of the dead soldiers were returned in two ways: those draped with red were martyrs for the country, while those draped with white were killed by their own when they tried to run away. Moreover, in every purge, officials are given quotas to fulfill: they *must* arrest a given number of people in their exercise of duty. Very possibly, the number of death sentences was also fixed beforehand, and did not remain contingent upon the merits of the case and the judicial process. The state has always "killed chickens to show monkeys," like the Chinese story that monkeys in the wild willingly enter the hunters' nets or traps when they witness the slaughter of chickens who refuse to obey. It is a far cry from the spirit of true law, of constitutional guarantees for the citizens' rights.

Chinese Communism and Taoism

Are there Taoist strands in Chinese Communist ideology? We are speaking here of Taoism as a philosophy, the philosophy of Laozi and Zhuangzi, who lived roughly two thousand years ago. We are not speaking so much of Taoist religion, which refers more to an organized movement that started in the second century as a healing and immortality cult.

At first sight the question itself appears naive, since Taoist philosophy, which exalts nature rather than culture, has often been associated with escapist philosophy and retreat from political life. It is possible to envisage that such love for nature and political "escapism" has served as a consolation to those who suffered political repression. Several intellectuals who suffered imprisonment acknowledged such. But what else?

For those who study the history of Chinese thought, Taoist philosophy has long been regarded as having lost its own distinctiveness while becoming one strand in a total world outlook. Taoist philosophy has been appealing to the young in the West, since it prefers the individual to the group, and nature to society and its constraints. But the realities in China are quite different. China is known as a highly collectivized society. If Confucian dominance had always supported the family over the individual, Communist dominance had replaced the supremacy of the family with the supremacy of the state.

Taoist philosophy is also not that simple. Indeed, it is full of contradictions. There is political concern also in Laozi's Taoism, manifested as preference for a "back to nature" small government, but definitely an authoritarian government, an isolationist government.

> Though adjoining states are within sight of one another, and the sound of dogs barking and cocks crowing in one state can be heard in another, yet the people of one state will grow old and die without having had any dealings with those of another.[10]

And last but not least, in its irreverence for social values, Taoism has expressed an anarchist bent. Sometimes described as a Confucian patriarch figure, Mao Zedong had actually shown himself to be very Taoistic in his visionary utopianism with its anarchist streak. He ruled a large country as though it were a small village state, with methods derived from his guerrilla experience as well as from his disdain for law and order. He had the strange conviction that good government would itself issue out of chaos. On balance, Mao Zedong made good use of his own status as the Confucian father figure for the People's Republic, in mobilizing the masses to carry out his own will, such as in seeking periodically to put into effect his Taoist-inspired vision of a "quick socialism." To the extent that his dreams were directed to a socialist future, he was also a communist. Obviously, he was selective in his intellectual preferences. He was no orthodox Confucian or Taoist; neither was he an orthodox Marxist-Leninist. Impatient about the slow process of historical materialism, he tried, time and again, to impose his own will, not only on the people of China, but also on history itself—to bring about a modernized, industrialized China, which would be at the same time a communized China.

Of course, Mao all his life was the great rebel, an individualist who could not conform to the general will, but who sought to have the general will conform to his own will. He was often on the side of protest, first against the Nationalist government, and then against the party itself when he found its apparatus thwarting his wishes. To that extent, he had the style of a Taoist, a man who did not fear to be different. He cannot be said to have also possessed at heart the aspirations of a philosophical Taoist, of a person accustomed to harmony with nature and escape from society. But Mao did share in some of the aspirations of a religious Taoist: he desperately wanted to live on. He longed for immortality, physical as well as "revolutionary." Mention has been made in chapter 3 of Mao's persecution of the playwright Wu Han, who had criticized him, under the veil of history, through the play *Hai Rui Baguan*, which depicts a good official, Hai Rui, being dismissed from office for seeking to prevent the emperor from overindulging in "elixirs of immortality."

Mao also wanted adulation as a wise man and as a ruler. Unlike Confucius, he had a disdain for learning. He approved only of "knowledge of the struggle for production and knowledge of the class struggle." As he put it, "a great many so-called intellectuals are actually exceedingly unlearned and the knowledge of the workers and peasants is sometimes greater than theirs." His great arrogance, as well as his own lack of preparation for statesmanship, played a role in his misgovernment, as these also did in the party's misgovernment. He was, in essence, neither a Taoist nor a Confucian.

Chinese Communism and Legalism

The term "Legalism" should not be confused with a rule of law. It refers rather to an ancient school of thought that (among other things) advocates the use of penal law to enhance and maintain political power. Legalism has been a favorite of despots. It was the official ideology of China's First Emperor. Following the downfall of the Qin dynasty (207 B.C.), many Legalist ideas infiltrated Confucianism as the latter philosophy gained dominance in the Han dynasty (206 B.C.–A.D. 220).

Taoist philosophy has also contributed to Chinese Legalism, that philosophy of power sometimes cloaked in a mysterious language. Laozi has said: "The best of all rulers is but a shadowy presence to his subjects."[11] Perhaps Mao Zedong had learned from this to remain mysterious during his rule. Lauded as the "reddest sun in our hearts," the Chairman actually was mysterious and capricious like the moon. He had periods of withdrawal from government and society, making his occasional public appearances all the more fascinating. He was also adept at manipulating the masses, at using them to accomplish his own ends: "When his task is accomplished and his work done, the people all say, 'It happened to us naturally.'"[12]

The Legalist, Han Feizi, offers the mysterious Tao as a model to the ruler, instructing him to remain secretive, and never to pour out his heart, not even to those closest to him.

> The Way lies in what cannot be seen, its function in what cannot be known. Be empty, still, and idle, and from your place of darkness observe the defects of others. See but do not appear to see; listen but do not seem to listen; know but do not let it be known that you know. . . . Hide your tracks, conceal your sources, so that your subordinates cannot trace the springs of your action. . . . Destroy all hope, smash all intention of wresting them from you; allow no man to covet them.[13]

In these words of tactical advice, we can see a reflection of Mao the leader, exceedingly crafty and often mysterious, both in his periodic disappearances from public view as well as in his abrupt about-faces. Mao was a man of contradictions, and these contradictions were manifested in his "Thought" as well as in his actions and orders. While a visionary, he was also pragmatic, and it is his pragmatism that comes through in these words about Marxist-Leninism, in which he compares the ideology with Taoist religion:

Our comrades must understand that we do not study Marxism-Leninism because it is pleasing to the eye, or because it has some mystical value, like the doctrines of the Taoist priests who ascend Mao Shan to learn how to subdue devils and evil spirits. Marxism-Leninism has no beauty, nor has it any mystical value. It is only extremely useful.[14]

In mainland scholarship, Legalism is often regarded favorably as a "progressive" school of thought, whereas Confucianism has been previously described as "reactionary." During the anti-Confucius campaign (1973–74), Legalism was exalted as the "ideological hero" that had always engaged Confucianism in a life-and-death struggle. The anti-Confucius campaign has been officially discredited under Deng Xiaoping, but what has persisted is the policy of using the juridical system to impose severe punishments for crimes real and imagined, high and low.

Mao has been seen as a peasant rebel who made good, someone who had learned a bit of Confucianism and Taoism, but even more from Legalism, and who was also able to use to advantage certain ideas coming from Marxist-Leninism. "Democratic dictatorship," for example, is Lenin's idea and Lenin's terminology, but one that Mao also used. Such a mixture is Mao Zedong Thought. Like every earlier peasant rebel made good, however, Mao believed in his own supreme rights—and so did Deng.

And what more can we say of Deng Xiaoping? He was even less of a theoretician than Mao Zedong. Neither understood or appreciated ideas of freedom or democracy. Deng is no romantic, even if he enjoys visiting "mountains and rivers" in the company of his family. He is even more pragmatic than Mao. This is exhibited in his famous saying that a cat's color, whether black or white, does not matter, provided the cat catches mice. He relies on the party apparatus, but only to do his own bidding. In all this, he shows himself neither Confucian nor Taoist, but a Legalist.

In the past few decades, Western scholarship has given some attention to another Legalist text, also a favorite of Mao Zedong's: *Xunzi binfa* (The art of war). It insists on the importance of knowing the facts, both about oneself and about the enemy. Naturally, the most important chapter in this treatise concerns the use of military intelligence, considered the secret of success on the battlefield. Military strategy favors secrecy. During the Vietnam War, Asian analysts commented on American openness, since many military reports were published by major newspapers and thereby made available to the enemy. Military strategy favors manipulation and even conspiracy. In traditional China, strategists were often called conspirators (*yinmou jia*). Mao Zedong was an avid player of Chinese chess (*weiqi*) and Deng Xiaoping an equally avid player of bridge. For both, these games are an exercise ground for political manipulation as well.

In this context, I am of the opinion that the worst of the Marxist-Leninist police state has worked in collusion with the worst of the traditional heritage, a theory about power called Legalism, or even truer to life, the "conspiratorial" theory. To the extent that Legalism has perverted Confucianism during the ages, and only in this sense, it may be said to have also drawn Confucianism (as a "minor" partner) into the conspiracy.

What Is Chinese Communism?

There is little in the traditional literature of China that prepares the researcher for grappling with Communist China. One can look far and wide in the traditional literature for discussions on leadership, whereas the literature of Communist China often consists of nothing else. In preparing the manuscript for this book *Ideology and Organization in Communist China* I was repeatedly impressed by how little "Chinese" it appears to be. Where is China in all these processes? Chinese culture has not disappeared, but China's traditional social system has. Revolutionary changes, which began more than a century ago and were brought to completion by the Communists, have profoundly altered the substance and form of Chinese society.[15]

I was impressed with a French film on China, *A Tale of the Wind*, which was shown at the September 1989 film festival in Toronto. It was Juris Ivens's last work, codirected by his wife Marceline Loridan, and features him, as an old man, aged ninety, revisiting China in search of something we may call Chinese wisdom. What he found was state bureaucratism, and an incongruity of the past mixed with the present. The film juxtaposes myths and reality, beauty and ugliness, and leaves it to the viewer to draw the final conclusion.

This image, of course, is what most people find in China. For those who knew the country four decades ago, there is much that is now missing. The visitor no longer finds "the flavor of human feeling" (*renqing wei*) so characteristic of the Chinese people. Rather, one has to face up to proscriptions about everything. "Thou shalt not. . . ." And this comes not just from the central government, but from every level of the bureaucracy. For a traveler, it is difficult to be told at the railway station that tickets can only be purchased at the hotel, and then be told at the hotel that these can only be purchased at the railway station. In my experience, one could only get to places, traveling as an individual, by constantly arguing with the petty bureaucracy, by complaining and yelling at the irrationality of it all. I remember as well my trip to Moscow in 1978 with Intourist. The driver sent to the airport to pick me up made me wait for a long time, while he carried on a casual conversation with someone else. Neither country's service personnel appear eager to please the customer. On one occasion, I was pushed to one side by a Chinese airline stewardess who wanted to have the Caucasians behind me go up first into the aircraft. On another occasion, when the China Travel Service personnel were unusually uncooperative, even my normally calm brother Frank was feeling frustrated. He had traveled even more extensively in the Soviet Union, and exclaimed: "This is just like in the Soviet Union." The woman working there was not happy with that description. "No, it is not," she said. "But it is," said Frank, "I have been there too." And so the argument went on for a short time, while we hoped that something might dawn upon the bureaucrats.

The events of May and June 1989 were all the more impressive because they lifted a curtain from repressed Chinese emotions. The hunger strike galvanized popular support for the students, who received daily supplies of food and drink from the Beijing populace. Also heartwarming were the efforts of the people to keep away the military, to reason with individual soldiers. Here we see *renqing wei* at its best, directed not just toward one's family members or friends but to the peaceful demonstrators. The city of Beijing acted as a big family, as it gave, each according to ability, to those in need.

Chinese Communism was a beacon of hope to many people in 1949. With time, it turned into a despotism. Mao Zedong lost the intellectuals during the Anti-rightist campaign. He lost the peasants when he communized the land that he had earlier distributed to them. He further lost the workers during the Great Leap Forward, which had set ridiculous work targets. The ideals of communism were betrayed in practice in China, as elsewhere. After June 1989, we have unabated Stalinism allied with Oriental despotism. That is Chinese Communism today.

Have There Been Benefits?

What have been the benefits of the Communist Revolution? In the previous chapter we mentioned political independence and unification, as well as a sense of self-respect in the family of nations. There have also been material benefits to those dispossessed persons, whether in the cities or in the countryside, who have experienced a "turnover" (*Fanshen*), who are no longer in daily fear of starvation and despised for their poverty or lowliness. It should be noted that these benefits all refer to "collective liberation" of one sort or another, rather than to the liberation of the individual.

William Hinton, a social scientist and for years a constant friend of the People's Republic, published a famous book under the title *Fanshen*. In it, he uses the term to explain the success of the Communist party in the countryside:

> Every revolution creates new words. The Chinese Revolution created a whole new vocabulary. A most important word in this vocabulary was *fanshen*. It means "to turn the body," or "to turn over." To China's hundreds of millions of landless and land-poor peasants it meant to stand up, to throw off the landlord yoke, to gain land, stock, implements, and houses. But it meant much more than this. It meant to throw off superstition and study science, . . . to learn to read, to cease considering women as chattels. . . . It meant to enter a new world.[16]

Indeed, there is a whole class of people, those who were oppressed and downtrodden under the old regime, who have gained self-respect and a decent livelihood under the Communists. Under Mao Zedong especially, a new class structure had replaced the old one of pre-Communist China. Those who were the poorest became the most trusted of the new regime. Those who belonged to the bourgeois classes, or had ties to the Nationalist government, became the new social outcasts. The problem was that Mao did not secure to the landless peasants the redistributed land. He moved quickly to collectivization and communization, thus jeopardizing the gains of the landless peasants. Under Deng Xiaoping, the situation was once more ameliorated with the dismantling of the commune system. The peasants have him to thank, even if the implementation of a continually changing official policy has continued to harass those who work the land. And the number of unemployed in the countryside is in the millions.

It appears that the situation in China has been more volatile in the cities than in the countryside. Following the crackdown, the regime has placed severe constraints on those *getihu* ("individual households") who work on their own rather than for a collectivity. This was a punitive measure, since many such entities had assisted the democracy movement. But it is not known how the people involved should continue to live, were they to be deprived of their means of livelihood. Another big question is: Will the rural policy also undergo serious change?

I have brought up this question, while discussing the benefits of the

Revolution, because it has been reported (September 1989) that William Hinton, who had been living in China for some time, decided to leave the country after the crackdown. Reports say that he too had been unhappy with recent developments. So has Edgar Snow's widow, Helen Snow, who has said that she is in mourning after the crackdown, as though someone in the family has just died. The present regime has lost some of its firmest friends.[17]

Indeed, "liberation" (*jiefang*) itself is an ambiguous term, since one may be liberated from one kind of bondage only to be submitted to another one. "Collective liberation" especially is an ambiguous benefit, since it does not necessarily entail the liberation of the individual within the collectivity. As we shall see in chapter 5, the Chinese people had wanted *both* collective liberation from the dominance of Western and Japanese imperialism as well as individual liberation from the dominance of the collectivity called the Confucian family and society. The liberation represented by Chinese Communism has so far substituted a new bondage for the old one, replacing the family and society with the state, the party, and the party leader, for everyone's absolute loyalty. Everyone is now being treated as a minor, subordinate to the bureaucratic apparatus called the party government, to the surveillance of the secret police, and to the personal dictatorship of the leader.

"Oriental Despotism"—of the Worst Kind

It has always been recognized as ironic that the communist states, whether in Europe or East Asia, should have produced such huge bureaucracies and so many laws and decrees governing every aspect of people's lives. Has Marx not spoken of the "withering away of the state" as the final goal of socialism? This is, of course, known to the Chinese people. In taking over power in China, Mao Zedong advocated the "people's democratic dictatorship" as the best form of government for the country. He answered questions about the ultimate Marxist dream:

"Don't you want to abolish state power?" Yes, we do, but not right now; we cannot do it yet. Why? Because imperialism still exists, because domestic reaction still exists, because classes still exist in our country. . . .

The state apparatus, including the army, the police, and the courts, is the instrument by which one class oppresses another. It . . . is violence and not "benevolence."

"You are not benevolent." Quite so. We definitely do not apply a policy of benevolence to the reactionaries.[18]

Mao knew he was no benevolent dictator. He stood, rather, in the tradition of Oriental despotism, with the difference that his despotism represents *total* power, to the extent that this is possible for any one individual to exercise. He had his real or imagined political enemies, but he had no institutional constraints on his power. The Oriental despotism that Communists have inherited has been expanded and transformed into a totalitarianism that uses the party as an instrument to oversee and control every aspect of the citizen's life. George Orwell's *Animal Farm* (1945), which uses Stalinist Russia as a model, also tells us much about Communist China.

Here, we are touching upon *the* basic problem with so-called Oriental despotism. In his classic work, *Oriental Despotism: A Comparative Study of Total Power* (1957), Wittfogel puts forward his thesis that the needs of an ancient hydraulic society for organization and bureaucracy set China on the road to Oriental despotism. I do not wish to pass judgment on the controversial thesis, but I find his description of total power very relevant today. Under the chapter title "Despotic Power—Total and Not Benevolent" Wittfogel examines the absence of effective checks on the exercise of such power, whether in the written constitution or in the society at large. He also develops the concept of a "beggars' democracy," stating that total power does not necessarily imply that the state succeeds in asserting its authority in everything.

> In modern totalitarian states the inmates of concentration and forced labor camps are permitted at times to gather in groups and talk at will; and not infrequently certain among them are given minor supervisory jobs. In terms of the law of diminishing administrative returns such "freedoms" pay well. While saving personnel, they in no way threaten the power of the commandant and his guards. The villages, guilds, and secondary religious organizations of agro-managerial society were no terror camps. But like them they enjoyed certain politically irrelevant freedoms. These freedoms—which in some instances were considerable—did not result in full autonomy. At best they established a kind of Beggars' Democracy.[19]

Until very recently, Western as well as expatriate scholars of traditional China sought to see the best in the tradition itself. Many objected to the philosopher Hegel's assertion that only one man in China was free—the emperor. Recent events have provided a shock impetus for a careful reevaluation of history. In my opinion, Chinese history has been moving toward *more* rather than less concentration of power in the hands of the few. For example, the Song dynasty (960–1279) exercised more centralized power than the Tang (618–907), the Ming dynasty (1368–1644) was more despotic than the Song, while the Qing (1644–1911) also surpassed the Ming in this respect. In our own times, the Communists have exceeded the Nationalists in replacing an authoritarian government with a totalitarian one, supported, as this is, with all the experience of the Soviet model and all the military technology of the twentieth century. To compare today's despotism with that of the past, Wittfogel gives the example of how today's state intrudes upon family life to secure its own purposes:

> The traditional Chinese family, whose head enjoyed a particularly distinguished position legally, was not forced by political and police pressure to set one family member against another, as is the case in modern apparatus states.[20]

In the days just following the military crackdown of June 1989, the Chinese government paraded on television a student activist who had been "surrendered" to the state by his own sister and brother-in-law. Later reports (September 1989) indicated, however, that the sister had not done so voluntarily and is suffering internally from a guilt complex and externally from social opprobrium, even if that is not publicly articulated.

Chinese intellectuals appear preoccupied with the problem of despotism to the extent that they almost overlook its existence in other parts of the world, whether that be the Islamic Middle East or countries in Eastern Europe. Wittfogel had this to say in 1970 about social revolution in China:

> Marx found that the atomisation in Asiatic society left man no choice but to vegetate. As a young man, he had already postulated that despotism forces man to live in a political "animal kingdom." The implications of these ideas are frighteningly meaningful. As a retrogressive social revolution that moves toward the *total* alienation of man, the Chinese Communist revolution is catching up with, and indeed surpassing, the retrogressive social revolution that is occurring in the Soviet Union and in other parts of the "socialist" Communist world.[21]

The years 1978 to 1988 appear now in retrospect to have been a hiatus, a pause between the much condemned Cultural Revolution of the past and the regime of terror of the present. Even if some scholars had discoursed on the "irreversibility of change" in the People's Republic, the facts seem to show otherwise. And the reason is clear: the Chinese leadership resists the modernization of politics.

True, things could have been different. Had Zhao Ziyang's side won in the recent power struggle at the top, democratization might have set in. However, the fact that it takes someone at the top to initiate this process is itself proof that the system resembles a pyramid—with one man at the top, whose word is command for all. This, however, is parallel to the situation in Eastern Europe. If popular protests are reaping political benefits in Poland, Hungary, East Germany, Czechoslovakia, Bulgaria, and Romania the people in these countries have Gorbachev to thank.

The Lost Opportunity?

In evaluating China's recent past, many people agree that the best years were the decade of 1978 to 1988, which witnessed reforms and an increasingly frank discussion about Marxism itself. I regard these years as presenting a last chance for Chinese Communism to redeem itself after having made numerous mistakes that had so shaken its credibility.

In fact, following at once upon the fall of the Gang of Four in 1977, the country's educated people were immersed in discussions regarding what "truth" is. At the beginning, the followers of Hua Guofeng insisted on an unswerving loyalty to the deceased Chairman Mao Zedong's policies and directives. The followers of Deng Xiaoping proposed something different. Having witnessed Mao's many mistakes and the obstacles that insistence on his "infallibility" would pose to the path of modernization, Deng Xiaoping and his followers preferred the formula "practice is the only norm for the test of truth." In asserting this, they also referred to Mao's example. As Deng put it in 1977:

> Let us reflect on this, comrades: to take practice as the point of departure for everything, to unite theory and practice—is this not the basis of Mao Zedong thought? Is this basis now out of date, can it ever become out of date? Should we oppose practice as the point of departure and the union of theory and pactice, how can we even speak of Marxism and Mao Zedong Thought?[22]

In supporting Deng's stand, Hu Yaobang spoke of how he had personally been disillusioned by mistakes made by incorrect party lines. He criticized blind obedience, urging the need to continually learn from practice, discussions, and dialogues with the masses.[23]

The problem, however, is: What about Marxism itself? Does it not remain the norm for the test of truth? One answer is that only practice can test truth—including what true Marxism is.

These discussions came to a head in late 1978, when Deng Xiaoping affirmed the importance of liberating thought:

If a Party, a country, a nation should . . . be rigid in its thinking and permit superstitions to prevail, it would be impeded in its progress and lose its life and creativity. Only by liberating thought and by insisting on finding truth in practice, can we carry out smoothly our socialist modernization.[24]

In the decade 1978 to 1988, Chinese intellectuals boldly extended the "liberated" area of political discussions. They returned to the origins of Marx's thought. They rediscovered the young Marx, the humanist. Su Shaozhi, a Marxist theoretician, speaks of learning socialism and Marxism all over again, rather than blindly accepting what has come to China from the Soviet Union:

People of our age learned what "came to us" from the Soviet Union or what we "have taken" from it. . . . Actually, it should be called Stalinist Marxism, or just Stalinism.[25]

Claiming that Marxism is born of practice, Su insists on the primacy of freedom in Marxist thought:

Human liberation includes the liberation of labor and political liberation. . . . Liberation means liberating the human being from all alienation. This is the ultimate goal of Marxism. But we often regarded political power as the ultimate goal and the establishment of proletarian dictatorship as the final goal. Actually, all this should only be the means for liberating the human being.[26]

According to him and others, the survival of Marxism requires a brave grappling of the past and the future.

If the Soviet Union has [problems with] social stagnation and political and economic crises, it is because a state that contols and determines everything is led by a party that controls and determines everything . . . and a Stalin who controls and determines everything.[27]

For Su Shaozhi, Yu Haocheng, and many others, the future of economic modernization cannot be separated from the implementation of political democratization. They accepted the insistence on a Marxist vantage point and methodology, but not particular Marxist ideas. They called for more rationalization in the reform of political structures, in permitting a free press and democratic elections.

Once more, in light of China's crackdown on dissent and the political protests in East European countries, we cannot but reach this conclusion: that the common malaise in East and West is due to the common political structure, the despotic regime that goes by the name of the "dictatorship of the proletariat." The Chinese embarked on a path of economic change and openness to the outside world. They actually started *perestroika* and *glasnost* before the Soviet Union, and they were beginning to reap some benefits from this policy, while experiencing as well some problems. The Chinese intellectuals, especially the party members among them, could have been the best friends and allies of the government. Had the leadership heeded their voices for more reform, the party itself could have earned new respect and credibility.

Unfortunately, Deng had seriously compromised himself by his suppression of the 1978 Xidan democracy movement, an action that in retrospect serves as a beginning of the end to the "liberation of thought." Deng has shown the world that "truth" means, to him, what serves the interests of his power. And "practice" has shown him that the liberation of thought is dangerous to his power. In 1989, the guns of Beijing silenced the voices for reform. But they have thereby compromised the future of Communism in China as well. With the end to the liberation of thought, however, has come as well the end to hope: the hope that a reform under the banners of Marxism may yet preserve some role for the Communist party in China's future.

It should therefore be no surprise to us that many of the intellectuals who had joined in such discussions regarding the truth of Marxism have been, since the events of June 1989, either under arrest or in exile.

They are now regarded as enemies of the government that had initially encouraged freedom of discussion.

Is Despotism China's Destiny?

True, freedom and democracy are both Western concepts, unknown to the people of China (and of Korea and Japan) before the twentieth century. True, the Confucian tradition, especially in Mencius, advocates that the ruler give first priority to the people rather than to himself. But this is not democracy, only "benevolent government." The dissident Liu Xiaobo and others in China are correct to assert that even if Confucian ideals are reached, there will only be a benevolent despotism, not a democracy.[28] However, I disagree with him and with others who tend to blame all the evils of the recent past on a now moribund Confucian order. Confucianism did not know of freedom and democracy, but Confucianism is also opposed to repression and tyranny. John Locke and Jean-Jacques Rousseau were Western thinkers, but they both spoke from experience when they discoursed on the natural liberty of human beings, and the need of popular consent for a government to rule effectively. In that sense, even their ideas echo in part the Confucian concept of benevolent government (*renzheng*). Besides, modern Chinese intellectuals, including especially those who were Communist sympathizers before 1949, and others who grew up under the Communist regime, have all read the writings of such persons as Li Dazhao, a founder of the party, and Karl Marx himself. They know that Marxism began as a philosophy championing human liberty, especially those of the have-nots.

One does not have to be educated in the liberal West to desire liberty. One knows that liberty is desirable, especially if one lives under fear and terror, experiencing the deprivation of liberty. One does not even have to be a Taoist philosopher to recognize that animals in the wild enjoy their freedom, while also having to cope with the uncertainties of life itself. Human rights and democratic government may be Western ideas, but human beings everywhere have a natural right to personal freedom as well as to freedom from tyranny, to human dignity and self-respect, and to an adequate measure of self-determination. Communist governments have sought to manipulate these feelings by promulgating constitutions that enshrine some of these values when in fact they have served themselves badly by not adhering to their own enshrined values.

But then, is despotism China's destiny, as many seem to fear? Could it be overturned by a strong democracy movement?

Could the student demonstrations alone have brought about democratization? Obviously not. In the context of Communist China, the student movement could only succeed if the party leadership had agreed to the students' petitions. This was recognized by the dissident Bao Zunxin, also now under arrest. In an interview on May 31, 1989, Bao asserts, nevertheless, that while the movement might be quickly suppressed, and a period of political darkness might ensue, the demonstrations would still have sown the seeds for a future movement. In his words:

> The biggest advantage in this movement is that it has exposed what the Communist party has called its insistence on tradition. This tradition is despotism and dictatorship. It has been completely unveiled. All the disguises of the past have been torn up.[29]

To speak here of exposing the truth about communism is more than to name it a despotism, to affirm the belief of Marx in the inability of China to produce a true social revolution, and to confirm the prediction of Lenin that the failure of such a social revolution would spell the return of Oriental despotism. It is also to say that Chinese Communism today has abandoned all its ideals, including those of bettering the people's livelihood. It is basically to say that today's rulers are concerned only with their own power and interests.

But what about the people? Are the people really unable to ever adapt to new life in new times, and to take their destiny into their own hands? In gloomier moods, the Chinese dissident intellectuals seem to say this. But of course, their actions and their sacrifices belie such a belief.

> There is no inherent reason why Chinese civilization should not effectively adapt to modern life. . . . Indeed it is clear that in Asia the peoples who were most influenced by the basic qualities of traditional China have been the leaders in successful modernization. . . . China's tragedy has been that none of its rulers, from the last of the Ch'ing through Mao Tse-tung, has been able to give the nation's very talented people the kind of government that could maximize their great capacities.[30]

These words were said eighteen years ago. They are still true today. China's Communist regime has been harsher than those of Eastern Europe, in some ways harsher even than that of Stalin himself. But we cannot blame all this on a legacy of Oriental despotism alone. We have to take into account the evil fruits of a marriage of convenience: that of Communism *and* Oriental despotism.

■

CHAPTER 5

Student Protests in Modern Chinese History

Student protests as we call them were not known in the old days, but students from the schools did things like kneeling at the palace gates to present their petitions, refusing as a group to sit for examinations, and dispersing to their homes, which was analogous to what is today known as student protest.
— LIU YIZHENG, 1925

I remember a conversation with a young Japanese scholar who had spent some years as a student in Beijing. "The Chinese students and intellectuals have such a sense of mission regarding their country and its politics," he said. "There is no such parallel in Japan."[1]

My immediate reaction was that there is no parallel in Japan, because the Japanese have a high overall level of education. In China, where 30 percent of the one-billion population is still illiterate, the educated continue to regard themselves as the conscience of the nation, the mouthpiece of the people. In this, they also follow an age-old tradition, to consider "the affairs of the world as their own responsibility."

I should explain here that the word "intellectual" is not an adequate translation for the Chinese term *zhishi fenzi* (literally, people with knowledge), which has a wider application, referring basically to "informed persons," or "the educated"—the equivalent of the professionals in non-Communist societies, including leaders in educational and literary circles and university students. They constitute an elite with a history of political consciousness and social responsibility, nurtured by the tradition called Confucianism. Their numbers are not so large, but their influence extends further. Their ancient models are Confucius and Mencius, each of whom wanted public office to serve the people. As a group, they have a strong sense of mission toward the country and the society, combined with an awareness of the difficulties inherent in such a mission. Throughout history, China's educated have been aroused by these words of Mencius:

> When Heaven is about to confer a great office on anyone, it first exercises his mind with suffering, his sinews and bones with toil. It exposes his body to hunger, subjects him to extreme poverty, and confounds his undertakings. By such methods, it stimulates his mind, hardens his nature, and makes good for his incompetences.[2]

An article by Liu Yizheng, published in *Xueheng*,[3] was written at the time of the May Thirtieth Incident of 1925 in Shanghai's international settlement, when police under British orders opened fire on three thousand students and workers protesting certain inequities and mistreatment by both their Japanese employers and the British police. Eleven Chinese were killed, dozens were wounded, and dozens of others arrested, all of which in turn provoked nationwide protests, strikes and boycotts. Disorder continued until the British officers involved were dismissed and the victims were given compensation. This incident contributed very much to anti-imperialist sentiments in China at the time, although the violence involved pales by comparison to what the Communist "liberators" have done to their own people during a period of forty years.

The reference to tradition in that article was to past precedents that go back to nearly two thousand years ago, to the Han dynasty, as well as nearly one thousand years ago, in the Song dynasty. In the first instance (A.D. 2nd century), a greatly expanded imperial college (*taixue*)—an institution that had as its aim the training of future bureaucrats—had an enrollment of 30,000 students, who were understandably concerned about their future career possibilities at an uncertain period of history and were given to mass protests and demonstrations. In the second instance, the Song dynasty, the number of students at the imperial college was much smaller, and the issues had to do with curricular matters, the examination system, and politics—at a time when the country was much pressed by outside invaders. On several occasions, both as individuals and as a group, the Song students had presented petitions to the court. The best-known occurrence was in February 1126, when a group of several hundred students under their leader Chen Dong knelt before the palace gate in Hangzhou to protest against "evil ministers" as well as to petition for the restoration to office of Li Gang, a much-loved general. They were joined by a crowd, possibly tens of thousands of sympathizers who rioted on the sight of soldiers and caused the death of a dozen or more eunuchs. The government proceeded to reinstate the general, debated the question of punishing the students for causing the riot, but decided in favor of a pardon, since it judged that the students' motives were "loyal and righteous." Later, under a different emperor, the same Chen Dong was executed after making further petitions. His last words were "If I were afraid of dying, I would not have dared speak out."

Perhaps history would have known more and greater student activism had the imperial college always been important to the education and training of future bureaucrats. But most dynasties preferred to make use of the civil service examinations, with candidates coming from local and provincial schools, to a strong imperial college at the capital whose students were exempt from civil service examinations.

I am not seeking so much to claim continuity between student protests in imperial China, whether of two thousand or of one thousand years ago, and those of the twentieth century, as to discern parallels between the past and the present. I believe also that the most recent student demonstrations draw their inspiration especially from the May Fourth Movement of 1919, which offered a model for subsequent student action. There are, besides, other lessons to be learned from history, not the least of which is the fact that, unknown to the outside world, students have protested time and again under Communist rule, and have met with suppression each time. Nevertheless, the scope of the protests has only grown in the course of the decades, so that we may say with some confidence, that the worse the oppression, the stronger will be the revived protests.

While we are mainly dealing with students here, we shall also include in our discussions the role of the broader educated class, or the "intellectuals," who have served as informal mentors and devoted collaborators. For the Communist dictatorship, China's educated have been a necessary evil and a source of trouble. While some of them have joined the ranks of the regime's faithful "echoes," many have kept their independence of mind and spirit, and have suffered various types of brainwashing and class struggles. Ironically, it was this very circle that gave birth to the Communist party and nourished it in its infancy. I am now referring to the broad intellectual circle of teachers, students, and their sympathizers whose combined strength gave rise to the May Fourth Movement, a watershed in modern Chinese history.

It is useful to say a few words here about the status of education in modern China. The world knows of the fervor for education of the Chinese outside the mainland, whether in Hong Kong, Taiwan, or overseas. Such a zeal is rooted in the Confucian tradition. But even before the fall of the Manchu dynasty in 1911, the civil service examinations had been abolished and Western-style higher education had been introduced. In the years that followed, the country developed its fledgling university system, including over a dozen tertiary institutions set up by Christian missionaries. Under the Communist government, all universities became state-controlled, and an effort was made in the fifties to model higher education after the Soviet style, with certain institutions concentrating on science and technology and others on the social sciences, and including on every level (primary and secondary schools as well as tertiary education) political indoctrination. All this ideological control is remarkable, especially when we turn to an examination of the May Fourth Movement, and hear some of its original demands for intellectual openness and pluralism.[4]

The "Original" Student Protest: The May Fourth Movement (1919)

The date of May 4, 1919, is very special to modern Chinese students and intellectuals. It is the date of the student protests that began in Beijing and spread to other cities and to other social sectors, and that initiated labor unrest and sent shock waves to the rulers of the time — the warlords of China.

The May Fourth Movement of 1919 occurred at a time when China was divided among warlords and threatened by Western and Japanese imperialists. It began with a demonstration in Beijing by five thousand students from thirteen colleges and universities. They were protesting the agreement, made at the peace treaty of Versailles following the First World War, to transfer Shandong from German to Japanese hands. China had worked on the side of the Allies during the war, but found itself impotent at the hand of the Great Powers, as the warlord government needed Japanese acquiescence for its own survival. The students took up the cause and protested against the pending transfer of Chinese land from one colonial power to another. The demonstrations turned violent when students broke into the house of the foreign minister and beat up a houseguest, another minister. Protests and strikes ensued all over the country, pressuring the Chinese delegation at Versailles to reject the treaty — although the humiliating transfer took place anyway.

While thirty-two students were arrested at the time, the movement led to the founding of student unions for both university and middle schools in Beijing and elsewhere, the founding as well of teachers' unions, and student strikes in more than two hundred cities. After the mass arrest in Beijing of 1,150 students (June 3), workers and merchants went on strike in many cities to signal their support.

What happened on May 4 that year served as a catalyst for a new sociopolitical consciousness, a new sense of nationalism objecting to foreign imperialism as well as domestic corruption and warlord opportunism. A national desire for modernization, for individual freedom, intellectual pluralism and national independence came to the fore. Students cried slogans asking for "Mr. Science" and "Mr. Democracy" (personifications of their objectives) and protesting a fossilized social order without individual freedom represented by the establishment called "Confucius & Sons." In its wake came a literary renaissance spearheading the use of the vernacular in literature, as well as the founding by a group of intellectuals in Shanghai of the Chinese Communist Party (1921).

The popular demands of the May Fourth period have been well summarized by Chen Duxiu, one of the movement's leaders who subsequently helped found the Communist party only to leave it in later life:

> To oppose the aggression of the Japanese imperialists and the [Chinese] traitors.
>
> To oppose the bondage of the old ethics and promote the emancipation of thought and women in order to wipe out the remnants of feudalism.
>
> To promote science, the destruction of superstition, and the construction of industry.
>
> To oppose the classical literature and promote the vernacular as a means of educational and cultural popularization.
>
> To promote the people's rights and oppose bureaucracy.[5]

Until rather recently, the May Fourth Movement had been eulogized by Communist scholars on the mainland and ignored by the government in Taiwan. Mention of it was absent for a long time from Taiwan textbooks, because of its association with the origins of the Communist party. At the time of its occurrence, the students' iconoclasm regarding the Chinese tradition had also alienated many intellectuals attached to traditional culture. But the road traveled by some of the best known among them—many were professors at the University of Beijing—was a clear one. They moved from an initial interest in Western Europe and the United States, in science and democracy, and a desire for intellectual pluralism to a single-minded commitment to Marxist values. The reasons were political as well as psychological: disillusionment with Western imperialism, and inspiration received from the successful Communist overthrow of Czarist Russia. At the time of crisis, when the survival of the nation was in the balance, they chose ideology over freedom. The choice was momentous.

The May Fourth Movement itself unleashed a nationalism that continued to manifest itself in numerous student protests and workers' strikes, including the May Thirtieth Incident of 1925. Students demonstrated many times under the warlords and while the country was facing the Japanese threat. In December 1935, student demonstrations in Beijing (then called Peiping) met with clubs and water hoses ordered by Chiang Kai-shek's government, but the casualties were generally low (by comparison with what happened after 1949), even according to Communist reports. A total war between China and Japan soon became inevitable, and this broke out officially at the Marco Polo Bridge outside Beijing in 1937. Many patriotic students and intellectuals joined the Communist guerrillas or the underground under Japanese occupation in northern and southeastern China (1937–45), when the Nationalists moved their capital to Chongqing (Sichuan) after the Communists had made their "Long March" to Yan'an (Shaanxi).

"The Storm in the Universities" (1957)

The Chinese Communist Party began in 1921 initially as a party of intellectuals started by university professors, but became successful under Mao Zedong, a normal school graduate, as a party of peasants supporting a guerrilla-based revolution. After consolidating its mass base, the party never demonstrated very much confidence in students and intellectuals. There had already been rectification campaigns during the Yan'an days. From its very beginning, the new government in Beijing (1949) worked hard to stifle dissent and demolish all possible opposition to its rule. Campaigns for "thought reform" were already instigated in these early years (1951–52). Their first victims were university professors, their later victims were middle and elementary school teachers as well as students, writers, and artists. Confessions and self-criticisms were extorted from all these people, on the ground of helping to transform their political behavior. As was the custom, one brainwashing campaign was barely terminated before another one began. In more recent years, the question has arisen as to why Communist China has not produced a single Nobel laureate for the arts and letters or even science, although American citizens of Chinese origin are among those who have won the award. Students and professors have given the numerous political campaigns, as well as other constraints on their time and energy, as the principal reasons. It seems that politics has been hampering a nation that, without doubt, includes much hidden talent.

The next blow was struck by Mao himself. A restless man, curious about his own degree of acceptance by his people, especially by the intellectuals among them, he first cowed them into silence during the "rectification" campaigns and then decided to test them with the "Hundred Flowers" movement (February 1957). The reference here is to the slogan "Let a hundred flowers bloom, let a hundred schools contend," meaning, let a diversity of opinion be voiced, about Mao and his rule. It was officially launched as an invitation by the Communist party to invite non-Communists, especially intellectuals, to offer criticisms. I am told that many people were initially reluctant to criticize the party and its leader, but were urged to do so by party functionaries. Perhaps Mao had hoped to hear happy voices. He received instead a torrent of criticism, first mildly proffered, and then presented forthright. These ranged over a spectrum of issues. The party was said to lack a proper governing apparatus; the National People's Congress was not being taken seriously, even by party members, since decisions were generally reached first inside the party, with the standing committee of the congress serving as a rubber stamp. The criminal and civil codes, the police regulations, had not till then been enacted. Food and other commodities were in short supply, although party cadres were living well. And the question was posed as to whether it had been necessary to punish landlords and other groups with such indiscriminate vengeance and brutality.

The fifties are considered in retrospect to be the golden age of Communist rule in China. Looking back from the eighties, that earlier age is now regarded as a period of stability and of constructive activity. But the Chinese Communist Party was no longer a party of intellectuals. Since Mao took over the reins, it had slowly become a party of the backwaters, of the semiliterate. He was able to seize China with these cadres; he sought also to govern with their assistance, without utilizing the talents of those from the newly won urban centers. Already then, the party was being criticized for not properly putting to use the skills of the educated class:

> There are students of philosophy who work on the compilation of catalogues in libraries . . . , students of dye chemistry who teach languages . . . , students of mechanical engineering who teach history. . . . There are also returned students from Britain who earn their living as cart-pullers and returned students from the United States who run cigarette stalls. . . .

> [Primary school teachers] are required . . . in some places to do odd jobs . . . , to drill wells and build dykes . . . , to dry grain and to keep watch on granaries.[6]

Moreover, it was said:

> We have applied to intellectuals methods of punishment which peasants would not apply to landlords and workers would not apply to capitalists. During the social reform campaigns, . . . intellectuals . . . chose to die by jumping from tall buildings, drowning in rivers, swallowing poison, cutting their throats. . . . Comparing our method of massacre to Auschwitz, the latter appeared more clumsy and childish . . . but more prompt and benevolent.[7]

While their teachers were speaking out, students were not exactly keeping silent. In May and June 1957, the country witnessed what it called "the storm in the universities," beginning at Beijing but spreading elsewhere, as thousands of university students on different campuses in many cities, followed later by middle school students, joined the "blossoming and contending" of opinions and ideas and even took to the streets with rallies and demonstrations. They complained about incompetent administration, low allowances, slander in the press, and asked for more freedom and democracy. The sociologist Fei Xiaotung is later quoted as having said:

> The students are looking for leaders everywhere. If teachers join in, there will be a bigger trouble. Of course it is easy to put it down. Three million soldiers will put it down but public support would evaporate and the Party's prestige among the masses would be finished.[8]

Perhaps Mao himself would agree with the following assessment of the Hundred Flowers: "It was not thought that the Party could have committed so many mistakes. The problems brought to light have far exceeded the estimate, and really the 'task has been over-fulfilled.'"[9]

Most probably, the Hundred Flowers movement was not a government trick to smoke out the opposition. But the government did become alarmed about the sentiments of opposition it heard, and it was mindful of the Hungarian uprising of 1956. Mao and his followers decided on another repression: The Anti-rightist campaign. A principal organizer of this campaign was Deng Xiaoping. That summer, the standing committee of the National People's Congress postponed its meeting, first from June 3 to June 20, then to June 26. Those people who had poured out grievances were subjected to denunciations. Some student leaders were sentenced to forced labor, and three students from a Wuhan middle school were condemned to death and executed for leading a riot. Those among party officials who had sympathized with the "rightists" were dismissed from their positions and expelled from the party. Writers and artists advocating more freedom were also punished, as the hope that China might proceed on the path of intellectual freedom and popular democracy vanished.

While purging intellectuals, the Communist authorities encouraged them to "give over their hearts" to the party, to be honest and forthright in examining their consciences and ackowledging their mistakes and faults. The party promised pardon, so that people could start with a clean slate. Many believed in this promise and unburdened themselves in making confession after confession. But alas, all this material was recorded, and included in people's "dossiers." Every adult has a political dossier in China, and life is often conditioned according to this dossier and the interpretation given to it.

A tragedy for students and intellectuals, the Anti-rightist campaign was also a lesson that they apparently never took to heart, if we are to judge from the Tian'anmen crackdown. Because of the even greater mistake of the Cultural Revolution, the Anti-rightist campaign has often been forgotten. But it still stands as a landmark of Mao's mistakes as a dictator, mistakes for which the people and the country had to pay a price.

Students as Ultra-Leftists: The Red Guards (1966–68)

The period of the late sixties saw worldwide student protests, in Paris, New York, Berkeley (California), and Tokyo. The European rebels, the Berkeley hippies, and the Red Guards were all desirous of changing an imperfect world—a reason why the Red Guards, who had a head start, initially aroused so much admiration outside China.

But there are both similarities and differences. If all were to a large extent young and naive, the Red Guards were basically tools in the hands of a political struggle. Having grown up in a simplistic and idealistic atmosphere, these young Chinese hardly knew what the feudalism and capitalism they were so eager to demolish were. While acting lawlessly and creating social havoc, they sincerely believed they were obeying the commands of Mao from on high. Their collective experience deeply scarred their generation as well as the country itself. Their Western counterparts, on the other hand, were opposed to all authority. At the Sorbonne in Paris, the slogan was "Il est interdit d'interdire" (It is forbidden to forbid anything).

An important difference is the Chinese sense of patriotism: to save

China. Since the May Fourth Movement, China's students had been in the vanguard of political and cultural reforms. They attempted to demonstrate their strength and articulate their ideas during the 1957 "storm in the universities," and had been suppressed by the party. However, in the years that followed, Mao Zedong felt himself increasingly alienated from his own party, because of criticisms of the Great Leap Forward. He was looking for allies from outside the party apparatus. At that time, his chief enemies were Peng Zhen, mayor of Beijing; Liu Shaoqi, chairman of the the People's Republic; and Lo Ruiqing, chief of staff of the Army. With the support of Lin Biao, the defense chief, he was successful in first purging Peng Zhen (summer of 1966). But he was concerned about a move against Liu Shaoqi, who was, after all, head of state, with wide support in the bureaucracy and the armed forces.

Mao decided to look for support from two sources: the military and the students. He thought of turning to the students as to a tool, mainly to supplement the military, because he was not certain of the extent of his support in the entire army. This was how the Red Guards movement got started. Students, first from universities, and then also from secondary schools, were told that "it makes sense to rebel"–against the country's bureaucracy. They were given the task from Mao himself to strike against his own political enemies in the party. "Bomb the Headquarters!" he told them in a wall poster penned by himself (August 5, 1966) that was later carried as an editorial by the *People's Daily*. Inexperienced and naive, the young people responded enthusiastically in the beginning, regarding themselves as youthful revolutionaries, a shock force with the mandate to carry Mao's movement from the capital to the provinces.

It was a messy war, pitting the party chairman against the chairman of the People's Republic and, ironically, the entire Communist party itself. Dedicated to the elimination of "old thought, old culture, old customs, and old habits," the young people were fanatically committed to Mao's thoughts, and determined to make China safe from allegedly bourgeois influences and revisionist tendencies. Thousands of them marched by Liu Shaoqi's house demanding his resignation from office. Liu was accompanied in his fall by many party stalwarts, including Zhu De, the People's Liberation Army's founding father; Lo Ruiqing, the Army's chief of staff; and Bo Ibo, vice-premier. One by one, party and government officials were paraded in the streets, wearing dunces' caps and carrying boards that announced their alleged crimes.

The young people also served Lin Biao's all-out effort to rebuild Mao's image, tarnished since the mistakes of the Great Leap Forward. It turned into a process of deification, of the rote memorization of his words and the worship of his pictures. Everywhere, Red Guards wrote big-character posters, ransacking private properties and rampaging through the cities. Many got on the trains free of charge and traveled the length and breadth of the country preaching Mao's revolutionary message. With the support of both workers and students, the city of Shanghai even turned itself into a Commune (February 1967), supposedly modeled upon the Paris Commune of 1871. When the people of Shanghai petitioned Chairman Mao to turn the entire country into a commune, their request alarmed Mao, who wondered openly how such a country would be accepted by other nations of the world. He had never dreamed of a country without a head. From then on, he would move away from some of the excesses that he himself had unleashed.

So even Mao found the young difficult to control, and feared their excesses might make the country ungovernable. Once he had achieved his aims of disposing of his personal foes, he turned against the Red Guards and disbanded them. The students' experience of the Cultural Revolution was therefore that of being manipulated, used, and then discarded—by Mao Zedong, their idol.

The ferocity of the Red Guards waned by autumn of 1967, when the group was disbanded. The students were first sent back to school, while the army was given the task of keeping some order. The country, however, remained divided between Mao's supporters and Liu's followers, who continued to resist a total purge. Street fighting and bloodshed occurred in many places, as the country sank into chaos. By autumn of 1968, Mao had decided to send the young people down to the countryside, "to learn from the peasants." Their usefulness to him was over.

It has been said that seventeen million urban youth, willing or not, were sent to live in villages during the years 1967 to 1976. For them, feelings of revolutionary idealism would give way to those of betrayal and political cynicism. Deprived of the possibilities of higher education or better employment, many of these young people eventually made up what has been called "the lost generation."

An interesting case of someone who *was* admitted to tertiary education during those years is that of Zhang Tiesheng (1973). As a young peasant he achieved nationwide fame for allegedly submitting a blank piece of paper for his physics test in university entrance examinations, and, after complaining about the failing grade he received in return, was admitted to the institution of his choice in Liaoning on the basis of his "political" merit. Made into an instant hero, he was sent to Japan to represent China's youth! No wonder teachers were unwilling to give or mark tests afterward.

In the meantime, a reform of the country's education was put into effect. Put briefly, the entire policy of the preceding seventeen years was declared to be mistaken. Revolutionary committees took over the task of administering schools and universities, abolished examinations, shortened the length of schooling on every level, and reduced all theoretical education to the study of Mao's own "Thought." Under their administration, the study of literature would have been eliminated except that the chairman had written some poetry, which students were made to study and memorize. Otherwise, most of their curriculum was replaced by "productive activities." In this way, the new system favored the political "Reds" over the experts. These Reds, selected from worker, peasant, or military background, were enrolled in schools and universities, often without a proper previous education. This practice opened the door to favoritism and nepotism, abuses that still survive today in the bureaucracy.

During the Cultural Revolution, the group that suffered the most were the educated—the more educated were the most humiliated. In the past, during the dynastic cycles, scholars were at the top of the social ladder. Under Communist rule, this changed radically. Branded as "stinking number nine"—that is, the bottom layer of the entire society—many scholars were arrested, sent to "cowsheds" or labor camps, or exiled to the frontier regions. The professional services of teachers were hardly missed, since many schools and universities had been emptied of their students, and resumed function only partially, under military supervision (1970–72). Virtually all academic, scientific, and cultural publications had been suspended since 1966, and what did appear in print had political indoctrination as its content. Here, too, one can imagine the thirst for information that such a situation created, especially for people who could read. Red Guards who ransacked homes frequently kept books they found and read them; people considered themselves fortunate when classical novels were being attacked for their purported political messages, because this gave them opportunity to first read what they would then have to criticize during political sessions.

The Cultural Revolution continued in its course to devour its own children: the ultra-leftists, now judged to be the nuisance. Chen Boda, Mao's personal secretary, was the first to get the ax, and then Lin Biao, the designated heir (1971). It is significant for those times that ultra-leftists could be punished only as "wolves in sheep's clothing," that is, as "ultrarightists," as "bourgeois careerists" and as "counterrevolutionaries."

Dictatorships are frequently amusing because of their reliance on the irrational. There was, for example, the custom of making confessions of one's own mistakes, which was so often done in the fifties. During the Cultural Revolution, such activity grew feverish and created a new demand in society: that of writing "confessions" or "examinations of conscience" for others. Experts rose to the occasion and charged for their services. Signs could be found on streets, saying: five cents for an ordinary confession, RMB 1 for a thoroughgoing confession.

Students as Liberals: The 1980s Protests

In a totalitarian state, the man at the top makes all the important decisions. When Mao's mantle eventually fell upon Deng Xiaoping, a man whom he never really trusted, the Chinese government was given an entirely new direction. Denounced earlier by Maoists as a "capitalist roader," Deng would prove them right. Communist China was to turn into a country Marxist in name only, but remaining Leninist in the structure of its bureaucracy, under the rule of "get rich quick" cadres.

Under tremendous odds, the country picked up the pieces left behind by Mao and the Gang of Four, to start life anew. Educational institutions received a shot in the arm as examinations were reinstated in 1978 and the old curriculum was revived and broadened. As I remember, when China first opened itself to the world in the late seventies, many of the university campuses were literally under army occupation, and many of their administrators were army veterans, frequently without university (even without senior middle school) training. Touring with a high-power education delegation from the United States in 1979, I was amused to find the group entertained by individuals with a ninth-grade education representing the education ministry, the provincial boards of higher education, and the universities. I was also shocked to meet academics still bearing the signs of their sufferings and too reticent to speak to outside guests.

Of course, irreparable damage had been done to the country. An entire generation of young people had suffered grave cultural deprivation, and their losses can never be recovered. I remember meeting many young people working in service positions in the country's hotels and stores who were barely literate. Besides, during the days of turmoil everyone was told that courtesy is a decadent bourgeois vice and a sign of hypocrisy. Words like "thank you" and "please" vanished from the lips of the young of the nation. A civilization that had been characterized by its devotion to ritual and etiquette appeared dead and gone, as were many of its historical monuments, statues and artwork, burned as trash or thrown into the rivers.

The outsider comparing the situation just after the Cultural Revolution with the situation to follow in the ensuing years (1977–89) can find much improvement. After an initial period, during which grievances concerning the Cultural Revolution were publicly aired, Chinese scholars and intellectuals gradually came back into their own. Even postgraduate education was reinstated within the country, as thousands of students were sent overseas for further training. At learned conferences, one noticed the Chinese colleagues becoming once more human, capable of exhanging ideas with one another and with the outside, and increasingly free of political slogans in their publications.

In the name of promoting the Four Modernizations, higher education in China improved appreciably during the eighties, especially when compared with the time of the Cultural Revolution. A more rational and methodical approach was reinstated, with regular classes and examinations. Educational administrators were no longer junior high graduates sent from the People's Liberation Army, as was frequently the case during the Cultural Revolution. Instead, people with proper university training were appointed to such posts, and made serious deliberations on important issues like curricular flexibility, institutional autonomy, and career placement.

Then, over the years, one noted something very wrong. It was the sense of powerlessness, of destitution, and of humiliation. The educated people complained that the government continued to disregard their needs and frustrate their legitimate desires, while returned scholars from overseas found their newly acquired skills often misplaced and misused. At a time when everyone was being urged to "get rich," education on every level remained seriously underfunded. But enrollments were dropping because the young and their families found education useless, perhaps an obstruction, to career advancement. It is widely known that the Shanghai Sheraton attracted several graduate students and a younger lecturer from the prestigious Fudan University as applicants for service staff positions (1986). The students' reason for turning to the hotel: a higher wage. Until the Tian'anmen events, schools were known to rent out spare rooms to local visitors to earn much-needed cash.

An article in the New York Times, written by Fox Butterfield (November 15, 1987), also sounded the alarm. According to his information, the number of high school graduates in China dropped from 7.2 million in 1979 to 1.96 million in 1985, while the number of high schools declined from 192,152 to 93,221. The 1982 census had found that 236 million of the country's one billion people were illiterate or semiliterate. With these problems, China ranks 132 out of 149 nations in spending per capita for education.

The well-known dissident Fang Lizhi is an eloquent critic of the Communists' education policy and their continually shabby treatment of the educated people. He points out that the government's spending on the remuneration of teachers and of other intellectuals in the work force is next to last on the world's scales: just above Cambodia with regard to the renumeration of teachers and other intellectuals in the work force, and just above Haiti with regard to the funding allotted to education. For a country with more than four thousand years of cultural heritage, built upon traditional respect for education, this is quite an indictment.

In 1981, during a lengthy stay in China, I had occasion to meet with some individual students. They were hesitant to speak to an outsider, but once the ice was broken they showed themselves very eager to learn, and were concerned about making up for the lost years. In 1987 I found the situation quite different. Students were no longer afraid to speak to outsiders, but their tales were of frustration. There was no motivation for studying, they said, since job prospects were dismal. It is well known that barbers and peddlers earn more than professors or physicians. Most recently, foreign language teachers coming back from the disturbances in China also report (to their surprise, due to the "studious Chinese" stereotype they had known) the lack of incentive on the part of students they encountered in their teaching experience. One visiting professor reported having told the students of their own future importance in the country. Speaking as she would have to her students back home, her words were: "You will be the agents of change in your society." After class, a woman student came up to her in tears and said: "This will never happen. You don't know the system here. Our country is being ruled by very old men. We can never really matter."

Even more serious is the moral vacuum of the nation. The old morality is gone, having been discarded by the Communists in power. The new morality is nowhere to be seen, as the so-called revolutionary or Communist morality has become a laughing stock. In telling the country that "getting rich is glorious," Deng's regime has encouraged the worst kind of individualism, without freeing society of the fetters of socialism. It has become a situation of "every man for himself," as teachers spend more time earning money outside of classes while physicians also prefer patients who pay more. Like the relationship between the government and the people, human relations in general (the cornerstone of the traditional Confucian order) face the crisis of a loss of trust. The old are uncomfortable with the young, whom they find nihilistic, concerned only with the pleasures of the moment. Despite all this, the journalist Wang Ruoshui was criticized for his defense of humanism, of human values and human dignity, in the monthlong "campaign against spiritual pollution" (1983).

Against this background, we can examine the student protests of the eighties, and appreciate the spirit of sacrifice with which the young people declared their patriotism as well as their love of freedom and democracy. For seven weeks in the spring of 1989, the demonstrators were actually proving their elders wrong, by showing the world that they did have their ideals! And their countrymen responded. Reports say that the city of Beijing took on a special life of its own during the length of the student protests, that people removed their usual masks of rudeness and passivity, and displayed an enormous concern for the students and for one another, increasingly as tension grew and crisis approached. It is as though they had forgotten their individual miseries and joined in a common cause that was greater than themselves. And then, when the tanks were sighted and the soldiers were approaching, nearly the entire population participated in peaceful resistance, only to be confronted with shots and bayonets.

Perhaps it takes a crisis of such proportions to assure us that there is still hope for the country. However, since I have already given an account of the 1989 events, I shall concentrate in this chapter on the monthlong protests between mid-December 1986 and mid-January 1987, which were especially intense in Shanghai, although these spread also to Beijing and elsewhere. The 1989 protests may be regarded as a continuation of the 1986–87 protests, since they both voiced the same demands for freedom and democracy.

The student protests in 1986 to 1987 were heard in twenty-nine cities, involving 150 tertiary institutions. Signs of the unrest were first manifest in Hefei (in the province of Anhui) on the campus of the University of Science and Technology, but reached world headlines when it spread to Shanghai and other major cities. On December 15, 1986, the security police arrested students in Shanghai for taking part in a dance with American visitors. This had followed a performance staged by the foreign guests, and had taken place on their initiative. Complaints about the illegality of arrests without warrants and without cause were met with beatings, so fellow students demanded, through their university authorities, the release of the victims as well as an apology from the police. The mayor, Jiang Zemin (recently made party general secretary), ironically himself a student activist in the 1940s, sought personally to stop students from taking to the streets. But he met with student resistance and the reminder that he lacked a popular mandate, since his position was by appointment from above rather than by election from below! The mood of the students can be inferred from that. In the following days, thousands from different institutions (the numbers reaching 30,000 on December 20–21), took over nearly all the city streets, where they met with applause and food offerings from fellow citizens. To their earlier demands, the students added that of accurate news reporting, since they considered themselves to have been slandered in the official press, which alleged student brutalities against the police!

In the People's Republic, the citizens have "constitutional guarantees" of the freedom of speech, the freedom of assembly, and by extension, the freedom of demonstrating in public. These rights, however, are circumscribed by many police decrees. In 1986 as well as 1989, for example, students were supposed to register their demonstrations before the event. But the authorities made it known that police permission would not be forthcoming. It was under these circumstances that the demonstrations grew and spread to many other cities, including Hangzhou, Wuhan, Kunming, Shenzhen, and even Beijing, while teacher groups also joined their students. Television viewers in the West saw the massive numbers marching peacefully with their hands joined and with banners waving: "The Future Belongs to Us," "We Want to be Human Beings." The marchers also cried pro-democracy and anti-bureaucracy slogans—including calls for freedom of the press.

In January 1987, the central government stepped in with the well-known measures of suppression. Many student leaders suffered arrest; others were dismissed from school. Several leading intellectuals in sympathy with the students were expelled from the Communist party. These persons included the physicist Fang Lizhi, the journalist Liu Binyan, the literary critic Liu Xiaobo, and the writer Wang Ruowang. More serious was the removal from office (through extra-legal means) of the general secretary Hu Yaobang, on the ground of improper handling of student unrest. All these persons, victims of the official "anti-liberalism" campaign, became instant heros in the hearts of the educated classes. But little did people know that the seeds were being sown for another protest movement—which was to exceed in its own scope and in the brutality of the repression it met, any previously known protest. According to the latest figures, the April–May 1989 demonstrations involved students from over six hundred institutions in 84 cities spread through 29 provinces, municipalities, and autonomous regions.[10]

Conclusion

Guo Yitong, a dissident who had suffered imprisonment in Taiwan, is the author, under the pen name Bo Yang, of the controversial book *The Ugly Chinaman* (13th ed., 1987) that took both sides of the Taiwan Strait by storm until it was banned in the mainland. Guo visited the mainland in the late eighties, and was shaken to hear students and others ask him on campuses: How can we save China? How can we modernize the country, and make her free and democratic? The questions were identical to those asked at the time of the May Fourth Movement in 1919. Hearing these questions made him reflect: So China has not moved any nearer to these goals after seventy years.

True, students today have been asking for the same things as their counterparts did seventy years ago. But that is because the original ideals of freedom and democracy have been sacrificed in the name of an ideology—that of Marxism—for the sake of "saving the nation" from imperialism and feudalism. That was why the Communist party was founded. The first generation of party members were men like Chen Duxiu and Li Dazhao who were little accustomed to the ways of power. The second generation included a different breed: men like Mao Zedong and Deng Xiaoping who learned more from Lenin and Stalin than from Marx, and more from the ancient Chinese Legalists than from Confucius. These men never understood science and democracy, but turned ideology into a tool for political control. The rest is familiar history.

True, other governments are known to have used violence to clamp down on dissent and student demonstrations. The best-known instance in Asia is the Kwangju Incident in South Korea (1980), where the number of deaths and casualties was also very high (allegedly at least two hundred deaths), although what transpired in Rangoon, Burma, in autumn 1988, resulted in over two thousand killed. It is also known that the elders in the Chinese government look to authoritarian regimes like the South Korea of the past for their inspiration. But the students of South Korea were armed; their counterparts in Beijing were not. Besides, even South Korea has begun a process of democratization that appears to be irreversible.

The hopes and promises of the May Fourth Movement have never been fulfilled in China. That is why, time and again, students and intellectuals have taken to the streets. And they have to struggle against greater odds than their earlier counterparts. Seventy or eighty years ago, there were one hundred newspapers in Beijing alone, and five hundred in the whole country, enjoying various degrees of liberty. Today, there are only official organs, whether of the central government, or of the local governments, or of the various units within the government bureaucracy. In this, of course, China shows herself to be part of the entire communist world. But repression in China has usually been worse than elsewhere, a reason why intellectuals claim they never produced, even secretly, any works like Pasternak's *Doctor Zhivago* and Solzhenitsyn's *The Gulag Archipelago*, even though there are plenty of parallels to Soviet camp life. The best stories about the Cultural Revolution have been written by expatriates.

There are, however, important factors that distinguish the more recent protests from the May Fourth Movement. Besides the greater magnitude of the most recent protests, the desire for freedom and democracy has taken priority over the motif of a narrow patriotism, even when these are voiced in the name of patriotism. The students and their supporters are now capable of looking beyond mere patriotism; they affirm universal values, especially the protection of human rights and freedoms, as symbolized by a replica Statue of Liberty. To a government that had just removed from Tian'anmen Square the portraits of foreigners like Marx, Engels, Lenin, and Stalin, the Goddess of Democracy had a special message. It is the preference of one set of universal values over another.

The student demonstrations in the last decades sadden us because of the repression that has so far always followed, that appears to take away the few gains in freedom that were previously tolerated. But the truth is not so simple. The demonstrations of 1986–87 and 1989 show a surprising discipline and maturity that have not been seen anywhere else in the world. While students may have erred strategically in prolonging their peaceful occupation of Tian'anmen, they never gave real cause for a crackdown in the name of law and order. Rather, it was the ruthless military that acted lawlessly, and the world knows it.

The struggle for freedom and democracy will be a hard one, all the more because the country is now under a centralized police state, free from foreign interference. Where, for example, can anyone hide from the authorities, who are looking, not only for the body, but also for the soul?

More than a decade ago, Wei Jingsheng had predicted a tough struggle for democracy involving bloodshed. His words have come true:

Will democracy emerge by itself at the end of a natural and necessary evolution? Certainly not. On the way toward democracy, the smallest victory will exact a terrible price; let us have no illusions; democracy will be reached only after bloody sacrifices. . . .

Genuine democracy, the only valid democracy, is nourished with the blood of martyrs and with the blood of tyrants. Every step forward toward democracy must overcome the frantic counterattacks launched by reactionary forces. . . . The Chinese people fear nothing; once they have clearly recognized which orientation they must follow, they will be able to overthrow their tyrants.[11]

This is a cry of patriotism. But even more, it is a cry of the human spirit. Only the next time, give liberty, not death!

■

CHAPTER 6

Is There Religious Freedom in China?

Communists may form an anti-imperialist and anti-feudal united front for political action with certain idealists and even with religious followers, but we can never approve of their religious idealism or religious doctrines.

—MAO ZEDONG, 1940

The role that religion and religious people played in the events of 1989 is still unclear to us. What is known and clear is that religious people in each of the major religions in China joined demonstrations and supported the students. This brings to mind two questions: how important is religion to the Chinese people? and is there religious freedom in China?

Are the Chinese a religious people and is their civilization rooted in religious beliefs? Had they gods, myths, and heroes as did other peoples—Greeks, Hindus, and even Japanese? These are the questions with which I began the first chapter in the book *Christianity and Chinese Religions*, written jointly with Hans Küng (1989). These questions are often answered negatively by China scholars who specialize in one or another aspect of the country's traditional and modern culture. In the past, the image of China in Western scholarship was that of a civilization that entered history full-grown, not having passed through a childhood of dreams and heroic exploits but rather appearing from the very beginning with a humanistic face and rationalistic outlook, as reflected in its classical texts and the persons to whom these were attributed: Confucius, Laozi, and others.

Against this background, it is interesting that Communist Chinese scholarship has assisted us in identifying the presence of religious beliefs and sentiments, as well as the survival of religious communities in mainland China. It has done this in two ways. First, the promotion of archaeological research has shed light on the religion of antiquity, with its mythology, its practices of divination, and its sacrifices. Is not the terracotta army of the First Emperor of China itself evidence of a belief in the afterlife? Have not goddess figures unearthed in western Liaoning in 1979 indicated a mother-goddess cult in a remote past (4,500 or more years ago), while a bronze figure coming to light in Sanxingdui, Sichuan (1985–86) has been described as a sage or god figure of 4,800 or more years ago who accepted sacrifices? Second, Marxist scholars have shown sensitivity for discerning religious directions and sentiments in traditional philosophical teachings. Presumably, this effort is motivated by the insistence on atheistic humanism, accompanied as this is by the need to search out religious trends if only to manipulate or oppose them.

I come from a family more secular than religious, even though I can say with some pride that my stepfather is a devout Buddhist, and I have Muslim ancestors on my mother's side. I myself am a Catholic married to a Presbyterian. Being religious, I have especially sought out religious places to visit during my frequent travels to China, and I have been saddened many times by the state of disrepair in which things stand, or by the sorry looks and stories of the clergymen I happen to meet. When one compares China with India, one cannot escape the conclusion that the Hindu civilization is much more religious in character than the Chinese. On the other hand, when one sees the temples and churches, and witnesses the fervor of individuals and communities in worship, one cannot but admit that religion is also alive in China.

The Cycle of Tolerance and Repression

In today's China, there are five officially recognized religions. Buddhism and Taoism are so-called native religions, even though Buddhism came originally from India and Central Asia. There are also the two forms of Christianity: Catholic and Protestant, both introduced from outside, and then there is Islam, which came to China earlier. In the language of political ideology, Buddhism and Taoism have been associated respectively with the forces of feudalism, while the two Christian religions are associated with those of imperialism. Islam defies labels, but is usually considered to be more on the feudal side. As such, none of these religions is desirable in a Marxist China, but may be granted tolerance by a regime that believes in the historical triumph of dialectical materialism. In actual life, their treatment by the government has varied, depending on the religious body as well as on the period of time in recent history. But here too, we can discern a pattern parallel (and subordinate) to that discovered in political history for greater tolerance of, or tighter control over, people's thinking. Basically, this is also a cyclical alternation between tolerance and persecution. I shall speak of the "good years" and the "bad years"; readers may find that the "good years" are, at most, the "less bad years."

The "Good Years"

During the period 1949 to 1966—that is, until the outbreak of the Cultural Revolution—the government made some efforts to honor the guarantee of freedom of "religious belief," enshrined especially in the 1954 Constitution, but without mention of "religious activities." Such freedom was extended to those who consented to collaborate with the authorities. To further that end, an official Bureau of Religious Affairs was established in the fifties, directly affiliated to the State Council, while each religious group was encouraged to set up its own association. But such "freedom" was limited and short-lived, as the Korean War furnished occasion for all kinds of suspicions, and as the Anti-rightist campaign (1957) put an end to many dreams.

Collaboration with the government meant accepting the "Three Self" principles (self-administration, self-finance, self-propaganda), that is, abandoning ties with the outside world. Many mainline Protestant denominations accepted these principles rather quickly in the Three Self Movement (1951), although some more evangelical groups, like the Little Flock and the Jesus Family, resisted. It was especially difficult for Catholics, who regarded the Roman pontiff as the head of their church. At a mass meeting in Chongqing (Sichuan) arranged for the denunciation and expulsion of the papal delegate, Archbishop Riberi, Father John Tung had this to say (June 1951):

> Gentlemen, I have only one soul and I cannot divide it; I have a body which can be divided. It is best, it seems, to offer my whole soul to God and to the Holy Church; and my body to my country. If she is pleased with it, I do not refuse it to her.[1]

These words are indicative of the conflict in which individual Chinese found themselves over and over again. While Catholics were among the first to experience the inner conflict, nearly all educated Chinese now share the distress of having to choose between body and soul, between a government that claims to represent the entire country and the conscience or a higher power. Father Tung was arrested in Chongqing about a month after his speech (July 1951).

Another clerical victim from Shanghai was Father Beda Chang, a

Sorbonne graduate and highly respected Jesuit. Chang died in prison (November 1951) three months after his arrest, possibly after torture. His tomb was not marked because the regime insisted that the word "convict" be attached to his name, even though he was never tried. Four years later, Bishop Ignatius Gong (Kung) of Shanghai, along with about fifteen hundred Catholics, mostly lay people, were rounded up and taken to jail (1955). Similar arrests took place all over the country. These are the circumstances under which the Catholic "Patriotic Association" was set up (1953–55). The term "Patriotic Church" is often used to refer to the Catholic church in collaboration with the state. As the expulsion of missionaries and the imprisonment of other clergy meant a decrease in personnel, the Patriotic Association proceeded to request permission from Rome to consecrate bishops, and eventually carried out the consecrations (during which pledges of loyalty were made to both party and government) without ever getting such permission (1958).

True, the conflict between the Catholic church and the Communist government in China was one underscored by the Vatican, as Pope Pius XII condemned the "Three Self" principles from 1952 to 1954, and forbade the three-million-some Chinese Catholics any cooperation with the Communist regime, including membership in Communist organizations, and reading of Communist newspapers, magazines, and books. Those bishops consecrating others without permission, as well as those consecrated, were all excommunicated. This state of affairs persisted even after the end of the Cultural Revolution, and continues today.

Chinese Buddhists also experienced pressures from the government, and monastic life was infiltrated by cadres who persuaded monks and nuns to abandon a life-style of a "parasite." The Chinese Buddhist Association was formed in 1953, claiming to represent 500,000 monks and a hundred million lay followers, and with the aim of collaborating with the regime that proceeded to convert many temples to secular uses. The other native religion, Taoism, did not fare even as well since it was regarded as less scientific and more "superstitious." Even more Taoist temples were requisitioned by the state, and the Taoist Association was established later in 1956. Folk religion, often associated with Taoism, was singled out for special attack.

The "Bad Years"

With the beginning of the Cultural Revolution, all religious organizations and activities would go under, until it seemed as though China had no more religion. The Cultural Revolution had the designated aim of "Destroying the Four Olds" (culture, thinking, habits, and customs). All ancestral tablets and domestic shrines in peasant houses were destroyed and replaced by pictures of Mao Zedong. Red flags were placed over Christian churches in place of crosses, objects of veneration were removed from the premises and Bibles were burned, while busts of Mao Zedong were frequently installed in the middle of these places of worship. In the aftermath of Red Guard terror, all places of worship in the country were closed or put to other uses and religious personnel were made to do labor reform and sometimes were even tortured or killed.

I remember a building in Beijing near the Catholic Nantang ("Southern Church") near the old Xuanwu Gate that dates back to the time of Matteo Ricci, who died in China in the early seventeenth century. It was probably part of the old Catholic mission. Robert Ruhlmann, a French sinologist now deceased, pointed out the cross on its top that was literally dangling, evidence of an unsuccessful attempt to remove it. "It breaks my heart to see it," he said. "Someone should just take it away. It is so sad."[2]

While traveling with a group of Americans associated with Sargent Shriver and the Kennedy Institute of Ethics in 1979, I was requested to go and find the parish priest of that church. A group of us were taken to the church's parlor, where a very reluctant priest received us. He was obviously uncomfortable with our questions, including the one about what he had suffered during the Cultural Revolution. Just to give an example, he said, "I was made to walk on all fours in the streets, to show that I was a running dog of the imperialists."

A poster pasted outside the YMCA Building in Beijing (August 1966) announced:

> There is no God; there is no Spirit; there is no Jesus; there is no Mary; there is no Joseph. . . . Like Islam and Catholicism, Protestantism is a reactionary feudal ideology, the opium of the people, with foreign origins and contacts. . . . We are atheists; we believe only in Mao Tse-tung.[3]

Outside a Beijing mosque was another poster:

> Close all mosques;
> Disperse [religious] associations;
> Abolish Qur'an study;
> Abolish marriage within the faith;
> Abolish circumcision.[4]

In those days of rabid anti-religious feeling, clergymen suffered the most, even those who had collaborated with the government. A story was told to me about Li Chuwen, the deputy head until 1987 of the New

China News Agency in Hong Kong, which functions as the delegation of the People's Republic in the colony. Li had served as pastor of a congregation in Shanghai, where he gave weekly sermons and pious exhortations. When accused by Red Guards for carrying on religious activities, Li revealed that he was not really a Christian, but a Communist party member who had been told to infiltrate the community. My informant was himself a member of that shocked congregation. I mention this fact, which is now well known to Hong Kong residents, because it is an example of Communist suspicion of religion and anti-religious activity. The party is known to have sent people to infiltrate various religious groups, including the Tibetan monastic communities. Whether these individuals learn from these religions any respect for the faiths concerned, of course, is not known.

During the Cultural Revolution, people were made to demonstrate their devotion to Mao Zedong, the great leader, rather than to God or Buddha. Throughout the country, a new liturgy was carried out as people paid respect to their Mao portraits mornings and evenings, seeking daily instructions from him in a quasi-religious manner. This took place especially at Tian'anmen Square, to which soldiers, workers, and Red Guards went at sunrise every morning and returned at sundown every evening. Thus Maoism became a surrogate religion offering a new faith, elucidated in the Little Red Book, Mao images, lapel buttons, posters, songs, drama, and even "liturgy." The political leader had become a god.

A Red Guard has given poetic expression to a Tian'anmen rally at which the Chairman appeared:

> Suddenly, like the eruption of a volcano,
> Like the crashing of thunder in spring,
> Before Tien An Men
> Joyful shouts burst from our throats:
> "Long live Chairman Mao! Long, long life to him!"
>
> You are the lighthouse by the misty sea,
> The bright lamp showing us the way;
> You are victory,
> You are light!
> We will follow you.[5]

The Return of the "Good Years"

The fall of the Gang of Four signaled the return of the "good years." As the country opened to the outside, visitors to China were treated with stories of persecutions suffered during the "ten years of turbulence." It appeared that everyone had been a victim: the party member as well as the religious believer. For a while, it also appeared as if common suffering might create a bond of understanding and sympathy between the rulers and the ruled. In this context, the government's new constitutional guarantee of freedom of religion has been more visible than that of many others. Marxism was in principle atheistic, and the Cultural Revolution had virtually removed all signs of religion and silenced all believers. As a new leaf was turned, however, outsiders learned that worship had never ceased, as, for example, with Christians who had gone underground and held home services. This continues to take place in villages as well as in cities. In the case of Catholics, we have heard of priests going around with small paper kits containing the essentials for the Eucharist, and celebrating it here and there. Such stories always made me think back to the Elizabethan times in England, when Catholic activities also went underground.

I remember meeting a Chinese professor, a man in his late thirties. He had no idea that I was a Christian. However, in the course of our conversation, he disclosed to me that he and his wife were married for more than twelve years before he found out that she was a Catholic. "She came from a Catholic family," he told me, "but did not dare tell anybody. Only at the end of the Cultural Revolution did she dare to come out in the open."

Believers are still very aware of political pressures suffered in the past and fear for the future. I understand that Catholics hesitate to go to confession to priests who have collaborated with the government. They prefer those who have not. People remain very loyal to Rome in their hearts, and even those serving in the Patriotic Church would like to settle things with the pope, in return for the recognition of the People's Republic, of their own election as bishops, and church autonomy.

The past decade has seen the reopening of thousands of Christian churches as well as Buddhist temples, and the recruitment of religious personnel by all the recognized sects. But I have been told by a mainland researcher in 1986 that there are still more Christians who worship at home than those who worship in the open (and the churches are always full). Another Chinese researcher, whose name I do not even know, once approached me and said: "I am going to a certain town. I am doing research there on a strange phenomenon, a real problem. There have been mass conversions there to the Catholic church."

For the reassurance of believers, the new Constitution of 1982 is very specific about their rights:

Art. 36.   The citizens of the People's Republic of China enjoy freedom of religious belief. No state agency, public organization or individual may compel citizens to believe in, or not to believe in, any religion; nor may they discriminate against citizens who believe in, or do not believe in, any religion. The state protects normal religious activities. No one may make use of religion to engage in activities that disrupt public order, impair the health of citizens, or interfere with the educational system of the state.[6]

A more comprehensive attempt to deal with the religious question is found in a document, number 19, which was issued by the Party Central in March 1982. The document acknowledges that major mistakes had been made in the implementation of religious freedom, not only during the "ten years of turmoil," but during the entire span 1949 to 1966. However, it also gives a positive appraisal of the official policy of maintaining autonomy in the religious communities. The essential task is described as rallying all people to work for the construction of a modernized, socialist state in which religious belief is a private matter, for citizens to decide individually from age eighteen on. The various religious associations that had been disbanded during the Cultural Revolution were all permitted to reorganize under the government's leadership. No religious education of the young would be permitted outside of homes, and no religion would be allowed to control the work of education. The document also names the Vatican and some Protestant missionary societies as objects of suspicion.[7]

And so, after the devastations of the Cultural Revolution, religious faith is still present in the People's Republic, and is in fact growing, even if *knowledge* about religion is very limited. In 1982 the official figure puts Catholics and Protestants at three million each, which implies a large growth rate during the years of the Cultural Revolution. In 1987 Protestants claim to have reached four million, a quick rise indeed, with new recruits coming especially from the educated circles. Speaking generally, Protestants no longer have denominational cleavages, although in fact sectarian loyalties remain. There is a prestigious Union Seminary for Protestants in Nanjing, and there are seven Catholic seminaries in operation, of which the best known is in Sheshan outside Shanghai. Buddhists and Taoists each have a headquarters in Beijing, for the advanced training of novices, while monasteries in the provinces are also known to be recruiting and training recruits on their own.

An interesting question is that of clerical celibacy, whether for Buddhists, Taoists, or Catholics. Buddhism has always been a monastic religion, whereas Taoism is represented in recent history by two sects: the southern Heavenly Masters sect, which permits a married clergy, and the northern Perfect Truth sect, which enforces celibacy. I have been told that many Buddhist monks and Taoist priests are known to have married during the Cultural Revolution. In many cases, they have returned to active service in their congregations, without always leaving their wives and families. When visiting the Jade Buddhist temple in Shanghai, I was told of this by someone there: that some of the monks put on monastic garb at the temple, and remove it to return home at night. It appears, however, the Buddhist novices are trained to be celibate. Taoists seem to have decided in favor of "nature," without formal proscriptions. In the case of the Catholic church, some clergy, including some bishops, are known to have married. They are permitted now to help with church work, but not to celebrate the Eucharist.

If Christians in China feel that they belong to a larger entity that is world Christianity, Buddhists and Muslims are also aware of fellow believers in the faith outside. Japanese Buddhists have especially made their pilgrimage to many Chinese temples where famous Japanese monks had lived. Chinese monks have also become aware of the fact that celibacy has long ceased to be an issue in Japanese Buddhism. Certainly, the universal character of all these religions has helped the Chinese believers to get recognition and tolerance from their own government. The Venerable Hsin-yun (Xinyun), well-known Buddhist monk from Taiwan and founder of the new temple outside Los Angeles, visited China in April and was received in "personal audience" by President Yang Shangkun, who even indicated to him, at that time, that a petition coming from religious groups in favor of amnesty for Wei Jingsheng might be reviewed more positively than a similar petition from Fang Lizhi and thirty-three other intellectuals. Presumably, Yang is signaling a preference for a petition on the ground of compassion over a request from the intellectuals as a pressure group.

Buddhists in China, on the other hand, suffer from the lack of a visible leader. They do not really have anyone of the stature of Bishop K. H. Ting (Ding Guangxun), the head of the Three Self movement as well as of the Christian Council. Zhao Puchu, a layman and the head of the Buddhist Association, is well respected for his knowledge of the religion. He has always collaborated with the party and is presumed to be a party member. In a Chengdu temple, I found the portrait of the Tibetan Panchen Lama, who is usually considered as second to the Dalai in spiritual influence. I was impressed by this respect extended to a Tibetan monk in a Han temple. However, the Panchen Lama died suddenly in 1989; he remains unreplaced and irreplaceable.

Taoists are even more of a deprived community, without a visible leader, and without international links. It has been reported that a young boy from the Heavenly Master's family was being trained as a priest, and one wonders whether this was in competition with the lineal heir recognized in Taiwan. (I refer to the current Heavenly Master, descended from the Zhang family of the Dragon-Tiger Mountain in Jiangxi.) Presumably, such a visible religious leader would be useful as a government collaborator. The Taoist religion should also be helped by the knowledge that it is respected outside China, and receives quite some scholarly attention even in the West. A young German scholar, Thomas Hahn, has done extensive research on the Taoist religion in China from 1984 to 1986. He visited thirty-eight temples and noted many manifestations of old beliefs and practices.

Though an outside visitor may be limited to seeing churches and temples, China's researchers know more. I have been told that as much as 80 percent of China's population may be called religious. In the countryside, the hold of popular religion is still strong, though hard to discern. Besides, many peasants who were formerly Buddhists and Taoists now call themselves believers in Jesus, since Christianity to them sounds like a "modern" religion. I have heard about faith-healing sessions at which the sick gather to read passages from the Gospels about Jesus' healing miracles, and to have someone claiming special healing powers hold hands over their heads. I am told that some of the former "shamanesses" (*wupo*) now call themselves Christians. People are converting one another, even baptizing one another.

Occasionally, the outsider has since heard about violations of the constitutional guarantee of religious freedom, mostly on the regional and local levels, sometimes resulting in illegal arrests and even deaths. The outsider has often presumed these to be specific cases of abuses of power. Compared to the days of the Cultural Revolution, China's mini-religious revival, even in Tibet, has been an encouragement to those who wish her well.

Opium of the People?

During the past decade of relative openness or *glasnost*, there have also been lively debates and discussions on two subjects in China's academic circles: practice as the test of truth, and the distinction between "religion" and "superstition." In chapter 5, we reported discussions on the first of these topics. We turn here to the second subject.

Ren Jiyu, the former head of the Institute of World Religions in the

Chinese Social Science Academy, has always defended an orthodox line: namely, that religion is the opium of the people. His basic assertion is that "all religions are superstitions, but not all superstitions are religions." In practice, this means that religion is superior to pure superstition. According to this view, atheism is superior to all religion, but some religions are superior to others. Christianity, for example, is often regarded as superior to Taoism, which is associated in people's consciousness with practices like divination and exorcism that are said to be superstitious. Having been received in audience by Mao Zedong shortly before the Cultural Revolution, Ren regarded himself as having been given a mandate to study religion for the sake of criticizing it.

During the past decade, Ren Jiyu has been involved in several related academic debates. One is about Confucianism: whether it is a philosophy or a religion. Even in the West, scholars differ in their responses to this question, since Confucianism may be described as a mere ethical and social teaching, and may also be described as having been associated with a ritual system and having performed certain religious functions. In China, the same debate goes on, with some variations. Basically, following Marxist ideology, philosophy is regarded as superior to religion, which is usually defined as the "opium of the people." Hence those who call Confucianism a philosophy esteem it more than those who call it a religion. The best-known spokesman for Confucianism as a religion, Ren Jiyu has published multi-volume histories of philosophy, used as university textbooks. Ren asserts that "Confucius wanted to maintain the then-weakening divine authority of the Lord-on-high (or God) in philosophy."[8] There are many, nevertheless, who disagree with his description of Confucianism and emphasize Confucius's focus on the human rather than the divine. Feng Yulan has always maintained that Confucianism is strictly a philosophy; Kuang Yaming, former president of Nanjing University, voices a similar opinion. He has been active in the Confucius Foundation, which sponsored an international conference in 1986 in Qufu, Confucius's native place.

The Communist government has adopted Ren's view: Religion is subordinate to philosophy; religious belief always indicates a philosophical position of "idealism" rather than "materialism," whereas philosophies may be of one or the other kind. In the mid-eighties, there was a debate over the nature of religion, with Ren Jiyu insisting upon the definition that it is the "opium of the people." Zhao Fusan, the former vice-president of the Chinese Social Science Academy, asserted that in its functions, religion is *not* just the opium of the people. In the aftermath of the military crackdown of the pro-democracy demonstrations, Zhao

Fusan did not return to China after attendance at a UNESCO meeting in Paris (July 1989). He has not declared himself a member of any democracy alliance; however, he is reported to have said that he did not wish to participate in any "struggle meetings," whether to attack others or to be attacked himself.

The irony of these debates about religion and superstition is that Marxism has served *both* as religious truth and as supersition for the people governed by Communist rulers. Chinese intellectuals are well aware of this irony. For this reason too, they have shown a real tolerance and openness for that enemy of militant atheism: religion.

Personally, I have much respect for Feuerbach's characterization of religion as a projection of one's psychological needs. The problem with Communism, as many people would agree, is that it promises its own "pie in the sky" (the withering away of the state in a future utopia), which remains too inaccessible, and it also deprives people of the consolations of religious faith. Even architecturally, Communist structures look monstrous and ill-planned, while traditional Chinese temples offer a depth of discovery with their successive courtyards and rich iconography. Going up a Taoist sacred mountain (for example, the Qingcheng in Sichuan) is also a delightful experience, as one visits the many shrines along the way and meditates on the ascent to Heaven as did the priests.

Religion and the Ethnic Minorities

An interesting community within China is the Chinese Jews. The presence of Jews in Guangzhou is mentioned in a tenth-century Muslim chronicle, but the community we are discussing is distinctive, and goes back at least a thousand years. They have been especially numerous in the ancient city of Kaifeng (Henan). Where the West is concerned, they first came to light when the Italian Jesuit Matteo Ricci was living in Beijing in the early seventeenth century. He had a visit (1605) from someone he deemed to be a long-lost Christian, who turned out to be of the Jewish faith. Three years later, the chief rabbi of Kaifeng even offered to have Ricci succeed him in his office, provided the priest would give up the practice of eating pork! After the departure of Jesuit missionaries from China, the Jewish community was once more lost to the outside world until the early twentieth century, when it was re-introduced to the outside world by the Anglican Bishop William C. White. This Canadian missionary in Kaifeng set up his mission on what had formerly been synagogue ground (1912) and wrote a book about the Chinese Jews.[9]

When my husband, Will Oxtoby, and I were in Kaifeng (1981), we interviewed a middle-aged Chinese, a descendant of the original Jews. He told us the story of his Jewish forebears, known to the Chinese as believers in a religion that "picked the sinews" from the meat. According to him, there were about two hundred families in Kaifeng who still remembered their origins and who, though they now eat pork, still do not raise pigs. When I asked him where the old synagogue used to stand (the first one was built in the twelfth century, the last one in the seventeenth), he said, "You are sitting on the site itself." So the Chinese Jews are still living in houses constructed on the very site of their old synagogue, even if they no longer know Hebrew and hardly keep any of the observances of the law. They have intermarried so much with the local populace that they are hardly recognizable as a distinct ethnic group. However, there are claims that the community received new immigrants via the Silk Road even as late as the seventeenth century or after. It is also thought that many of China's Jews became absorbed by the Muslim population, which has similar beliefs and customs.

A monument to a long-lost religion from the outside is the tiny Manichaean temple outside Quanzhou (Fujian). In available Chinese texts, Manichaeism is first mentioned in an eighth-century imperial edict, and last mentioned in a late-sixteenth-century Fujian gazetteer. Somewhere between the two dates is the little-known history of a syncretistic religion that operated very much in secret and is regarded as having influenced, and been influenced by, Buddhism and Taoism. I visited the former temple (1987), which holds the portrait of Mani, honored as the "Buddha of Light," and witnessed a devout Buddhist nun reciting her prayers at the site.[10]

Among the various *living* religions present in China, Islam and (Tantric) Buddhism are each associated with particular ethnic groups: Islam with the Hui population dispersed in various regions (descendants of Arabs, Persians, and other converts to that religion), and with the Turkic peoples of Chinese Central Asia or Xinjiang (Uighurs, Kazakhs, Uzbeks, Kirghiz, and others), and Tantric Buddhism with the Tibetans and Mongols. It is difficult to give correct statistics for these peoples: we hear of two million Tibetans and of ten million Muslims—the latter figure is definitely on the low side.

Islam started early in China—probably in the mid-seventh century, although the exact date is difficult to establish. An old tradition even claims that Mohammed's maternal uncle (whose "sepulcher" stands today in Guangzhou) brought the religion to the country. This cannot be taken seriously, as it would date the beginning of Islam in China to the time before the Hijra (A.D. 622). Most probably, the sepulcher in question is that of an early Arab trader. In the course of centuries, Chinese Islam absorbed certain features of Confucian philosophy, especially its ethics and cosmology, with ideas of good and evil as well as *Taiji*, *yin* and *yang*. Both the Sunni and Shi'i traditions are present in Chinese Islam, and Sufism has been active in special regions. Under Communist rule, a Chinese Islamic Association was established in 1953, a parallel to the Chinese Buddhist Association and to the Christian counterparts.

Muslims in China, as elsewhere, advocate "holy war" (*jihad*) for the defense of their faith, and have always given trouble to their Communist overlords. The Kazakh revolt (1950–51) was put down with difficulty, and a great number of them sought later to flee China. Communists sought here as well to infiltrate Islamic schools and to persuade Muslims to become party members. Sporadic insurrections took place in different parts of the country, for example in Gansu (1952) and in Yunnan (1972), in each case with thousands of deaths and casualties and after the annihilation of whole districts or villages. Although socioeconomic grounds exist that cause discontent, religion is also a factor. Muslims, for example, are insulted if they are asked to raise pigs. Except during the Cultural Revolution, select Muslim groups were permitted to make the pilgrimage to Mecca.

In Tibet's case, the Communist army first entered there in 1950. Both the Dalai Lama and the Panchen Lama, the two highest spiritual leaders, received government protection and promises of religious freedom. A few years later, however, taxes were increased, estates confiscated, and land redistributed, while lamas were sometimes assaulted and killed. In the aftermath of a 1959 uprising, which was quickly quenched by the government, the Dalai Lama and his entourage escaped to India, where he still remains. Harsh repression followed in Tibet itself as monasteries were destroyed and secularized and monks were rounded up and forced to work and marry.[11]

I visited Xinjiang together with my husband in 1981 and was generally impressed by the open welcome offered us by the Muslims there in the often dilapidated, newly opened mosques. My brother Frank reports on his visit there a few years later that he found a Catholic church in Urumqi with a parish priest who had no ties with the Patriotic Church. We heard later, however, that he had been arrested. My husband and I both visited Lhasa for a few days in 1987, together with the theologian Hans Küng. We found nomads obviously on pilgrimage to the Jokhang temple (the holiest shrine in Tibet) from the villages, moving on all fours, holding on to small pieces of wood while making obeisance by full-length prostrations. Indeed, we had difficulty not stepping on them as we visited that same temple. I was very much reminded of the faithful at the cathedral in Mexico City. I have been told that St. Joseph's Oratory in Montreal, with its memories of Brother André, witnesses the same devotion from people going there to worship.

During our visit to the Sera monastery just north of Lhasa, we witnessed groups of Buddhist monks sitting on the ground, rehearsing "debates." This was a kind of scholastic exercise during which one monk would stand at the edge of the circle making dramatic arm gestures to prove his point. At particular moments he would clap his hands with a flourish. Obviously, it was a practice session, since the monks were all laughing. The pace and gestures of the debate appear ritualized; however, my friends in Tibetan studies say that the form is still important and can contribute to creative thinking about the old scriptures. Later, at an official dinner we hosted to thank members of the Tibetan Academy of Social Sciences for their help, we also met an old monk from that monastery. He was much venerated for his learning, and respected also because he had remained celibate whereas so many of his contemporaries had married. (The Panchen Lama, who died suddenly in 1989, is known to have married a Han Chinese after the Cultural Revolution.)

In the case of both Xinjiang and Tibet, a major cause for discontent was the influx of many Han Chinese, that is, the majority population of the country. Many of these were exiled to these frontier regions, giving rise to increasing ethnic as well as religious conflicts because of different life-styles. Muslims claim that refusal to eat pork or raise pigs frequently played a role in these conflicts, especially during the heat of "political campaigns," such as during the Cultural Revolution. For the Tibetans, the flight of the Dalai Lama and the dispersal and secularization of monks caused the strongest resentment. Everywhere we went, monks were asking for pictures of the Dalai Lama from outsiders. At that time, however, we saw no sign of discontent. We were surprised at how tourists could purchase souvenirs directly from the street vendors, using U.S. dollars. My surmise is that they would not be able to make much capital out of foreign currency, but would have to change it to domestic currency at official rates. The army was not very visible during our visit, although individual soldiers we saw all looked like ethnic Hans. A friend of ours lost several thousand dollars to a pickpocket at the Lhasa post office. He was quite sure the culprit was a Han Chinese speaking with a Sichuan accent.

During the Cultural Revolution, these remote areas and the ethnic minority groups all suffered religious repression. This was lifted by 1981, as a certain number of temples and mosques were reopened and the recruitment and training of religious personnel was once more permitted to all religious groups. I remember how on our way back from Urumqi, we stopped at many places, visiting the mosques as well as the Dunhuang Caves. Frequently, people thought I was a Chinese Muslim and my husband was an Arab. In a small Muslim eatery, we met a Uighur family: father, mother, and infant. We started a conversation in Chinese. They were on their way from Kashgar to Beijing, as their child needed medical care that was not available back home. It was practically the longest rail journey possible in China. When the man showed pleasure at Will's recitation in Arabic from the Qur'an, we asked him whether children were allowed to study the holy book. Instead of answering us openly, he switched to hand gestures, as though reading a book, and then made a signal of a gun shooting. Then, as the waitress was approaching, he took a piece of paper and showed us how the Uighur language is written. On it he wrote, in that language, for her to see: Long live Chairman Mao.

Even very recently (1988–89), the bloody repression of people, including monks, asking for more autonomy in Tibet alarmed world opinion, while stirrings were heard as well in Xinjiang for real autonomy (1986–87). On this account, the party secretary there (Saifuding) was transferred to Beijing. Interestingly, several students from ethnic minorities (Wu'er Kaixi, a Uighur; Nixi, a Tibetan) were elected by their fellows as leaders during the most recent demonstrations in Beijing, where a female student, Chai Ling, was also prominent at Tian'anmen Square. Buddhist monks, including those in Tibetan costumes, are known to have participated at the demonstrations in Beijing, as did Taoist priests and Christian recruits, including seminarians. From exile, the Dalai Lama made several statements, first to support the demonstrations and later to condemn the military crackdown.

Ethnic conflicts and hostilities between the Han population and the others are real, especially in the frontier regions where there is little true autonomy, and where the minorities are rightly anxious about being overwhelmed by the forced influx of the Han. On the other hand, the unfolding of the drama at Tian'anmen also revealed that the deeper cause for disunity was the repressive regime. With the process of democratization, many problems can be resolved with relative ease, not only with regard to Tibetan Buddhists and Turkic Muslims, but also with regard to Hong Kong and even Taiwan. Some people have recently spoken in favor of a federal system for China, to replace the centralized administration. Certainly, the country's vastness, its cultural and religious diversity, as well as the difference between economic systems (between the mainland and Hong Kong), justify much more political and administrative pluralism.

A New Religiosity

In the past, Chinese intellectuals have usually been proud of their culture's predominantly secular attitudes toward life and the universe. The names of contemporary philosophers and historians such as Hu Shih (now deceased) and Ch'ien Mu (now living in Taiwan) come to mind in this regard. It comes therefore as some surprise to hear words such as the following from Liu Xiaobo, a lecturer at Beijing University who (before his arrest in June 1989) attracted thousands of hearers to his talks:

> The Chinese believe that they themselves are the center of the world, and that human beings are omnipotent. But to be omnipotent is actually to be impotent, as the human being is [really] limited. Whether physically or spiritually, the human being is not the center of the universe, and no nation can become the center of the world. . . . The tragedy of the Chinese is the tragedy of not having a God. Because of the lack of light from beyond, the darkness on this shore has been mistaken as light. . . . [12]

Although I know little about the Soviet Union and Eastern Europe, and have visited only a few places there, I have always felt that the Iron Curtain served as a mask for a people that never forgot its spiritual roots, despite all the corruption that has been associated with the older forms of Christianity that their fathers and grandfathers had known. This feeling has been proven correct, as Gorbachev's *glasnost* policy lifted the curtain on Soviet life. I surmise that the Bamboo Curtain has served the same function, that the people would gladly have the freedom to read the old classics again, and rediscover pride in their old heritage.

I have, however, discovered that the facts are not so simple. On the level of the less educated, it appears that the old religious (and, some would say, superstitious) beliefs are still important. Burning firecrackers outside Taoist and Buddhist temples, for example, remains a popular custom—for chasing away demons—but can literally backfire in accidental hazards. After the religious repression of the Cultural Revolution, people have returned to their places of worship, even to practices of divination and faith healing. Impressively, the children of religious parents, whether Buddhist or Taoist or Catholic or Protestant, have usually returned to the practices of their respective religious heritage. But I have also found, largely to my amazement, that an immense number of people show an interest in a non-Chinese heritage: the Christian religion. It is indeed ironic that the breast-beating of many ex-missionaries over cultural or religious imperialism has not found much echo in the country, except in official circles. Despite the available literature in mainland China on this subject, people (especially the younger set) appear not to concern themselves with such accusations, but express strong interest in *Western* religion. No doubt, they associate it in their minds with the modern (rather than the medieval) West. Protestant Christianity seems to attract the most people, but many find the Catholic liturgy appealing. The churches are full especially at midnight masses every Christmas, so that priests have to devise ways of turning away the non-Christians. One way is to ask people to give their Christian names. One young man wanting very much to get in declared: "My name is Maria." He didn't make it.

While we who live in the West are conscious of the diminishing statistics of our church attendance, Chinese visitors to our countries still manifest astonishment at the strength of religion in our societies. The dissident astrophysicist Fang Lizhi is an example. He has recorded his own impressions of an Advent service at Cambridge, England, in 1979, during which he kept asking himself: Why has Christianity been so influential in Western society? Why does it attract so many scholars and students? In a student newspaper article on Fang Lizhi published at Beijing University in 1985, we also read:

> Our attitude toward the entire religious question bears rethinking. We naively assume that Western religions reveal ignorance, but fail to realize that modern Western religion is a vigorous tradition infused with contemporary meanings. Western religion is also a means of experiencing such emotions as love, friendship and compassion.[13]

If Fang's first impression of a religious service was a positive one, his consciousness was also of his own experience of pseudo-religion in China during the Cultural Revolution. He recorded asking himself during the service: Have I not been attending like services every year of the Cultural Revolution, singing hymns praising my "Lord" (Mao Zedong)? Is not expulsion from the party very similar to excommunication from a church?

> What I should repeat once more is that I do not believe in God. I also appreciate how the leaders of the Renaissance transformed the god of religion into a human being in an art filled with the spirit of humanism. This deserves to be called a high point in the history of development of human civilization. On the other hand, the Cultural Revolution, which calls itself something that greatly surpasses the Renaissance, wanted to transform an individual human being into a god. . . . [Its] inferior songs and shouting tunes cannot help but make you feel that it has reduced Chinese civilization to a very sorry state.[14]

After the nihilism of the "ten years of turmoil," the novelist Li Ping broke taboo by publishing a short story with religion as its main theme: "*Wanxia xiaoshi de shihou*" (Twilight hour). In it, the young hero, Li Hui-ping, a Communist party member proud of his family background and convictions, learns from mistakes and painful experience that the truth is not so simple. He hears about Christianity through a girl from a family that had earlier served the Nationalist cause. And he later meets a Buddhist monk with whom he discusses the true (science), the beautiful (art), and the good (religion). He is thus led to realize the inadequacies of his own man-made categories of right and wrong, truth and falsehood, good and evil, as well as the capricious character of society's own judgments, which led to so many tragedies during the Cultural Revolution. Through the monk's words, the author voices ideas about religion that are characteristically Chinese: that all religions seek the good, and that what is good is more important than what is true. "Religion is basically made for people's hearts. It exists if you believe it; it does not exist if you do not believe it. What is important is being earnest and sincere." Of course, this is an idealist conclusion, and one accepted by a humbled mind.

Conclusion: What Next?

An American teacher in China, John Shillington, reported the following story of what he witnessed, presumably on June 4, 1989, a Sunday:

> As I walked into church I saw the young teacher at the altar. He was from our college, about my age and wearing a black mourning arm band. The elderly church members were gathered around him in a heated argument. The young man had made a tape of a prayer he had composed for the students and soldiers who had died in Beijing.
>
> The people around him were urging him to sit down, begging him not to speak for they knew he would certainly be arrested and possibly killed for asking prayers for students who are now referred to as hooligans and counter-revolutionaries. . . . Surrounded, silenced, the young man finally collapsed on the back pew of the church and wept convulsively. Intense sobs racked his whole body.
>
> As I went by the teacher I stopped and stared. I'd never witnessed such intense pain. The teacher wept so bitterly, sobs which did not sound human, as if the screams and cries of those in Beijing were carried inside his body. It was beyond grief, the sound of injustices so large that they could not be overcome or humanly forgiven. Sounds of such empathy bordering on the brink of insanity where humanity merges with God.
>
> A policeman waited outside of the church to take the teacher away.[15]

By June 27, 1989, the various officially recognized religious groups in China had all come out in support of the regime and its crackdown. They had no other choice. But what future can we forecast for the religious situation in China? Will religious life continue to prosper and develop, or will there be greater harassment and even renewed persecution? At present it appears that religion is both surviving and prospering, while a certain measure of harassment and persecution is also persisting. Obviously, Maoist ideology failed to replace religion during the Cultural Revolution, and has in fact left a real spiritual vacuum that is being filled by the revival of religious life. With the greater efforts at modernization, it appears that the people have found the Western religion, Christianity (in particular Protestant Christianity, called the *Xinjiao* or "new religion," especially attractive.

Will the guarantee of religious liberty survive the tragic end to the student demonstrations? Will not the support (food and water, among other things) offered to the demonstrators by believers of religion offer an excuse to the regime to limit the exercise of even this newly won freedom? The answer to this question is still being awaited. The mass arrests, the quick judgments, the reports of torture all indicate a return to the methods of the Cultural Revolution. Journalists who had shown their courage in demands for greater freedom for the press are once more reduced to repeating official statements of the "truth." In this political climate, it is difficult to depict much freedom or even tolerance for religious activities.

I am convinced that freedom of religion is an issue that cannot be separated from freedom of thought and expression, freedom of speech and association. The virtual suspension of these constitutional freedoms has now rendered the 1982 Constitution a dead letter. Has religion also entered a new dark age? We hope not, but we fear Yes. We have witnessed the cycle of good and bad years in the past. Quite honestly, the "good" years were never so good, whereas the "bad" years were very bad indeed. When will this cycle of tolerance and repression be broken by democratization? This is the question on everyone's mind.

CHAPTER 7

■

The Two Tian'anmen Incidents: 1976 and 1989

Do you know under Heaven

· How many twists and turns there are in the Yellow River?
· How many boats there are on each of the twists and turns?
· How many poles there are on each of the boats?
· How many oarsmen there are on each of the twists and turns to pole the boats along?

This is the refrain so often repeated in the six-part, four-hour 1988 television series produced in Communist China called *River Elegy*, a work considered to have artistic value and a political message.[1] The river is none other than the Yellow River, known for having nourished the "cradle" of Chinese civilization, and yet, at the same time, having been so deadly in its periodic flooding. Culturally iconoclastic, *River Elegy* becomes more comprehensible to the outsider when taken as a political metaphor. Then the river that is being mourned is only superficially Chinese civilization, and represents more fundamentally the capriciousness of the Communist regime, to which the country is bound, apparently more for worse than for better. The rule of the party floods periodically, devouring those whose lives depend on it. This understanding of history as cycles of progress and decline seems to give mass appeal to Jin Guantao's "ultrastable system" of prosperity and decline, discussed in chapter 4.

Coming back through Hong Kong after my first trip from the United States to China (1978), I remember how our group met and spoke with a successful businessman in Hong Kong. We were enthusiastic about the places we had visited and seen in three weeks of travel up and down the country, and excited about a future when China would become more open and accessible to the outside world. His remark was simply: "China changes every ten years or so. . . . We have seen the Great Leap Forward campaign (1958–62), the Cultural Revolution (1966–76). It is opening now. But what will be happening ten years down the line?"

"China changes every ten years." Whether we regard the ten-year cycle as an absolute is not as important as the fact that a cycle, a periodicity, exists. Indeed, when we examine the historical facts closely, we find many repetitions of events, many smaller cycles within the bigger, roughly ten-year cycles. Every period of relative openness has been accompanied by demands for freedom and democracy and followed by severe repression. The death of Mao was preceded by demonstrations and a massacre, and the awaited death of Deng is apparently following the same course. China is a totalitarian dictatorship with power concentrated at the top—and frequently, the top is represented by a gerontocracy, or one single old man.

"China changes every ten years." The calculation may not be exact, but the periodicity that characterizes the flooding of the Yellow River characterizes Communist rule in China as well. The twists and turns refer to its history, basically a chronicle of power struggles; the boats refer to the various regimes (there have basically been only two, but who knows how many more will follow?); the oarsmen refer to the leaders at the top.

"China changes every ten years." This indeed has been the watchword of the expatriate observers and China-watchers, now again that the promises of stability of the Deng era have turned, so very recently, into false hopes. This has also been the reason behind the disquiet in Hong Kong even before the most recent events, as its people are bracing themselves for eventual reunion with the motherland in 1997. The cycle has once again caught up with us. But why this cycle? If we had just about forgotten it this time (1989), what can it tell us about the future?

I believe that the best example of such cyclical change, of the periodic and capricious flooding of the Yellow River, has been given to us by the recent Tian'anmen Square Incident. It was actually foreshadowed by an earlier Tian'anmen Square Incident, that of April 1976. True, the interval was longer than ten years, but we should not forget that huge student demonstrations had erupted already in December 1976 and January 1977, and that the 1989 protests might be considered a renewed version of that earlier, if abortive, effort. Chinese Communist history has been full of historical repetitions of hundreds of political campaigns aimed at suppressing the expressions of dissent. These have generally been unsuccessful, if we are to take the present student generation as a sample, for the present generation consists of young people who have grown up entirely under the Communist rule. But the swing of the pendulum, from the loosening and tightening of thought control, to the public outburst of protest sentiments, to the bloody repressions and the executions and harsh imprisonments—all this has been seen over and over again in recent history.

A comparison of the two Tian'anmen Incidents is still significant because of the dramatic quality each displayed, and because there may yet be a lesson the first incident might impart to those of us who are wondering now what else will happen after the second.

The First Tian'anmen Incident
(March 28–April 5, 1976)

The first Tian'anmen Incident is little known in the West because it predated the arrival of Western tourists and journalists. But written accounts are available, by Chinese as well as Japanese eyewitnesses, including those by newspaper correspondents, such as those from *Asahi Shimbun*. From these, we have pieced together this account of what happened that April, 1976.

In the night of January 7, 1976, Premier Zhou Enlai, the one beloved figure of Communist China, passed away after a long illness. He and his wife were childless, although they are known to have accepted over eighty adopted children (to this group belongs the present premier Li Peng), many of whom held high positions in the military. The announcement of his death was made in the morning of January 9, and the flag flew at half-staff at Tian'anmen Square. On January 10, the newspapers announced the official mourning for Zhou's death, which allegedly occurred among a small circle at the Beijing Hospital. It was strange that there had not been a bigger, public service, but the Cultural Revolution was a time of strange political happenings. So, in the afternoon of January 11, a huge crowd of a million people lined the streets in sub-zero temperature to say farewell to the hearse, followed by about eighty Red Flag cars, which were driven to the cremation grounds in the western suburbs. The cremation took place despite many objections on the part of the assembled crowds; indeed, over 10,000 letters had been received by the government requesting that the body of the deceased be preserved. However, as Zhou's widow explained, it was the wish of the deceased that his ashes should be strewn over "the country's mountains and rivers." In any case, the people at large, who were devoted to his memory, were not given any opportunity to mourn his passing and remained dissatisfied at the manner by which he had been laid to rest. Rumors were all over the country about his having been poisoned by Mao's wife, Jiang Qing.

At that time (as is once more the case), politics in China was shrouded in mystery. Mao was growing older and presumably getting senile. Jiang Qing and her ultra-leftist supporters were doing their best to exploit an ambiguous situation. The government bureaucracy that Zhou had sought hard to hold together was itself divided. Zhou himself had remained the voice of rationality and moderation in a sea of radicalism and extremism. He was known as the "beloved" Premier. Shortly before his death, Zhou had launched the policy of the Four Modernizations and placed it under the direction of the vice-premier, Deng Xiaoping. The population at large was opposed to Jiang Qing's clique but dared not express opinions aloud. Even sentiments of sorrow at Zhou's passing, and of anger at the lack of public memorials, were being suppressed.

Between early February and late March, during the month following Zhou's death, articles appeared in the *Wen Hui Bao* (Shanghai) and elsewhere, and *dazibao* were affixed on university campuses in Beijing and in other cities. They were presumed to have been written at the order of Jiang Qing and her cohorts. Their message was to continue the Cultural Revolution and bring it to another, higher level. Their targets were the deceased Zhou Enlai (criticized as the reactionary "Confucius"), his colleagues (described as "capitalist roaders"), and their policies, especially the Four Modernizations. To those who had eyes to see and ears to hear, it was a concerted effort to remove from power such individuals as the vice-premier Deng Xiaoping, and to prepare for Jiang Qing and her associates to succeed to Mao's position in the event of his death. Since the memory of Zhou Enlai was sacred to many people, these actions had an aggravating effect. The Shanghai paper's office was attacked in a riot, and nine people in that city committed suicide by pouring gasoline on themselves in front of the municipal building and at the People's Square. The flame was already ignited; it would be fanned further in early April.

About two months after Zhou's death, late in March, on the approach of the Chinese feast of the dead (*Qing-ming*), wreaths started to appear at the Monument to the People's Heroes at Tian'anmen Square in Zhou's honor. The first wreath, presented by a group of teachers and students from a Beijing middle school, is alleged to have been placed there on March 25, the day the hated article appeared in *Wen Hui Bao*. Other wreaths followed quickly, presented by political and military personnel.

The honor being paid to Zhou Enlai, on the part of the grass roots as well as of a "silenced" bureaucracy, was regarded by the Gang of Four as a challenge to their authority. But the movement was not limited to Beijing itself. In Shanghai, expressions of mourning were aired more quietly, usually within the factories and other work places. In Xiamen, Chengdu, Kunming, and Wuhan, university students are known to have conducted memorial services on campus.

By April 1, despite official prohibitions, more and more wreaths were appearing at Tian'anmen Square, and larger crowds were gathering there to look at the wreaths, on which were attached expressions of respect for the dead premier. Ten thousand people were already gathered at the Square on April 2. On April 3, the accumulated wreaths measured fifteen meters high, and the newer ones were accompanied by more or less explicitly political messages. *Qing-ming* arrived on April 4, and slogans like "Down with the Empress Dowager" appeared—using the hated female ruler from the late Manchu dynasty to represent Mao's wife, and showing the people's deep discontent with Jiang Qing's role in politics.

The Security Bureau's policemen were already circulating among the masses on April 3, warning them against being "used by class enemies," but to no effect. Wreaths were being removed in the dead of night, so some people started tying them with wire to the railings around the monument, with notes attached saying "Keep till April 6" or "Keep till April 7. We shall come to remove them." And the wreaths presented were getting bigger and bigger. That afternoon, a Saturday, over 10,000 people were there. In the evening, people used megaphones to express their devotion to Zhou Enlai and to recite their poems aloud.

On April 4, the security police started to arrest the leaders of this rally, but found themselves encircled by tens of thousands of people, and some of them were even beaten by the mob. By then, thousands of *dazibao* were posted on the monument and nearby. Overnight, however, more than a hundred trucks were mobilized, allegedly under Jiang Qing's orders, accompanied by armed militia forces. They removed all the wreaths and tore up the posters. It is reported that she had first turned to the Beijing Garrison for help, but it had refused to comply.

On April 5, near 6 A.M., large crowds started to assemble at Tian'anmen Square. When they discovered that the wreaths had all been removed, their mood turned angry. The armed militia tried, in vain, to prevent people from approaching the Monument to the People's Heroes. Shortly after 7 A.M., a huge portrait of Zhou Enlai was brought over by a crowd from West Chang'an Street to the Square. Students from Middle School 173 followed, carrying their wreaths. By then, the assembled crowd had increased to about 50,000.

At 8:30 A.M. open conflict took place between the crowd and the militia with casualties on both sides. The crowds pushed away the militia and marched on to the Great Hall of the People, the site of the meetings of the People's Congress, the supreme legislative body. More militia then arrived together with soldiers from the No. 8341, allegedly Mao's elite guards, then under the command of Wang Dongxin. In the ensuing conflict there were hundreds of casualties, as the masses who had entered the Great Hall were pushed back. The mob then set on fire a propaganda vehicle from the Security Bureau and also overturned some fire engines. By noon, after this melee, people started to disperse. But at 2 P.M., Zhou's portrait and the remaining wreaths were all removed. The crowd that stayed behind then attacked the militia's nearby barracks and set it on fire. They also burned other militia vehicles before dispersing. Security police started confiscating cameras and even identity cards from the Japanese reporters present, telling them to leave the area, although several remained. Around 6:30 P.M., the Beijing party secretary Wu De arrived at the Square and addressed the crowds, censuring them for the actions that had taken place and asking them to leave. But over three thousand people stayed behind, with hands joined, singing the "Internationale." Around 9:30 P.M., the lights were suddenly turned on, as tens of thousands of militia arrived with truncheons in hand, followed by the armed police, making up a force of roughly 40,000. All that time, Wu De's speech was being broadcast, asking the "revolutionary comrades" (the "good guys") to leave, saying that the Square was full of "counterrevolutionaries" ("bad guys"). The final confrontation then began. Over three hundred people are known to have been arrested, although more probably died. By midnight a convoy of trucks arrived with cleaners, and the entire Square was being washed down with water. In the days of repression that followed, from 40,000 to 50,000 people were arrested in Beijing alone.[2]

This first Tian'anmen Incident occurred in the space of about one week, during which a million and a half people had been present at the site. The political sentiments that emerged on that occasion are best discerned in some of the poetry that was published afterward. The writers used historical references to vent their anger at contemporary politics, calling Mao Zedong the Qin emperor (China's first unifier in the third century B.C., known for his ruthlessness). They also supported "true Marxist-Leninism" against its alleged opposite, the Marxist-Leninism then in power, and advocated continuing the policy of Four Modernizations. Here are some of the best-known verses:

> China is no longer the China of the past:
> The people are no longer so foolish,
> The feudal days of the Qin emperor are gone forever.

We believe in Marxist-Leninism,
Let those who castrate this Marxist-Leninism
Go to Hell!

We want true Marxist-Leninism,
We do not fear the shedding of our blood
    or the loss of our lives.
On the day of the Four Modernizations,
We shall once more offer our libations.[3]

Although history will associate this first incident with Tian'anmen, the expressions of discontent were not limited to the capital. On roughly the same days, crowds had gathered in many other cities, including, for example, Zhengzhou (Henan), Nanjing (Jiangsu), Shanghai, Hangzhou (Zhejiang), Nanchang (Jiangxi), Kunming (Yunnan), and Guangzhou (Guangdong). The crowds in Beijing were apparently made up of workers, students (from universities and middle schools), and the unemployed young people who had secretly returned from the countryside; the crowds elsewhere were frequently led by students. In all these places, there were casualties following crackdowns.

The immediate political result of the incident was a second setback for Deng Xiaoping, who was made into a scapegoat for the riots. An emergency meeting of the Politburo (April 5) concluded that what happened was a counterrevolutionary attempt against the Revolution itself. Chang Chunqiao and Wang Hungwen both went to examine the site and reported such to Mao. This judgment was endorsed by the full Politburo two days later.

On April 7, Hua Guofeng, security chief and a dark horse in politics, was made the first vice-chairman of the party as well as premier, while Deng was removed from office but was allowed to keep his party membership. All this happened under Mao's orders (in an unconstitutional manner), but was ratified by the Politburo.

After that, on July 28, a devastating earthquake took place in the Tangshan/Fengnan (Hebei) region, killing probably nearly half the population there, that is, at least 600,000 people, and injuring even more. It was one of the worst in the world's history and the casualties were compounded especially because many workers were trapped underground in this mining region. Even the inhabitants of Beijing, fearful of aftershocks, left their houses to pitch tents in the streets. For a superstitious people like the Chinese, this was also a sign of worse things to come. They were, of course, awaiting the great Chairman's impending death.

Typically, the number of victims and casualties at Tangshan was not announced, and the press reported only the "brave efforts of the soldiers" in the aftermath. The same silence was observable with regard to that April's Tian'anmen Square Incident—even the number of those arrested came to light only much later.

By August, Mao Zedong's health was deteriorating rapidly. He finally died on September 9, aged eighty-four. He was succeeded by Hua Guofeng, who claimed the mandate from an alleged note in Mao's handwriting: "With you in charge, I can rest at ease." This note was later considered suspect, but the mode of power transfer was in any case unconstitutional. With the help of Marshal Ye Jianying and Wang Dongxing, the head of the elite No. 8341 guards (who had participated in the Tian'anmen crackdown), Hua Guofeng lost no time in arresting Jiang Qing and her cohorts, called the Gang of Four, on October 6, 1976, and eventually reinstated Deng Xiaoping on July 16, 1977.

In November 1978, a new official judgment was published on the 1976 Tian'anmen Incident. It is now recognized as "a revolutionary mass movement" that served as a "mass base" for the struggle directed against the Gang of Four. In time, Hua Guofeng would retreat from the scene while Deng Xiaoping consolidated his hold on power.

The Second Tian'anmen Incident
(April 16–June 4, 1989)

The First Tian'anmen Square demonstrations started out as a mass movement with participation of workers, students, and unemployed youths who had returned from the countryside. The Second Tian'anmen Square demonstrations were initiated formally by students, but received the support of nearly all sectors. According to statistics three months later (*The People's Daily*, September 6, 1989), the movement spread to over eighty cities, involving over six hundred tertiary institutions and 2,800,000 students. It also lasted four times as long, experienced an even bloodier crackdown with thousands of deaths, and was witnessed by the world media.

There were, nevertheless, many dramatic parallels, including the occasion and the timing (Hu Yaobang's death), the rallies at the Monument to the People's Heroes, and the triggering of a power struggle with the ensuing removal from power of Zhao Ziyang, the new scapegoat. And of course, all this happened as the prelude to a succession struggle, this time to follow Deng Xiaoping.

That 1989 should become an eventful year for China was inevitable. It was the year of the seventieth anniversary of the May Fourth Movement as well as of the fortieth anniversary of the establishment of the

People's Republic on the mainland. Early in the year, the dissident Fang Lizhi had written to Deng Xiaoping asking for amnesty for political prisoners, especially Wei Jingsheng. His action was supported by thirty-three other intellectuals in China in a signed, public statement, and even by many overseas Chinese. But such unprecedented boldness on the part of the intellectuals met with a stony silence. The Hong Kong "amnesty" delegation, carrying thousands of signatures, had met with many obstructions on the mainland. An atmosphere of tension permeated the country, with the reform movement stunted while official corruption and the rising cost of living were fueling mass discontent. That the students would take to the streets around the anniversary date May 4 was in any case predictable.

The first danger signal came on April 8, 1989. A Politburo meeting was taking place in Zhongnanhai (the former palace compound that is now the seat of the central government as well as the residence of its leaders). The topic of discussion was the many problems of education in China. During the heated debates, Hu Yaobang, the disgraced party chief, allegedly very sympathetic to educational reforms, experienced heart failure, and was sent at once to the hospital. He died seven days later, on April 15. Ironically, the news reached Beijing's students first through the Voice of America broadcasts around 3 P.M. that day, while the official Chinese broadcast came only at 7 P.M. Almost immediately, students made wall posters mourning his death and placed a wreath at Tian'anmen Square. The next morning, April 16, the Square was also symbolically full of broken bottles—a sign of discontent with Deng Xiaoping, whose name (Xiaoping) is pronounced like the Mandarin Chinese words for "small bottles," though written with different characters. Deng had ordered Hu Yaobang's removal from office in early 1987 following the student demonstrations in December 1986.

What followed is well known to the world, and related in chapter 1. I shall highlight only a few points.

First, the Western world was fascinated by the peaceful and disciplined demonstrations that offered a strong contrast to rowdy student protests elsewhere, often accompanied by violence. Chinese students were consciously following in the footsteps of Mohandas Gandhi and Martin Luther King, Jr., and they were asking for freedom and democracy. Toward the end, students revived flagging interest in their demonstrations with a replica of the Statue of Liberty that was erected near the Monument to the People's Heroes, across from Mao Zedong's giant portrait. Their boldness and initiative as well as the prolonged confrontation with the authorities created an atmosphere of false security. This offers a contrast to the later protests of October to December 1989 in East Germany and Czechoslovakia (where students were just as active), which were just as peaceful and disciplined but which benefited from Gorbachev's policies of noninterference.

Second, the Beijing demonstrations had been supported by mass student demonstrations, including hunger strikes, in dozens of other cities. Numerous students from the provinces (including very remote regions) had also joined the protesters at the capital, traveling there by train, frequently with the connivance of railway authorities who gave them free passage. (It is now alleged that more students from outside Beijing died at the Square that fateful night than students from Beijing itself, who could return to their campuses.) Suddenly, political consciousness swept across the globe wherever Chinese lived, as one million of them demonstrated in Hong Kong (May 21) and overseas students everywhere supported the Beijing movement, often crying the same slogans as those heard at Tian'anmen.

Third, the military crackdown was not unpredicted, since martial law had been in force for some time. What was unexpected, however, was the amount of popular support the students received from the workers and citizens of Beijing, including many members of the government and party bureaucracy and even civilians working in the military, who joined the demonstrations. Also unexpected was the deliberate brutality of the crackdown, unprecedented even in Chinese history.

Fourth, the world witnessed, to its edification and astonishment, the courage of the residents of Beijing, who clashed with the troops firing upon innocent and unarmed students and bystanders, and who were themselves shot upon. Moreover, immediately after the crackdown, news of the Beijing massacre reached many people in the provinces, and demonstrations protesting the massacre took place on June 4 in Shanghai, Nanjing, Chengdu, and many other cities, attended by hundreds of thousands. Such a spontaneous outburst of mass anger took place despite an armed presence very nearby, or, in some cases, right downtown.

At this point, I wish to offer a few possible answers to questions troubling the minds of many people who watched the events. These concern both the students' action and the government's reaction.

For people accustomed to the facts of repression in communist countries, the first questions that arise are: What is behind all this? Was it a spontaneous outburst, or an orchestrated one?

To the extent of our information, the demonstrations *were* initiated by the students themselves, that is, *in spite of* the repressive government, and *in order to* bring about more freedoms. One can feel the influence of their teachers, who insisted on a peaceful civil disobedience. But the teachers, or well-known dissidents like Fang Lizhi and his wife, did not take the first step of organizing the students. Groups of teachers and intellectuals did undertake hunger strikes of their own; some of them also distributed leaflets at the rallies. But tens of thousands of protesters would not have taken to the streets unless there was profound dissatisfaction. The week-long hunger strike actually reveals the amateur nature of student initiative, naive because of the debilitating effects of declaring an open-ended, round-the-clock fast on any protest group. Significantly, students gave up the hunger strike when the news of martial law broke. It was at that point that Zhao Ziyang's advisors tried to influence the rallies, according to the July report of Chen Xitong, Beijing's mayor, especially by urging an end to the fasting! If this report is correct, Zhao's action took place *after* his fate had been sealed.[4]

The week-long hunger strike appears quixotic in hindsight. After all, Chinese students had had small-scale "anti-hunger" demonstrations just a few months earlier to complain about the poor quality of campus food. For the emaciated students, the fast was debilitating and probably inhibited more rational moves. But such action touched the hearts of the masses, if not of the regime. Beijing residents, including many factory workers, and even members of the government bureaucracy, joined in the rallies and demonstrations in the wake of the hunger strike.

The confusion of the students' demands reflects a complex socioeconomic as well as political situation. They lacked a clear strategy, and did not initially call for workers and others to support their action. If they set up an "illegal" union of their own, it was because the official organization did not represent their interests and could not be trusted. As part of a democracy movement, students were committed to democratic procedures. According to published interviews with both Wu'er Kaixi and Chai Ling, two student leaders, their repeated calls to leave the Square went unheeded because the majority voted to remain there. As late as June 3, the Beijing group was outvoted by students from the provinces camping at the Square, who were less conscious of the possibility of dire consequences.

I believe it was not so much the temporary sense of euphoria, an illusory self-confidence in the power of numbers, that led the students and their supporters on to the chanting of anti-regime slogans and other bold action. It was, pure and simple, mass frustration seeking an outlet—all things considered, a *rational* outlet.

Of course, the students were aware that they were overstepping the limits of tolerable dissent in a totalitarian society. They knew of the possible and impending repression. They also made strategic mistakes, in seeking to arouse world attention and force the government to a compromise. From the brutality of the crackdown, the world can measure the regime's intransigence, and the futility of student efforts from the very beginning.

Taking Stock

Would it have been better for China if the students had not demonstrated, given the tragedy that ensued?

I find that scholars and students from the mainland, while mourning the students and workers who died, usually affirm the demonstrations as having contributed something to eventual democratization. This is not easy to comprehend, since the country appears now to be moving full throttle in reverse, enveloped as it is in a "white terror" of arrests, tortures, and fear. Many gains are now once more lost, including the "freedom" to criticize the government in the privacy of one's school or university. A motion that was to be debated in June 1989 by the standing committee of the National People's Congress concerned reforms of the press law, but the agenda was changed after the crisis. This committee met in the shadow of the military and concluded with statements of support for the hardliners. Of course, whatever "freedom" to criticize that was exercised before and during the demonstrations was only exercised with the government's tolerance rather than approval. Such tolerance was passive, a sign of a regime preoccupied with its own disunity. Ultimately, the responsibility to avoid a final confrontation with the demonstrators who were its own citizens rested squarely on the shoulders of the regime, rather than on those of the students.

To outsiders who have heard that China's youth were becoming nihilistic, uninterested in their studies, concerned about making ends meet, and anxious about the lack of a career future, the eruption of patriotism and political consciousness was a surprise. Eyewitnesses also reported a visible solidarity in the city of Beijing during the days of the hunger strike and martial law, with palpable concern by citizens for one another and for the students, and even with a drop in the crime rate. The young people's own sense of discipline and order contrasted sharply with a country mired in corruption and chaos.

Let us now move on to the political problems preoccupying many observers:

Why were so many troops from different military regions summoned to Beijing against unarmed students? Why did the government resort to military brutality of such scale, after weeks of threats and inaction?

According to the Chinese-language press, as well as recent visitors from Beijing, the troops were summoned not only to quell the students but to "guard against" one another. The leadership feared a mutiny from among the ranks of the Beijing garrison and the 38th Army stationed nearby, some of whom apparently refused initially to carry out a crackdown. The crackdown in 1976 was carried out by the militia and Mao's elite guards, apparently because the authorities at that time could not command the loyalty of the army. The troops who actually carried out the slaughter in 1989 were brought in from outside the city, after having been kept in ignorance about the peaceful character of the demonstrations. There is allegedly medical evidence of their having been drugged in preparation, according to information coming from hospitals that cared for the injured soldiers.

The official explanation that rubber bullets and water hoses were not available is unacceptable, since Tian'anmen Square is well equipped to handle fires. An inescapable conclusion is that the authorities wanted to make an example of the demonstrators, to create "stability" for their regime.

Was the government not fearful of international reactions, as well as a nationwide economic setback after a decade of relative prosperity?

It appears that the government was more concerned with the perceived threats to its own power from within the country. Reportedly, Deng Xiaoping and other elders concluded that there was no point to future economic development, if *they* were to lose the control and the benefits. The same could be said about any possible world reaction. Obviously, the regime had not reckoned with advanced modern technology, with which reporters could transmit news despite the satellite blackout.

The regime was *surprised* by the strength of world reaction: the condemnation by other governments, the economic sanctions as well as the protection offered to rebellious students and even defecting diplomats, accompanied by the lull in economic and other exchanges. A Chinese trade delegation was pelted with tomatoes by crowds in Mexico City (June 1989), a fact that surprised its members, who thought they could carry on "business as usual."

In his June 9 address, Deng Xiaoping raised the point that "the United States criticizes us for clamping down on students, but when they handle student protests within their own country, have they not also . . . made arrests and shed blood?"[5] Obviously, he had in mind the spring 1970 incident at Kent State University in Ohio, when the National Guard was called in to put down anti-war student protests, resulting in four deaths.

The differences to be noted include (1) the militant character and provocative actions of the U.S. peace activists; and (2) the American government's admission after the event that a mistake had been made.

Was there the possibility of a peaceful solution to the crisis? Could not the government have negotiated with the students, at least offering a compromise?

Here, I offer my own answer, as well as that of many mainland students and scholars. To my mind (and, I believe, to the mind of many others, including the demonstrators and their sympathizers), a compromise could and should have been made. In fact, it would have helped the country in many ways.

The student demonstrators in China differed from their counterparts, whether the Americans at Kent State (1970) or the South Koreans, many of whom were armed, at Kwangju (1980). A sensible government would have met them halfway, granted them a dialogue, and promised political reforms. The entire world expected the Chinese leaders to do just that, to demonstrate their own reasonableness and accountability.

The political changes in Eastern Europe in fall and winter 1989 show us that the Chinese government had been correct in its estimate of the gravity of its own situation in April and May. East Europeans have succeeded in overturning the Communist old guard in both Berlin and Prague. The trouble with demonstrations in both China and Eastern Europe is that they represent serious grievances that cannot be resolved by polite dialogues. Power has to change hands, and few dictators are ready to step down voluntarily to yield their places to their opponents. This does not mean one can condone the repressions in China. On the contrary, this only reinforces the conviction that the old guard is ruthlessly selfish, and unwilling, whatever the price, to share power with a people they claim to serve.

At the same time, this is not to say that the student demonstrations could have led the country directly to democratization. As the younger and more inexperienced members of a society, students can start a movement, but can seldom bring their ideals to fruition. The cause of democratization in China cannot move ahead without the involvement of workers and peasants. What the student movement has made public is the support of the urban workers, what Marx and Engels regarded as the most dynamic group in any social revolution. True, students have held many political demonstrations during the forty-year history of the People's Republic; but workers have also been important in spearheading the cause of democracy. Until 1986, the best-known dissidents, like Wang Xizhe, Wei Jingsheng, and Ren Wanding, were all workers rather than students. Peasants, too, are known to have made petitions and held protests. Indeed, several peasants were among those executed in the aftermath of the protests.

Another group of people that should not be forgotten in this context is the ethnic or "national" minorities. Interestingly, the students have elected some leaders from the Uighur (Central Asian Turkic) as well as Tibetan minorities, groups of people that had often been uncomfortable with the majority rule of the Han Chinese. Had the government risen to the occasion, it would have responded to the demands for democratization in the name of socialism and under the banner of its own constitution. Such a move would have helped everybody—not just the restless Tibetans and Uighurs, but also the Han people of Hong Kong—to accept Communist rule. It would also have impressed Taiwan, which the Communists desire to incorporate eventually into their own sphere of power.

By contrast, the repression galvanized sentiments of opposition, so that the future return of Hong Kong to the motherland will more likely resemble the occupation of Tibet in the late fifties. It is ironic that martial law has remained in force in two very different places in China: in the capital, Beijing, and in the remote region of Tibet.

Conclusion

Clearly China has changed far less in the past ten years than the joint ventures and the skyscrapers in Beijing suggested. For a hundred years, the military has played the decisive role in determining the outcome of power struggles. The rumbling of tanks into Beijing rudely reminded us that, beneath the surface, things are the same.[6]

Is Michel Oksenberg right to be pessimistic in the preceding passage? Apparently, to judge from the brutal crackdown, yes. But there is another way to answer the question of how much China has changed. It is that the outburst of demands for freedom and democratization shows the urgency of political reforms. A crackdown can bring about only a false impression of order and stability. But the anger will continue to seethe and ferment. There will be renewed protests and demonstrations, and eventually, the false stability will itself crack.

Is such ferment for change the result of China's contact with the outside during the past ten years? This tends to be the judgment of Western journalists.

My response is a qualified yes. The opening of the country to the West has certainly stimulated the intellectual ferment behind the protests. But other factors also played their part. Among the educated, urban people, many remember a time when the country was divided and at war, but enjoying more freedom than after liberation. Besides, China's recent history discloses a constant recurrence of student unrest, because the population cannot continue to take the lie that it is the "people's democracy." They have witnessed in recent years the ever-growing gap between the privileged and the underprivileged. They know that the system has become "socialist" in name only, since the leaders have been exploiting socialism for profit. The disclosures of corruption in East Germany in the autumn of 1989 reveal parallel problems in communist regimes, East and West. In the case of China, Hu Yaobang's death was only a catalyst, as Zhou Enlai's had been in 1976. The protesters could no longer wait for Deng's death to "stir the pot." This is the human factor in history. And if any regime, whether Deng Xiaoping's or his successor's, is to hold together a country like China, it must remember the important role of this human factor. Fewer and fewer people are willing to serve only as tools of the ruling class, which is what every communist regime expects of its governed.

Yes, Chinese observers of current events as well as Chinese historians are obsessed with cyclical occurrences, including the yearly seasonal changes and the traditional twelve-year system of the animal zodiac. And they see more historical repetition of events under Communist rule than ever previously in the rise and fall of dynastic cycles. Indeed, it may be called the "Dictatorship Syndrome," conditioned by a repressive government, a succession struggle, and irrepressible public anger.

Such a syndrome can be discerned in the events of Eastern Europe as well as in China, with the successive protests and repressions of the past. We need only mention East Germany in 1953, Poland in 1956, Hungary in 1958, and Czechoslovakia in 1968. The rise and resurgence of the Polish workers' union, Solidarity (1980–89), which had experienced many years of repression, has been particularly impressive. There, the dictator, General Jaruzelski, learned not only to tolerate dissent but also to collaborate with his erstwhile adversaries. For a time in 1989, he rode the storm much better than the hard-line communist chiefs of East Germany (Honecker) or of Czechoslovakia (Husak). Both in East Germany and in Czechoslovakia, demonstrators recalled the earlier protests in China on their banners and in their utterances. The unity of the communist world is reflected in the aspirations for freedom that have come to surface in both East and West.

At the close of the 1980s, relief came in sight for Eastern Europe with

Gorbachev's ascendancy in the U.S.S.R., and the success or failure of his reforms will determine the destiny of much of the world. The events of 1989 have been dramatic, but cannot yet be declared as final.

Ten years may be the limit of tolerance for the human psyche, whether in Eastern Europe or in China. Even in Czechoslovakia, barely nine years after the tanks of the Warsaw Pact nations had ended the Prague Spring, over seven hundred dissident intellectuals and other leaders signed a human-rights manifesto in 1977 ("Charter 77"), petitioning the government to respect its own constitution. Although suppressed at the time, many of these people have once more reemerged in the demonstrations of 1989.

For a long time, American observers and historians have found this heuristic device of identifying cycles "alien and confining," and have preferred to analyze social structures and economic developments or offer psychological interpretations for the changes in China. But the recent events of Tian'anmen Square, especially when compared with the previous Tian'anmen Incident that occurred in 1976, "suggests a new post-1949 cycle repeating itself in almost seismic fashion," says an American journalist.[7]

Offering an American analogy to this cyclical theory, this former Beijing correspondent of the *Washington Post* speaks of the great continental plates on the California coast grinding past each other at the San Andreas fault, and producing earthquakes at remarkably consistent intervals.

> There is a similar predictability in the way China and Marxism, pushed together for 40 years, have unleashed political earthquakes at the end of every decade since 1949. Two incompatible ideals forced to deal with each other apparently require periodic, essential and, unfortunately, often violent releases of tension.[8]

The exiled dissident Yan Jiaqi was active *both* in 1976 and in 1989 at the Tian'anmen demonstrations. He speaks of the "fresh air" he breathed there of "science and democracy," already in 1976.[9] It is indicative of the 1989 crackdown as signaling a step backward and the reinauguration of a "cultural revolution" that in December 1989 the repressive government announced the arrest of persons who had been active both in 1976 and in 1989 at Tian'anmen Square, for the very reason that they took part in both events. History in this instance seems to be deliberately reenacted.

In any case, the preferred Chinese metaphor is the flooding of the Yellow River. Not that metaphors make a big difference; it is the catastrophes represented that count.

We know under Heaven
- There are ninety-nine twists and turns in the Yellow River.
- There are ninety-nine boats on each of the twists and turns.
- There are ninety-nine poles on each of the boats.
- There are ninety-nine oarsmen on each of the ninety-nine twists and turns to pole the boats along.[10]

Ninety-nine represents a large number, even an indefinite number. If this is any prediction, at a time when it is rumored that the writers and producers of the television series *River Elegy* are being arrested and punished for their implicit criticisms of the powers that be, we may well expect a long "dark age" ahead for the people of China. On the other hand, can the Dalai Lama be wrong to predict for China, as he did on his reception of the Nobel prize in Oslo, Norway, in December 1989, that democracy will come about "within a decade"?

> A few days ago, the Tian'anmen Incident was rehabilitated, and this enhanced greatly the positive socialist sentiments of the masses of people. . . . A revolutionary political party should only fear not hearing the people's voices; it should only fear silence. . . .
>
> One should never use methods of repression against problems of thinking. . . . And the different levels of [political] leadership should never be polarized vis-à-vis the masses.[11]

These are Deng Xiaoping's words, said in December 1978, when he encouraged the liberation of thought. He was then referring to the Tian'anmen Incident of 1976. These may be the words of a new leader to come, vis-à-vis the Tian'anmen Incident of 1989.

■

CHAPTER 8

What of Moral Legitimacy?

> If a ruler regards his subjects as his hands and feet, then his subjects will regard him as their belly and heart. If a ruler regards his subjects as dogs and horses, the ministers will regard him as any other man. If a ruler regards his subjects as dirt and grass, the subjects will regard him as a bandit and an enemy.
> — *MENCIUS* 4B:3

There has been talk about the present Chinese government's having lost its moral legitimacy after the massacre of June 3–4. But what is "moral legitimacy"? The words suggest two sources for its meaning: morality and law. To fulfill the moral criterion, the governing power must be decent enough to keep the trust of the people. To keep the juridical criterion, it must also have and abide by reasonable laws. To quote briefly from the political philosopher John Locke:

> The natural liberty of man is to be free from any superior power on earth, . . . but to have only the law of nature for his rule. The liberty of man in society is to be under no other legislative power but that established by consent in the commonwealth, . . . [and] what the legislative shall enact according to the trust put in it.[1]

John Locke and others spoke as Western political philosophers, but they apparently felt that the truth they represented is universally applicable. In Chinese, there are no exact equivalents for the English words "freedom" or "liberty," now translated as *ziyou* (literally, self-determined). The closest classical term was *ziran* (literally, the natural), connoting more a sense of harmony with nature than of self-assertion. Another difficulty of translation is with the term "right" as in human rights. The modern Chinese term is *quan*, which also means "power" and can imply a threat to an established power. A less ambiguous term is the Chinese translation of "democracy," that is, *minzhu* (literally, the people as masters).

This linguistic digression points out a few difficulties in the Chinese struggle for freedom and human rights. The struggle is a modern phenomenon, but Chinese scholars in the past have long recognized the importance of a bond between the government and the people. Classical philosophers like Mozi (fifth century B.C.) discussed the origin of social authority through a form of consent on the part of human beings who gather together to prevent injury and disorder and to elect the wise to lead them.

Other ancient philosophers also spoke out on related questions. The best known is Mencius (fourth century B.C.). On the basis of the ancient classics and of Mencius's teachings, the Chinese long ago enunciated the doctrine called "the Mandate of Heaven," according to which every ruler receives his power to govern from Heaven, and keeps this mandate only to the extent that he practices humane government. If he or his heir becomes a tyrant, the mandate may be lost and given by Heaven to another. And Heaven decides the issue according to the will of the people, says Mencius, while quoting from the ancient classic, *The Book of History*, because "Heaven sees as the people see; Heaven hears as the people hear."[2]

Mencius insisted that the killing of a tyrant is no longer "regicide," but "tyrannicide." And the modern term for "revolution" is *geming*, that is, "changing the mandate." This is the reason why Chinese history has seen so many dynastic changes, and why even the Communist government fears the eventuality of *biantian*, or "Heaven changing its mandate." True, the government Mencius spoke about was essentially an absolute monarchy, but its absolutism was not unlimited. Mindful of the importance of keeping popular support and consent, the wise ruler practices benevolent government. As another Confucian scholar, Xunzi (third century B.C.), has said,

> One who truly undestands how to use force does not rely upon force. He is careful to . . . create a fund of good will. . . . is benevolence is the loftiest in the world, his righteousness is the loftiest in the world, and his authority is the loftiest in the world. . . . He need not wear out his men and arms, and yet the whole world is won over to him.[3]

A Moral Mandate to Rule?

Since the second century B.C., Confucianism has always been considered the dominant philosophy in Chinese history. Actually, it had to share the political arena with its arch enemy, Legalism, an amoral and immoral philosophy of power. According to this ancient tradition, the ruler uses "law" (*fa*) to strike fear in the hearts of his people. For this reason, the Chinese have always had a *negative* impression of law. All law has been regarded as punitive, rather than as protective of one's rights. As a people, the Chinese prefer arbitration to litigation as a means of settling disputes, basically because they do not trust the law or the courts, which are considered as supporting law-enforcement agencies. Let us quote from the third-century-B.C. Legalist philosopher Han Feizi:

> The tiger is able to overpower the dog because of his claws and teeth, but if he discards his claws and teeth and lets the dog use them, then on the contrary he will be overpowered by the dog. In the same way the ruler of men uses punishments and favors to control his ministers, but if he discards his punishments and favors and lets his ministers employ them, then on the contrary he will find himself in the control of his ministers.[4]

A well-known Legalist parable is that of a young boy who remained intractable in his misguided ways despite parental advice, the admonitions of teachers, and the counsels of neighbors. He was eventually forced to change his ways by the intervention of the local magistrates and the soldiers sent out to enforce the law.

> Thus the love of parents is not enough to make children learn what is right, but must be backed up by the strict penalties of the local officials; for people by nature grow proud on love, but they listen to authority.[5]

The Communist government does not follow the lines of Confucian political morality. Under Mao Zedong, it challenged time and again the moral authority of Confucius and of Mencius. It has been said, rightly, that Mao tried to establish himself as a "counter-Confucius," setting himself squarely against the Confucian virtues as well as against the entire social context in which they were expressed. But even Mao knew that the people retained a certain power, the power of the masses, which he sought from time to time to unleash and manipulate—to serve his own ends. And Mao also knew that the clever ruler must blend rewards and punishments according to Legalist advice in order to keep the people at bay. During the "Anti-Confucius Campaign" (1973–74) that vilified the ancient sage, the followers of Mao Zedong considered themselves also as followers of the ancient Legalists struggling against the followers of Confucius, whom they dubbed hypocrites. The Communist regime may indeed be regarded as manifesting a *mixed* heritage of selected Marxist-Leninist principles and Maoist strategies, which have been combined with the amoral heritage of Legalism.

The Cloak of Legitimacy

According to Fang Lizhi, the best-known Chinese dissident, who took refuge in the United States Embassy in Beijing shortly after the June 1989 crackdown, "The contents of our Constitution are quite good. Should we compare our Constitution with those of England and America, the difference is not so big. The problem is that we have not seriously enforced our Constitution."[6]

Those who consider Communist China to be a dictatorship may be surprised to hear that the government claims to rule with a constitution, and that the present constitution is rather well regarded, even by dissidents. As a matter of fact, in nearly forty years of rule, Communist China has promulgated many constitutions, beginning with the *Organic Law* (1949) and eventually wearing out three constitutions successively: in 1954, 1975, 1978.

Presumably, Communist China decided to give itself a constitution because such was the precedent set by the Soviet Union, its model, as well as by Nationalist China, its enemy. Moreover, what better way is there for legally establishing a government than giving it a constitution? Since the regime is not by definition an absolute monarchy, it needs a rule of law to show that it is what it claims to be, a people's republic. The constitution offers a cloak of legitimacy, in the same way as the imperial seals used to serve as the mark of legitimacy to the pre-modern governments, which ruled by imperial decrees.

The fact that a young republic has gone through so many constitutions may be puzzling to many people. By comparison, the United States Constitution has served well enough for two centuries, requiring on the average only about one amendment every ten years. In the case of England (despite Fang Lizhi's mention that is quoted earlier) there is in fact no "written" constitution to speak about, although the country claims to be the model and "ancestor" of Western constitutional democracies— Margaret Thatcher's dispute with the French at the time of their bicentennial in July 1989 being only the latest in England's claims to constitutional priority. Before examining the reasons for the rapid turnovers of Chinese constitutions, however, we should first look into the constitution now in force, to learn from it what the regime regards as its cloak of legitimacy.

China's newest constitution, now in force, is that of 1982. Speaking objectively, it represents a step forward. Among other things, it was actually drafted by a committee with the approval of the People's Congress rather than by a small clique appointed by the party or the Leader, as the preceding ones had been. Besides, the language is more precise and specific in setting forth the state's understanding of itself, and in detailing the rights as well as the obligations of the people.

The preface or preamble to the 1982 Constitution offers a survey of recent modern history leading up to the foundation of the Communist Chinese state in 1949. It is very similar to that preceding the 1954 Constitution, except for the addition of a paragraph about the Republican Revolution of 1911 under Sun Yat-sen. Presumably, it is put there as a token of good will to the Nationalists, now ruling Taiwan.

The body of the 1982 Constitution begins with a definition of the Chinese Communist state. It is the most important article in the whole document, and its dialectical language and stance make a special impression:

> *Art. 1.*   The People's Republic of China is a socialist state under the people's democratic dictatorship led by the working class and based on the alliance of workers and peasants.
>
> The socialist system is the basic system of the People's Republic of China. Sabotage of the system by any organization or individual is prohibited.

Only after this acknowledgment of the supremacy of socialism comes a second acknowledgment, in Article 2: "All power in the People's Republic of China belongs to the people."

After that comes the explanation of how this "power" is exercised, through the National People's Congress and the various levels of People's Congresses (*Art. 2*) and how these congresses are elected "democratically," "responsible to the people," and "supervised by the people" (*Art. 3*).

Article 4 outlines rather fully the equality guaranteed to the various nationalities or ethnic groups, whose rights and interests are all protected by the state, and how the minority groups enjoy autonomy in the regions where they congregate.

Article 5 stipulates, in strong language, that all law, and administrative and regional statutes must not be in conflict with the constitution, and that "no organization or individual can have privileges that go beyond the constitution and the laws."

These articles in chapter 1 of the constitution reinforce the "people's rights" promised and guaranteed in chapter 2. Essentially, the inclusion of "rights" is hardly new for the 1982 Constitution. The earlier versions all speak of people's rights. But the 1982 Constitution especially reinstated the basic principle that "all citizens are equal before the law." It then goes on to emphasize the balance between rights and obligations: "Every citizen enjoys the rights, and at the same time must perform the duties prescribed by the Constitution and the laws" (*Art. 33*).

Scholars have indeed agreed that the 1982 Constitution is much more comprehensive about "rights." In fact, we can compare, article by article, this constitution with the United Nations' Universal Declaration of Human Rights, and find real parallels. We shall quote first from the Chinese constitution:

> *Art. 35.* Citizens of the People's Republic of China have the freedom of speech, of the press, of assembly, of association, of procession (*yuxing*) and of demonstration (*shiwei*).
>
> *Art. 37.* The freedom of the citizens of the People's Republic of China is inviolable. . . .
>
> Unlawful deprivation or restrictionof citizens' freedom of person by detension or other means is prohibited; and unlawful search of the person of citizens is prohibited.
>
> It is prohibited to make illegal arrests or to use other means to deprive the citizens of, or to limit their personal freedom; it is prohibited to make illegal searches of the citizens' bodies.[7]

And now for the United Nations' Universal Declaration of Human Rights:

> *Art. 3.* Everybody has the right to life, liberty and security of person.
>
> *Art. 4.* No one shall be held in slavery or servitude. . . .
>
> *Art. 5.* No one shall be subjected to torture or to cruel, inhuman or degrading treatment or punishment.
>
> *Art. 9.* No one shall be subjected to arbitrary arrest, detention or exile.
>
> *Art. 20 (1).* Everyone has the right to freedom of peaceful assembly and association.

It should be mentioned that the 1982 Constitution deleted the right given to workers to strike, which was stated in two preceding constitutions. For a people's republic that defines itself as a state "under the leadership of the workers," the deletion must have been deliberate.

Let us for the moment reserve judgment about the ambiguous definition of socialism as a system. In that case, and speaking comparatively, the Chinese constitution would appear to cover the ground of "rights" rather well, with the exception of Articles 4 and 5 in the Universal Declaration. Of course, the Universal Declaration includes other articles as well, regarding access to a free press, and elections by universal and equal suffrage. Without stopping to examine these issues further, let us turn to the question of the observance of the constitution. After all, the proof of the pudding is in the eating.

The "Unwritten" Constitution?

I remember being impressed by a televised interview in the summer of 1989 of Yan Jiaqi, former head of the Institute of Political Science of the Chinese Social Science Academy. Speaking on the subject of constitutions, he said that there are two constitutions in China: a written one, which serves the people, and an unwritten one, which takes precedence over the written one, and serves the ruling group.

I have been thinking about what this "unwritten" constitution is: a kind of Chinese "common-law tradition," if we may call it that. I believe it comes from the ancient Legalist school, which teaches about how to acquire and maintain power. For the Chinese Communists, all law, including constitutional law, is an instrument of the power of the state rather than a guarantee of the rights of the citizens.

To understand Communist China, we must remember that it possesses a fundamentally dialectical and even contradictory structure. It is, first of all, a one-party government, with a certain built-in tension between the Communist party and the government, including its constitution.

The preface to the constitution also lays out the preeminence of socialism as a system and of the Communist party as the governing party of the country. These are two of the "Four Basic Principles" that Deng Xiaoping's regime has consistently insisted upon—the other two being the guidance of Marxist-Leninism and of Mao's thought, and the form of the government as a "people's democratic dictatorship," a phrase given in Article 1. Strange to say, however, the role of the party is not clearly defined in the body of the constitution itself.

But the exercise of power, including that of "enforcing the Constitution," demonstrates fully and well the pre-eminence of the party, and indeed its superiority to the constitution. This is exemplified in the most recent National People's Congress, which is nominally (that is, constitutionally) the supreme governing body of the country. In actual fact, it is also totally under the control of the party. Instead of carrying out elections for members to this congress itself, according to the literal stipulation of the constitution, the party (rather, the Politburo, or even its standing committee) actually recommends for acceptance the chief officers for both the congress and China's other large body, the Political Consultative Conference. It is in fact the party's Politburo that "nominates" the chairman or president of the standing committee of the People's Congress as well as the chairman or president of the Political Consultative Conference, together with their vice-chairmen or presidents and other members. The congress itself serves as a rubber stamp for these "appointments" as well as for "legislation" submitted by the Politburo for its approval. Exactly how the party controls the congress has been documented by the party-controlled newspaper, the *Wen Hui Bao* (March 1988), but it is not clear *by what power* the party does so.

In the 1980s, some openness was observed in the National People's Congress, which has served as a forum for rather energetic discussions and debates. These have included discussions of the lists of names submitted for consideration before final appointment, including those nominated to be cabinet ministers. Besides, at least on the "district" level, the country has held free elections, and even dissidents have run, and won. An example is Li Shuxian, Fang Lizhi's wife, who was elected to be a member of the district assembly representing the Haiding area, where Beijing University is located.

The problem is the lack of harmony between the laws and the constitution. My brother Frank, who served in China as a correspondent for the *Wall Street Journal* (1979–83), told me the story of how he was once briefly detained by Chinese security authorities. While walking by their office on a city street, he chanced to see a notice of certain decrees that had been published. He decided to take notes on what he saw, and this apparently attracted enough attention for him to be summoned inside for questioning. He was asked what he was doing, and why. He replied that he was taking notes of rules and regulations that had been published, which he found interesting because they limited the rights granted by the constitution—rights such as freedom of speech, of assembly, of association, of demonstrations. These were all limited by provisions of government security, and where assembly and demonstration are concerned, subordinated to specific case-by-case approval. When confronted with these laws and decrees, which could be found unconstitutional in a Western society, his interrogators were not amused; they questioned his motives in noting things down, as though this itself might be an act of sabotage. After an hour or so, he was permitted to leave, but because he was an American, not a Chinese, citizen.

If there is a moral to this story, it is that a Chinese citizen would not even have the right to note down in writing what the rules and regulations are that limit or prohibit him or her from exercising his or her constitutional rights. Presumably, only a fool would seek to challenge those laws that are not in conformity with the constitution. In the history of dissent in China, however, there have been many such "fools."

The Party and Legitimacy

In fairness to the Communist party, let us seek to understand its governing role as this is understood by itself and its own concept of legitimacy.

Both the 1954 and the 1982 Constitutions of the Chinese People's Republic begin with a lengthy preface outlining the historical process that climaxed in the Communist seizure of power. Although the process is distinguishable for being so un-Marxist, since China never passed from feudal to bourgeois to communist, it remains the basis for the Communists' claim to legitimacy: that history has made them the masters of China's destiny, and that they, in turn, will make future history.

We are using here the term "party"; the correct, technical term is "proletariat." In its originally Marxist context, the proletariat refers to the urban working class, destined to be bearers of a great historical revolution, against the ruling bourgeois class. Ironically, Marxist social analysis, based on the realities of Western European society, was transposed to pre-industrialized Russia and China. In the latter country, the revolution was only successful after Mao Zedong had turned to organizing a peasant base in place of an urban proletariat. With victory in the Chinese context, the proletariat, translated as the "unpropertied" (*wucan jieji*), represents essentially the party in power. Presumably, the mandate of the party is to liberate the oppressed from their oppressors; and this mandate, together with a combination of history and power, gives the party its legitimacy to rule.

According to such an ideology, the Communist party's manual of government should be its own party statutes or constitution. In fact, if the party occupies the position of the ruling group, it has to govern a massive population, the vast majority of whom are and shall remain non-Communist. Strategically, it is important for the party in power to rally to its support the people it must govern. This population turned out in 1949 to welcome with enthusiasm the Communist victors during the retreat of the Nationalists. And the fact is already impressive: that the smaller group of armed forces under Communist leadership was able to overcome a much larger Nationalist army, many of whom surrendered without fighting. For a people accustomed to the idea of a Mandate of Heaven that is granted to the more virtuous, this was the sign of moral as well as political legitimacy.

To consolidate this support, the new regime decided to follow the Soviet precedent of promulgating a constitution as a means of winning over the multitudes. It would declare itself to be a "people's democracy" as the Soviet Communists had before it. Such is the origin of the first Chinese constitution of 1954. The ideas it contains would be Marxist-Leninist, but adapted to Chinese realities by the Great Helmsman, Mao Zedong.

I believe that this brief explanation can help us understand the Communists' perception of their own legitimacy. Favored by the laws of history, they consider themselves endowed with legitimacy because they were the victors in 1949, and because their Communist party represents, and has put into effect, a "liberation" of the country from foreign imperialism as well as from the economic oppression of the landlords and other exploiters. Communists are republicans; they are by nature against monarchic restoration. Following the earlier efforts of the Chinese bourgeois revolutionaries, and to help gain acceptance by the multitudes, they decided to take on a cloak of legitimacy in the form of the Constitution of the People's Republic. But experience has repeatedly shown that the party, or its leader, would rule—with or without the constitution.

The problem, however, is that the Communist party in China has not enjoyed the same hold on power as has the Communist party in the Soviet Union. The latter was very much Lenin's creation, and has governed that country through the huge party machine that is also the government bureaucracy. In China, things have been at the same time more complex and more simple. The party and the party's leader have had many "conflicts of interest." Sometimes one wins, sometimes the other. This is remarkably different from how things happen in the Soviet Union. Lenin was the man who gave the party its disciplined and organized form. Stalin terrorized and decimated it, but never tried to govern without it. Mao did.

The Leader and Legitimacy

Who is the supreme leader of the People's Republic? According to the 1982 Constitution, this person is the chairman or president of the People's Republic, and is elected to this office by the National People's Congress (Article 79). This was also what the 1954 Constitution asserted.

When we examine the chronicles of history, we find that Mao Zedong was proclaimed the first president or chairman of the People's Republic as well as the Chairman of the Communist party in 1949. In 1959, however, after the Lushan party conference, he yielded the first title to Liu Shaoqi, who effectively replaced him as head of state. However, he remained the paramount leader, constitution or no constitution, and eventually the power conflicts between himself and Liu Shaoqi came to the surface during the Cultural Revolution, which can be understood as having been started by Mao to topple Liu. During the decade that followed, the country was being governed, in name, by Mao alone. It was a personal despotism of the worst kind, conditioned by his own caprices as well as the caprices of his collaborators, and by the vicissitudes of his failing health.

Under Deng Xiaoping, the exercise of power became even more ambiguous. Nominally, he is chairman of only the Central Military Commission. In actual fact, as revealed by Zhao Ziyang during Gorbachev's visit of April 1989, the party had secretly agreed that Deng should remain "paramount leader" even though first Hu Yaobang, and then Zhao Ziyang was made party chief, while Yang Shangkun was made president of the People's Republic. Although the secret was hardly confidential, the dichotomy between the nominal and the actual seat of power only increased. Thus two party chiefs, first Hu Yaobang in 1987 and then Zhao Ziyang in 1989, have been pushed aside, quite obviously by a decision process that excluded most members of even the party's Politburo, to be rubber-stamped by the proper agencies (in Zhao's case) only in the shadow of the troops in and out of the city of Beijing. We now witness the personal despotism of Deng Xiaoping, conditioned also by his caprices, and the caprices of his collaborators, and by the vicissitudes of his failing health.

If each leader's constitutional status has been ambiguous, his observance of the constitution has been an even more serious problem. By all accounts, the 1954 Constitution, which had been *selectively* observed, had lost all meaning by the time of the 1957 Anti-rightist campaign. Even after the military crackdown on the student demonstrators in June 1989, the Chinese authorities continue to assert that they have been acting "according to the Constitution." Presumably, therefore, they have been enforcing the second part of Article 1: the prohibition of any organization or individual from destroying the socialist system. But they have virtually suspended all the guarantees of citizens' rights and freedoms, including the right to personal integrity of life and limb. As new laws are now being enacted, limiting even further the rights of the people to freedom of speech, of assembly, of association, and of demonstrations, one wonders what good the constitution is at present serving, where *the people* are concerned.

The Record on Human Rights

What does the Chinese government mean by "rights"? This is an important question, if we are to judge the government by its own performance. Here, it is quite true, constitution or no constitution, that the Communist regime has always shown an uneasiness about *human* rights. Like the Soviet Union, it has not signed the United Nations' Universal Declaration of Human Rights. In fact, the rights mentioned in the constitution are considered to be *citizens'* rights, rather than *human* rights. There are certain differences that follow implicitly.

First, what is implied is the idea that these rights are not inherent to the human being. Rather, they are bestowed by the constitution, and by the power that "bestows" the constitution to the citizens.

Second, only citizens in good standing may claim to enjoy these rights. They are not recognized in the case of those considered to be enemies of the state. Such individuals are "non-persons," and can no longer appeal to constitutional protection. The relevant article is the following:

> *Art. 28.* The state maintains public order and suppresses treasonable and other counterrevolutionary activities; it penalizes actions that endanger political security and disrupt the socialist economy and other criminal activities, and punishes and reforms criminals.[8]

As liberators of the people, the Communist party presumably enjoys their support. Throughout its forty years of rule, the Communist government has consistently declared that it has very few enemies, or rather, that there are very few "enemies of the state." A percentage frequently offered is 5 percent, which, in a large country, means 50 million. The problem is enhanced by the fact that purges or political campaigns often use predetermined "quota targets"—so many people, or so much percentage of the population *must* be struggled against. The recent arrest waves may very well be based on this same principle, of getting rid of "a very small minority" of troublemakers—and this so-called small minority, in a big country, can be a sizable number.

Presumably, the government is concerned as well that the party itself, with about 40 million members, does not represent an adequate proportion of the total population. There is need therefore for constant watchfulness, frequent purges, and the threat of severe punishments to maintain control over the country.

The Second Emperor's New Clothes

We could go on forever, citing the selective enforcements of the constitution, as well as the more serious, selective transgressions of both the spirit and the letter of the constitution. The logical conclusion is that, protestations to the contrary, this constitution, like so many others that preceded it, is only a smokescreen for the exercise of power by the party leadership, or rather, by the "paramount leader" who delegates his power from time to time to this or that person.

This conclusion is especially supported by the most recent events. The student protests have emphasized the fact that Hu Yaobang's removal from office as party secretary general in January 1987 was illegal, since it was never ratified by the appropriate authorities, as the party's own statutes stipulate. The same, however, happened in the case of Zhao Ziyang, who was also removed from the same office by an act of will, apparently Deng Xiaoping's will. Legally, Deng's office was below Zhao's. Certainly, it was Deng Xiaoping, in association with other elderly comrades *no longer holding office*, who decided that Zhao had transgressed against the party—by exercising *his* free vote on the Politburo's standing committee. When the central committee did meet, nearly a month later, followed by the standing committee of the National People's Congress, both confirmed the decision made earlier by a small group—or rather, by one man acting with the consent of a few retired comrades. No doubt, among other things, Zhao's disclosure of Deng's paramount power during the Gorbachev visit was counted against him. Meanwhile, the military, also called in without proper observance of the constitution, continued to occupy Tian'anmen Square.

Before all this happened, Deng's China is said to have turned its back on Mao's totalitarianism, and to have come to represent instead a "post-revolutionary authoritarian model." Now, however, a reassessment is due. Clearly, the authoritarian model easily reverts back to totalitarianism, whenever it is found to be more convenient.

Such is a government of men, or rather, of the *one man*. In the cases of both Mao and Deng, each has proven to be an unbenevolent despot. Once enthroned, both emperors ruled without proper cloaks or vestments. In Mao's case, we may speak of a *charisma* of leadership, to the extent that he was considered the founder of the People's Republic, and had been exalted to the status of a near-god by a personality cult. In Deng's case, this is not so. Having promised a rational, institutionalized rule of law, he himself has trampled upon it.

Voices of Dissent

So far, we have sought to compare the regime's actions to its promises and guarantees, as these are laid out in what is alleged to be the supreme law of the land, the constitution. We have found both Mao and Deng seriously wanting in any respect for the constitution. But is this also the mind of the Chinese people?

Until the most recent events, the outside world had the impression that China had few dissidents, despite a long history of repression. The students' demonstrations and the sympathies they received were therefore an eye-opener. The truth, however, is not so simple. During the periodic thaws that occur in the long winters of Communist rule, many voices of dissent had emerged. The earliest were during the Hundred Flowers movement (1957). The people's genuine happiness in welcoming the arrival of the Communists to power in 1949 has on many occasions become their disappointment and disillusionment. In this regard, a university lecturer teaching in Beijing is quoted as having had the audacity to say:

> When the Communist Party entered the city in 1949, the common people welcomed it . . . as a benevolent force. Today, the common people choose to estrange themselves from the . . . Party as if its members were gods and devils. . . . The Party members behave like plain-clothes police and place the masses under their surveillance. If the Communist Party distrusted me, the distrust would be mutual. China belongs to 600,000,000 people, including the counter-revolutionaries. It does not belong to the Communist Party alone. . . . If you carry on satisfactorily, well and good. If not, the masses may knock you down, . . . overthrow you . . . , for the Communists no longer serve the people.[9]

Another criticism ran:

> Our Constitution provides that citizens "enjoy freedom of residence and freedom to change residence." In fact, we have not given any of the 500 million peasants the freedom to change their residence to a city. . . . Our Constitution provides that "freedom of the person is inviolable." During the campaign for the suppression of counter-revolutionaries in 1955, an untold number of citizens throughout the country were detained. . . . A great many . . . died because they could not endure the struggle.[10]

Hundreds of thousands, if not millions, were labeled "rightists" in the late fifties and suffered for this, some remaining in prison or labor camp for three decades. But few of them had even uttered such strong protests against Communist despotism. It took the Cultural Revolution and the impact it had on a long-suffering multi-million population to shake the people's fundamental faith in the good intentions of Communist rule—in this case, Mao's personal despotism, but something the party had permitted and even helped to produce. Writing under the pseudonym Li Yizhe, three young men in the south of China published a *dazibao* that is still remembered for its clear articulation of the problems of a regime without constitutional limits to power. They say:

> Do not our Constitution, the Party's constitution, and the instructions from central [authorities] speak of the democratic rights of the people? Yes, this is not only stated, but also given are such rules as "the people's democracy is to be protected," "attacks and vengeance are not allowed," "torture to extract confessions is strictly prohibited." But the fact is that rights are usually not protected, while the practice of Fascist dictatorship is often "practiced" with "permission" from above on both the revolutionary cadres and the masses: imprisonment, killing, making up false accusations, even many tortures . . . ![11]

These were accusations of gross violations of citizens' rights, permitted and even carried out under the aegis of the government.[12] These accusations were further echoed by an even more direct challenge, made in 1978 by the well-known dissident Wei Jingsheng:

> The Chinese have taken a path they should never have entered; if they followed it, it is because a despot, who knew how to peddle his trash shrewdly, simply took them for a ride. . . . Moreover, the people were kept in complete ignorance of all alternatives, and were persuaded that this was the sole feasible way. What a swindle! . . .
>
> Do the people now enjoy democracy? No. Is it that the people do not want to be their own masters? Of course they do! It is precisely for this reason that the Communist Party defeated the Kuomintang. After this victory, what came out of all the earlier promises? First they changed the slogan of "People's Democratic Dictatorship" into "Dictatorship of the Proletariat." And then the last democratic leftovers, which a tiny handful of people were still enjoying at the top, disappeared too, to be replaced by the personal despotism of the "Great Leader." . . .
>
> The inescapable truth is that today the people are more miserable, unhappy, and backward than before.[13]

Western scholars had not always regarded the "dissidents" as representative of the Chinese people at large. Only now, with the students' demonstration of spring 1989, has the world discovered that a large segment of the population has been seriously disaffected with the conduct of the government. In an address made to at least five universities in

Beijing between April 27 and May 4, Ren Wanding, the human rights activist who spent several years in prison for the part he played in the Xidan democracy movement (1978), points out that the Four Cardinal Principles, which are placed above the constitution, are unacceptable to the people:

> The party in power cannot represent popular opinion; the government cannot represent popular opinion; the National People's Congress cannot represent popular opinion. . . . To have the National People's Congress truly represent popular opinion, we must change the unity between the party and the government, between the party and the constitution.[14]

Even before the occurrence of the bloody crackdown, the people of Beijing were brought to a state of shock by the declaration of martial law and the sight of troop movements (May 20, 1989). All this had been done without consulting the channels provided by the constitution. From that date on, the demonstrators started calling Li Peng's government "illegal" (*wei*).

With martial law and finally, with the military crackdown, a confrontation turned into polarization. Survivors are also branding the regime an illegal one, and calling for its overthrow. Of course, even here the words remain ambiguous. Does the term "regime" refer to Deng's rule, or to the Communist rule as a whole?

It would appear that there was hope for change from within the system, until the system itself destroyed this hope. As far as the people are concerned, Deng Xiaoping's regime is finished. One cannot trust one's butchers, and he has publicly said that "a little bloodshed" was necessary to keep students in check! But then, judging from performance, the entire Communist system is also bankrupt. It was already hated by the populace long before the end of the Cultural Revolution. Facts have proved that it never really changed in essence. People's lives remain dispensable at the whim of the ruler, whose power comes fundamentally out of the barrel of the gun. In all but name, Communist China has shown itself to be a military dictatorship, and a despotic one.

A Kernel of Humanity?

Should we judge the Communist regime on its record of ruling according to its own constitutional promises and guarantees? If the party basically considers itself superior to the constitution, and regards the latter as merely an instrument of public relations or of "united front" strategy, then perhaps we are looking in the wrong place.

But then, where else can we look? Where else, indeed, can the Chinese people look? As people everywhere look to their governments, the Chinese measure the regime according to the fulfillment of its own promises. And these are enshrined in the constitution. The Chinese people, also like people everywhere, expect a *humane* government, based on rational premises. It is not necessary for their Communist leaders to act like the Confucian-educated rulers of the past. But there is need for a genuine kernel of humanity, for enabling the people to meet their basic needs, and for leaving them in peace to pursue their own lives.

Instead, the record has been entirely different. Not only has *survival* itself been difficult throughout the past four decades, but every dimension of life has fallen under Big Brother's ever-watchful eye. Everything has come under state supervision, including marriage and childbearing. I remember being told by a woman from China how she and her colleagues at work have to meet yearly to decide which family may bear a child that year. If the quota granted is not met, it may be passed on to another. But of course, even worse are the experiences of being penalized, should one have neglected to abide by these norms. What happens if a woman becomes pregnant without the appropriate authorization— whether in or out of wedlock?

The answer is usually abortion. For the married woman, this may be carried out with proper medical care. For the unmarried, it is done forcibly, without the benefit of anesthesia. "This serves her right" is the judgment of those who carry out the state's order. After all, in the official Chinese value system the interests of the state have always dwarfed those of the individual. Both now and earlier, this value preference is reflected at every stage of the criminal process. But the goals of the imperial dynasties and of the Nationalist party were far more limited than those of the Communist party. It has been determined for the first time in Chinese history to extend the power of the central government to the grass-roots level and to control virtually every aspect of human activity.

Reflecting upon the June crackdown, a Japanese scholar, Mizoguchi Yuzo of the University of Tokyo, a man known for his Marxist sympathies, remarked in conversation:

> If this hits Chinese scholars in their heart, it is hitting us in the head. We shall have to change all our principles of studying China, our whole

methodology. We have been mistaken, because we thought there was at least a kernel of "humanity" in the Communist regime.

We hardly need Confucius or Mencius to conclude that without this kernel of humanity, there can be no rightful government.

Of course, the people living in Communist China discovered this for themselves long before the rest of the world. In the darkness that was the Cultural Revolution, many learned the bitter lesson that their government, which was ruling completely through extrajudicial procedures—namely, whims and caprices—did not represent their interests and had therefore no legitimacy. To quote once more from Wei Jingsheng:

> The Chinese people docilely followed a "Great Helmsman" who fed them with cakes that he painted by using a brush called "communism" and who quenched their thirst by dangling in front of their noses plums that were called "Great Leap Forward." . . . After having suffered this regime with considerable fortitude for thirty years, the people eventually understood: like the monkey who attempts to grasp the moon, they were condemned to remain forever empty-handed.[15]

Even before the occurrence of the bloody crackdown, the people of Beijing were brought to a state of shock by the declaration of martial law and the sight of troop movements. From that moment on, the demonstrators started calling for Li Peng to step down. A flyer distributed by the demonstrators says:

> The ruling clique is busy sharpening its knives . . . , and has publicly rebelled against the standing committee of the National People's Congress, publicly trampled the Constitution of our republic, publicly declared itself an enemy of the People's Republic. Therefore we need to struggle, to force the entire ruling clique to resign as a group, to make them ask pardon of the entire population, and to get a thorough investigation of its political and juridical responsibilities involved. This is our only practicable choice (May 20, 1989).[16]

The Chinese government calls itself a government of liberators. But the very words "liberation" and "liberty" weigh heavy on the liberated, and those among them who ask for freedom are hunted down. Like Communist governments elsewhere, they have turned the principles of Marxist humanism into a nightmare. In the Chinese case, the breach of trust with the people was all the worse because of the brutality of the final crackdown. How could even martial law justify the indiscriminate slaughter that occurred?

There has also been another breach of trust: the trust of the outside nations, so carefully cultivated for the past twelve years by the Chinese authorities. China has become an outcast in world politics.

So What?

Deng's regime, and even Mao's regime before his, may be lacking in moral legitimacy. But the dictator may just reply: So what? There is, after all, a difference between legitimacy and power. The dictator has the power, and the trappings that come with power, such as the *de jure* legitimacy that a puppet constitution may give.

But the same government has also shown that it never had the sincerity of keeping its own word, of observing the letter of the law as laid out in the constitution. It prefers the "unwritten constitution"–basically a manual of power, and the many decrees and regulations that are issued by the State Council through its many organs, especially the security offices. The governing of China remains a matter of fiat; as we have been reminded most recently, it remains a matter of the will of *one man*.

This helps us to understand why the constitution has been replaced so many times in four decades. Indeed, the basic law of the land has been amended and replaced each time to suit the new party line: in 1975, it was during the Cultural Revolution, and in 1978, just after the Cultural Revolution. Of course, the changes represent political realities, since the 1954 Constitution was nearly suspended after the Anti-rightist movement, while the 1975 Constitution blatantly proclaimed a "total dictatorship" granting the right to the security forces to "permit arrests." All this has led to the common perception that the constitution exists merely to serve as a concluding statement to a political struggle, to become the tool of the new ruling group, to the extent that it finds this convenient. There exists no document or law that can limit the exercise of power.

But perhaps, power has produced its own predictable patterns. According to its cyclical movements, the Chinese leadership swerves like a pendulum, showing itself sometimes to the left of center, sometimes to the right of center. It will keep total control, but may exercise this sometimes by loosening, sometimes by tightening the screws. A strongman is in charge until his death, whether or not he occupies the *de jure* position of head of government. His heirs apparent are usually eliminated before he departs the scene. After that, there will be a collective leadership while a power struggle continues behind the scene, until another strongman emerges. This is the "dictatorship syndrome," called in Chinese a "malignant cycle" (*exin xunhuan*).

The Communist government seized power by right of conquest. It has tried to give itself a constitutional legitimacy; but it has never succeeded. Nevertheless it has been recognized by most of the world's governments and sits on the Security Council of the United Nations. Will it be able to last indefinitely even if it has lost the support of its own people?

Chinese history may be a good reference point here. China's first unifier and worst tyrant, the founding emperor of the Qin Dynasty, to whom Mao Zedong has frequently been compared, reigned eleven years over the entire Chinese empire (221–210 B.C.). This man built the Great Wall, unified weights and measures as well as the written script, burned books, and buried scholars. Three years after his death, his son and successor committed suicide, and the dynasty was soon over.

The Qin tenure of power was perhaps too brief to be compared to a regime that has already lasted four decades. Let us therefore invoke another possible parallel: that of the late Qing or Manchu dynasty. Faced with imperialist threats and domestic unrest, the ruling dynasty, often a gerontocracy, had attempted a few belated reforms between 1840 and 1900, especially in building up military technology and heavy industry, but always short of declaring a constitutional government until it was too late, and never giving total support to freedom of speech and of the press. The dynasty met its end in 1911 with the Republican Revolution. Mainland scholars have discerned parallels here too.

The problem with any Communist regime is its totalitarian structure, supported by the military as well as by secret police, which makes organized opposition extremely difficult. But the lessons from the rest of the Communist world demonstrate that no dictatorship can hold together an unwilling people, even with guns and tanks. This is not entirely on account of the moral strength of the masses, but also because such a regime will be gradually torn asunder by the forces inside itself: a dissatisfied bureaucracy, a reluctant military, a sullen population.

Power is now seen to rest basically in one octogenarian dictator, as it did during the last years of Mao's regime. Like Mao, Deng has not hesitated to resort to bloodshed in the face of purported challenges to his rule. Mao's regime collapsed quickly after the Tian'anmen Incident of 1976, following his own death. What will happen after Deng's death may be a historical repetition. He has seized and maintained power, like Mao before him, with the help of the barrel of the gun. The guns will decide the issue of succession.

On coming to power, Deng Xiaoping spoke of giving China law, order, and stability. It was because the country had been without law and order, and on the point of total collapse. In the ten years during which he had the reins in hand, he could have established a rule of law, but did not. Economically, he has been a modernizer; politically, he has been a feudal warlord. He relied on the army, not for external adventures, but to assure his own power base. A cultural revolution of sorts has already begun, ironically, because China has not been stabilized after eleven years of Deng Xiaoping.

What Alternatives?

What alternatives loom on the horizon, if the present Communist regime has forfeited its moral mandate to rule?

Theoretically, an alternative can be found from within the country, even within the party, or from outside the government, or even outside the country.

Taiwan

Of the forces outside China, there is Taiwan, which still calls itself the Republic of China and claims the legitimacy that comes straight from Sun Yat-sen and the Revolution of 1911. Taiwan has made great strides since the government was moved there from the mainland. Starting with a successful land reform, it has gone from strength to strength, and is now a mini-economic power with huge reserves of capital. Even more important, the government lifted martial law in 1987, permitting an organized opposition party to grow and function. Besides, the population is now free to visit relatives in the mainland, and many have gone to do business and even to invest there. At the moment of the bloody crackdown on June 4, 1989, there were about 10,000 people from Taiwan in various parts of the mainland, especially in the coastal regions. Despite its prosperity and reforms, Taiwan appears unsuitable as an alternative to the Chinese Communists, mainly because the Nationalists who are still in control there lost power on the mainland to the Communists, and many people still remember their corrupt government. Besides, Taiwan is too small in size when compared to the mainland.

Despite these odds, it should be said that more and more people on the mainland are now aware of Taiwan's political and economic progress. It is amusing to hear that the Nationalist Revolutionary Party, supposedly the successor to the former Nationalist party, and one of the mainland's twenty-odd "political parties" contributing to the Communists' window-dressing effort, reported receiving many requests for information from mainland youths impressed with Taiwan's efforts. (These so-called democratic parties have usually supported the party in power as a "United Front.") It is even more interesting to hear that among the three hundred mainland students in the United States who publicly gave up their Communist party membership after the June 3–4 massacres, many went to Nationalist representatives in the U.S. to ask about joining the Taiwan-based party.

Originally, the government in Taiwan had considered the island the base for an eventual strike at the mainland. Generations of young people were trained to cry anti-Communist slogans and pledge themselves to the eventual recovery of the mainland. Ironically, all this has changed with democratization. The militant mood has been replaced by an attitude of reserve vis-à-vis the mainland. The new approach is that Taiwan should continue on its own road to prosperity and democracy, to set an example for the mainland. Observers have remarked that Taiwan has been following in all but name the path of "Taiwan independence" or a formal declaration that Taiwan itself is an independent country, separate from the mainland.

At the same time, mainland students overseas involved in the democracy movement have been urging Taiwan for some time to show more interest in the mainland, to respond to mainland calls for reunification with counter-suggestions, such as permitting at once the circulation of Taiwan newpapers, and initiating more exchanges on every level. They have a naive hope that China's political scene might be enlivened by the presence of *another* active political party: the Nationalists. In return, Taiwan has remained very cautious, refusing any contact on the official level, while embarking on a "flexible foreign policy," which made possible its participation in Beijing at the Asian Development Bank meeting in early May 1989.

In military strength, Taiwan is no match for the mainland, and knows it. Despite the Communists' overture of "peaceful reunification," made since 1981, the mainland regime has never abandoned the option of resorting to force to recover Taiwan. That was why the government in Taiwan placed its own forces on alert after June 4, in case the Communists might launch an "adventurist" policy. By itself, Taiwan cannot undertake the recovery of the mainland unless a situation of chaos should develop over there. But the presence of Taiwan—its example and its rivalry—remains a challenge to the mainland.

Moreover, Taiwan has its own problems. Besides the constant threat from the mainland that hangs over its head like the sword of Damocles, Taiwan is going through a period of transition after the passing from the scene of the "strong men" who had ruled the island for so long: Chiang Kai-shek and his son, Chiang Ching-kuo. With the increasing democratization, the people are also increasingly taking advantage of the "soft" government that has replaced the earlier one. Taiwan is impressive for its rapid industrialization; it is also witnessing an increasingly unruly citizenry, interested only in the continual rise of the local stock market. For many, the mainland evoked a romantic nostalgia. In mid-1989, noises for reunification with the mainland were made through the formula: one country, two governments (a novel formula for international law), which of course would be an improvement on the assurance given to Hong Kong. But it appears not to be what Beijing would consider. After the military intervention in Beijing, even the nostalgic sense of romance is over, and people would rather forget the nightmare.

Hong Kong

Besides Taiwan, there is Hong Kong to consider. What can Hong Kong do to help democratization in mainland China?

Hong Kong is an example of freedom and prosperity. Although political participation has been minimal in Hong Kong, the colony serves as a challenge to the mainland's anti-imperialist propaganda, and to its claims of great gains made since 1949. Hong Kong's freedoms are ultimately guaranteed by Britain as a colonial power, because of its own political tradition, even though the population has little access to political participation.

Sad to say, despite China's pledge that Hong Kong will remain unchanged for fifty years, according to the "one country, two systems" formula, we have seen little progress toward representative government in the British colony. The Basic Law, itself only a piece of paper conceived as a mini-constitution for a future Hong Kong, is being drafted very much according to the preferences of Beijing, with the connivance of the Hong Kong government. Hong Kong has been witnessing a steady flow of emigration, as its residents prepare for the undesired reunification with the mainland in 1997. Three-and-a-half million of the 5.5 million people there have British passports, but as "Hong Kong residents." They would like to emigrate, but Margaret Thatcher's government has resisted granting the permission for them to go to the United Kingdom. Many of them feel trapped in the web of history. In late July, a *People's Daily* article threatened not to observe the Sino-British agreement for a continuation of the capitalist system in Hong Kong for fifty years after 1997, because of Hong Kong assistance to the Chinese democracy movement.

If Hong Kong cannot be certain of its own democratic future, how can it help the mainland's democratization? The answer lies in Hong Kong's very fear of a future tied to that of the mainland. Today, the 5.5 million people in Hong Kong realize that their destiny is tied to that of China, for worse—or for better. Democratization in the mainland will give hope to Hong Kong and permit the continuation of prosperity.

It is indeed ironic that while communism is manifestly losing ground in Europe, it still expects to gain more in Asia—by the eventual and very reluctant return of capitalist Hong Kong to the socialist "motherland." The world has been passively watching this reunion process as Hong Kong people continue their exodus to safer havens. One solution to the Hong Kong problem may be to have East European countries open their doors to Hong Kong capital and business expertise, much as Canada and Australia are doing. This could be extremely useful in East Germany, with its loss of valued citizens.

In the midst of despair, a third force appears to be developing. The opposition to Communist rule now taking root in Hong Kong is actively helping the democracy advocates who have successfully escaped from the mainland. When the Hong Kong movement is combined with the over 40,000 overseas Chinese students who have all arisen as one, together with hundreds of thousands of other expatriates, we get a combined force worthy of attention. If Hong Kong is awaiting with trepidation its scheduled return to the mainland in the summer of 1997, the Beijing regime can count on Hong Kong's 5.5 million population, accustomed as they are to freedom, to be a growing source of headaches. And this combined force may yet join strength with the 22 million people of Taiwan, whose anti-Communist consciousness has also increased. People still remember that the Revolution of 1911, which toppled the Manchu dynasty, was made possible especially by overseas Chinese support.

But these outside forces can only be effective when given collaboration from the inside. From all available information, we have assurance that the April–May protests in 1989 represented a nationwide movement of an unprecedented scale. These may have been silenced for the moment but cannot be totally snuffed out. The real force of this mass movement cannot be measured, except perhaps from the intensity of the government's repression: the killings, the arrests. The present estimate, according to Hong Kong reports, is that at least 120,000 have been snatched in the roundup of democracy sympathizers.

Besides, everyone knows that the present mainland regime is a "caretaker" one. At eighty-four, Deng Xiaoping cannot be expected to last long. He will have to go the way of Mao Zedong. And after that, it is anyone's guess what will happen.

In the meantime, China's multitudes can take consolation in the direction of history, especially communist history in Eastern Europe. In

June 1988, the police in Hungary used truncheons and tear gas to break up a rally of a thousand people in Budapest demanding a ceremony marking the reburial of Imre Nagy, prime minister during the 1956 uprising against Soviet domination. Just a year later, in June 1989, the desired ceremony took place, witnessed by a crowd of 250,000 that also commemorated executed freedom fighters. As Victor Orban, a speaker at the June 16 ceremony, told the assembled crowd:

> We are not especially thankful that we are not being massacred like those students in Beijing, since we could be massacred if the authorities wished. We need to create a situation in which they cannot oppress us, even if they want to.[17]

Hungary was, in fact, the first Soviet-bloc nation to denounce the Chinese crackdown, and the official spokesman was none other than its own Communist party chief, Karoly Grosz, who had ordered the police dispersal of the Budapest rally last year. His words were: "I firmly declare that we deeply condemn violence and fratricidal war. These methods have nothing to do with socialism."[18]

To many people, it is strange that the Chinese students, the meekest of protesters following peaceful methods, should appear to have "boiled the pot of democracy." Be that as it may, these students and their sympathizers can draw more lessons from the Eastern European experience. To quote once more from the op-ed piece in the *New York Times*:

> Eastern Europe has had its Tiananmen Squares and has learned its lessons from them. Even though the democratic movements of East Europe today are stronger than ever, with the experiences of 1956, 1968, and 1981 in mind, we don't have to be warned that post-Communist democracy is best when cooked on a low flame.
>
> Poland and Hungary are engaged in a conspiracy of caution. The democratic movements in both countries have decided to renounce the taking of revenge for earlier failures and to let the Communists retire from power step by step.[19]

China's students and freedom fighters should take note. Instead of an armed struggle, instead of asking blood for blood, they should continue to stir the pot, without forcing it to come to a boil. "By the turn of the century, we may well witness democratic reforms in China as unimaginable as this week's Polish elections would have been in December 1981."[20]

■

CHAPTER 9

Will "Mr. Democracy" Come to China?

"Democracy, democracy." "Democracy" is everything; everything is for "democracy." And to say that this "democracy" "met with catastrophe" during the Great Cultural Revolution, and therefore that "the revolution is dead." Is this not to twist and change what Chairman Mao and the party central have said about the nature and function of the Great Proletarian Cultural Revolution?

This was the critical response made by the authorities of the time to a *dazibao* published in Guangzhou in late 1974 regarding democracy and the rule of law. Except for the mention of the Great Proletarian Cultural Revolution, this response could have been made by the authorities today with regard to the student movement of April to June 1989.

The *dazibao* was the medium through which these early proponents made known their desires. Placed in public places where they can draw the attention of the crowds, some of the better big-character posters are aesthetically attractive in addition to being persuasive in content. The Chinese constitution of 1972 included a provision permitting this airing of opinion through the so-called four freedoms: to speak out freely, air views fully, hold great debates, and write *dazibao*.

Time and again, the Chinese people—students, workers, and intellectuals—have asked for democracy. They have suffered persecution, imprisonment, and even death in making this demand. But what kind of democracy do they really want, and are they ready for it? These are questions that have been asked in the West. These are very serious questions, since the answers to such questions will in large measure shape the success of any democracy movement.

The People's Republic as a Democracy

"Democracy" may mean different things to different people—as does socialism. It has an ideal meaning, as well as an actual meaning. Government by the people refers ideally to a government produced by direct, universal election. In practice, things do not always work that way, and candidates for elective office may be themselves from a more privileged segment of the society. All the same, for those of us used to a Western, liberal democracy, the system is based on a rather ordinary and practical foundation: on the morality, the preferences, and the sense of responsibility of the average citizen. The U.S. Constitution presupposes such an ordinary, average, imperfect person, rather than an "ideal man." That may be one reason why the ideal and the real are not so far apart in the actual experience of liberal democracy. People need not worry unduly about who their president is, since even an elected president can be impeached—although that does not happen often.

In traditional China, there was the consciousness that a government should have the consent of the governed; indeed, that the people—the governed—are those who reflect Heaven's mandate to rule. But traditional Chinese government was more preoccupied with the rationalization and routinization of its administration than with developing any theory concerning the rule of the people or democracy. The concept came from outside. It was the basis of Sun Yat-sen's political beliefs. It was also the stated desire of the May Fourth Movement, at a time when warlords were ruling by decree rather than by carrying out the wishes of the people.

For the Western world, a democracy is not necessarily associated with a republic. The United Kingdom is proud to be a constitutional monarchy with a democratic form of government that goes back many centuries—allegedly to an earlier time than that of the Republic of France. Japan, too, has a constitutional democracy—with an imperial system. But political democracy is not exclusive to capitalist societies. There are social democracies as well, for example, in Sweden, where the monarchy has also remained intact.

To the West, however, the word "democracy"—rule by the many—means the diametrical opposite of the word "dictatorship"—rule by the few, or just one man. But then we look at the dictatorship that is China's political leadership, and we may wonder what this word "democracy," which the leadership seems to dread, may actually mean in the Chinese context. If the people are asking for a democracy, presumably theirs is not yet a democracy; and yet when we examine the question, we find the disturbing answer that "the People's Republic" actually defines and considers itself constitutionally *both* a democracy and a dictatorship, in the first article of both the 1954 and the 1982 constitutions.

The term "democratic dictatorship" is actually borrowed from Soviet usage, coined as it was by Lenin himself. Accordingly, democracy is to be extended to the people, defined constitutionally as a coalition of members of the four social classes (the working class, the peasants, the petty bourgeoisie, and the national bourgeoisie). These are represented on the PRC flag by the four yellow stars, while the big yellow star represents the Communist party, their unfailing guide. Dictatorship, on the other hand, applies to the enemies of the people: the landlord class, the bureaucratic bourgeoisie, the Nationalist reactionaries, and their accomplices. Clearly, this definition is based on the Marxist idea of class struggle, and the opposition of the "people" and its enemies.[1]

According to the constitution, this "democratic dictatorship" follows a "socialist system," but this term is nowhere defined in the constitution proper, whether in 1954 or 1982. It is merely mentioned in the preface or preamble to both constitutions. In the later preface, we read about the Four Cardinal Principles: the leadership of the Communist party, the guidance of Marxist-Leninism and of Mao Zedong Thought, the Dictatorship of the People's Democracy, and the Socialist Road. These also are nowhere explained; the terms themselves overlap in reference (as intellectuals on the mainland have pointed out); presumably, they are self-explanatory—as is the precise relationship between the Communist party and the government structure, also not explained by the constitution.

In 1949 Mao Zedong explained the term "democracy" on two levels: in the conventional sense, as a society where the people enjoy the freedoms of speech, assembly, and association, and have the right to vote and elect their own government; and in the historical sense, as a distinctive stage in China's sociopolitical and economic development, which is technically "post-feudal and pre-socialist." He also called democratic dictatorship "democratic centrism," with the second word referring to a centralization of power in the Communist party.

In the preface to the 1982 Constitution, the post-Mao regime announced the socialist system as "already firmly established" with the transformation of the private ownership of the means of production and the disappearance of an exploitative system. But it continued to call the system of government "democratic dictatorship," and defined its goal as that of constructing "socialist modernization." By the decisive Third Plenum of the party's Central Committee in December 1978, this pledge was also made "to assure that everyone is equal before the law, and not to permit anyone to have supra-legal privileges." This was further confirmed by Deng Xiaoping's address to the plenum, in which he emphasized the importance of taking care of the material interests of the masses, and not merely demanding their collaboration in a spirit of sacrifice.

> It is necessary to truly protect the democratic rights of individual workers and peasants, including democratic elections, democratic management, and democratic supervision.[2]

The People's Republic as a Dictatorship

In speaking of the People's Republic as a democracy, we have to rely on the words of the constitutions and the promises of the various leaders. In moving to its status as a dictatorship, the concept becomes somewhat clearer. A dictatorship denotes rule from the top down, whereas a democracy suggests a rule from the bottom up. The two are hard to join. In the dialectical system that is a "people's democratic dictatorship," the resulting ambiguity has permitted the regime to define itself according to the needs of the occasion.

The People's Republic is actually governed by the Communist party, officially represented as the party of the proletariat, and this proletariat exercises the powers of the dictatorship. The party's structure is generally modeled on that of the Soviet Union. It resembles a series of concentric circles with a central committee at the middle (with forty-four members in 1949), which has a Politburo (with fourteen members), which in turn has its own standing committee (five members). Mao's term "democratic centrism" really means that power resides *nominally* at the periphery of the largest circle, but *actually* within the innermost circle. In the case of China, it frequently belongs only to the center.

The analogy is useful when we think of what sociologists have said about the center and the periphery. The recent student takeover of Tian'anmen Square is an example of how the people at the periphery took over the place that is symbolically the center of power in China. How this enraged the government is manifested by its own brutal recovery of this center. For the octogenarians, Tian'anmen Square had been polluted, its image had been literally defaced in front of the world. In fact, Mao's portrait at Tian'anmen was defaced by three young people from his own province who splashed paint on it, and these culprits were handed over to the authorities by the demonstrating students. The bloodbath permitted the "cleansing" of this image, in the eyes of the people in the innermost circle.

The party structure represents a Leninist bureaucracy, but it functions in China in a more Stalinist manner, tending toward total concentration of power under a one-man rule, whenever this strongman is around. On Deng Xiaoping's visit to the United States, American government leaders speaking with him were astonished at how readily he was able to make decisions and assurances, without referring to anyone back home, whereas the United States president would have the Congress to contend with. When the subject came up of permitting a number of Chinese to emigrate to the United States, Deng is reported to have said that since China was overpopulated, the Americans were welcome to add another zero to that figure (that is, increase it by ten times). This casualness in decision-making, displayed by a strongman in power, occurs again and again. Most recently, Deng is alleged to have used the argument of China's overpopulation once more to justify the deliberate butchery at Tian'anmen. Presumably, a few thousand less means less trouble for the overlord.

The *one man* may not always make all the decisions, since he may prefer to delegate, and at times he may even be blocked by various factions. But the "dictatorship syndrome" means a tendency to a one-man rule, to the rule of a center whose power and caprices are only checked by the innermost circle with a few others perhaps seeking to rival the one man. He is literally the "top gun," and is presented to the multitudes as a kind of patriarch figure overseeing the affairs of a large family. Such a nominally patriarchal style distinguishes Chinese leadership even from Stalinist rule. It is basically inherited from the imperial days, when the supreme lord or "paramount leader" had the power of life and death over all his subjects. Considering what happened on June 3–4, 1989, it is a frightening concept, especially as the Communist usage of such patriarchal power has stripped the patriarchy of any sentiments of paternalism that were supposed to inspire the earlier imperial despots. Besides, throughout history the imperial dynasties had developed their own rules of hereditary succession and their own systems of checks and balances, which the Communists have abandoned.

It is this patriarchy that today's Chinese intellectuals have identified as "feudal power," meaning a remnant of the past, when the country was an absolute monarchy. The more power the one strong leader at the center possesses and exercises, the less, of course, the country resembles democracy.

Power struggles occur at every level and in every layer of the concentric circles. But those that matter most take place at or near the center. These "fights between giants" (or "dogfights") have always frightened as well as fascinated the population on the periphery. For years, there had been the see-saw battle between Mao as party leader and Liu Shaoqi as head of state, with Liu's humiliation at the hands of the Red Guards and his subsequent death through neglect (1969). Before Liu, there had been General Peng Dehuai's challenge of Mao for his abuse of power and his mistakes in its exercise (1959); Peng too was purged and died in humiliation. After Liu, there was the dramatic rise and fall of General Lin Biao, Mao's "beloved comrade" and designated heir, who allegedly conspired against him and died in a plane crash (1971). But the best-known case was of course the rise and fall of the Gang of Four, accompanied by the several falls and final rise of Deng Xiaoping.

After the death of Mao and the fall of the Gang of Four (1977), it was a sad group of older comrades who reassembled to exchange their tales of woe. Every one of them (now belonging to the circle of eighty-year-olds around Deng Xiaoping) had suffered humiliation, had witnessed the sufferings of family and protégés at the hands of Red Guards running wild or from other henchmen of the Gang of Four. They had all lost their "democratic rights" during the Cultural Revolution.

Restored to power after the fall of the Gang of Four, Deng Xiaoping had a golden opportunity to return to the people their democratic rights through a proper system of government by law. At the Third Plenum (that is, plenary session) of the Eleventh Central Committee, he also warned the party against the dangers of exalting a leader above the country's constitution and laws.

> To protect the people's democracy, it is necessary to strengthen the rule of law. It is necessary to institutionalize democracy, give it the force of law, so that this system and this law will not change because of the caprices of the leader, the changes in his ways of seeing things and his [shifting] attention.[3]

These words may initially appear to echo those of the dissident Wei Jingsheng, who had earlier given *his* account of what happened:

> First they changed the slogan of "People's Democratic Dictatorship" into "Dictatorship of the Proletariat." And then *the last democratic leftovers* [italics added], which a tiny handful of people were still enjoying at the top, disappeared too, to be replaced by the personal despotism of "the Great Leader." . . . So it was that a new formula appeared: "Since the Leader is so great, a blind faith in his person could only bring increasing happiness to the people."[4]

However, in preserving the character of a "democratic dictatorship," the 1982 Constitution is also following the instructions made at the Third Plenum of the party's Central Committee. These maintain also that a "minority" of counterrevolutionaries who oppose socialist modernization is still around, and "class struggle" with such people cannot be relaxed. "We cannot weaken the dictatorship of the proletariat."

> Class struggles will continue to exist for a long time. . . . The Chinese people must fight against those forces and elements, both at home and abroad, that are hostile to China's socialist system and try to undermine it (Preface, 1982 Constitution).[5]

A humble electrician rather than a scholar, Wei Jingsheng voices the ordinary citizen's disaffection with such dictatorship. He expresses suspicion of what he was hearing about the new leader, Deng Xiaoping:

> The Chinese people need to be led by a strong man. If the modern despot is even tougher than his feudal predecessors, this merely shows his greatness. The Chinese people have no need for democracy, except when it comes properly "centralized"; in any other form, it is not worth a penny. You have little faith? As you wish. For your kind of people, there is always room in our jails.[6]

The last sentence proved self-fulfilling, in Wei's own case.

The problem is: For how long was the 1982 Constitution itself observed, whether in spirit or literally? I would answer: the *spirit of dictatorship*, of the struggles against political rivals and dissidents, was observed, even long before the crackdown of June 1989. But what was done was usually *against* the letter of the law as given in the constitution, and against the *spirit of democracy* guaranteed therein as well.

But democracy is not so easy to come by, and not just because the dictatorship does not permit it. Even if it can be established that the Chinese people want democracy, we may still have to show that they are also ready for it. What is essential is a certain political consciousness, a consensus of opinion regarding elective government, and even more, about the procedures by which such a government is to be formed. In recent Chinese history, there was experience of *mass* democracy during the early years of the Cultural Revolution—but without the legitimation and control of a rule of law. The Paris Commune of 1870 is an example of mass democracy; indeed, it was an example very much on people's minds during the Chinese Cultural Revolution when a parallel experiment was briefly envisaged: a state without a bureaucracy, a "Chinese People's Commune."

Mass Democracy: A Brief Experiment, 1966–68

An observation some have made about the 1989 student demonstrations is their superficial resemblance to the demonstrations of Red Guards in 1966. There has been the same mass spontaneity, the same ebullience and euphoria—followed each time by tragedy and disillusionment. Of course, the young people of today were not yet born in August 1966, and could only rely on their elders' memory of what happened over twenty years ago. In fact, there are serious differences between 1966 and the recent events. The Red Guards arose at Mao's summons, to do his bidding; when a million of them from all over the country rallied at Tian'anmen Square (August 18, 1966), they were reviewed by their god and idol, Mao Zedong himself. The demonstrators of 1989 initiated their own movement, and had a more sophisticated political consciousness. Their occupation of Tian'anmen Square never got the blessing of the man on top, even if Zhao Ziyang arrived belatedly to console them and bid farewell, after his own fate had been sealed in an inner circle of the party.

The movement of the Red Guards signaled a brief experiment in mass democracy. As there were real oppressors of the people in the party bureaucracy at the time, the young people took their mandate seriously and enthusiastically. From mid-August to mid-September, university and middle school students wearing red armbands went everywhere throughout the provinces, traveling free on the railroads, and putting the local authorities on trial for real or imagined crimes. This was the "free mobilization of the masses" so different from previous mobilizations or "rectification campaigns" that had been carried out by the party bureaucrats. To use Mao's words, their goal was to "bombard the Headquarters," namely, the top bureaucracy of the party itself. The goal, they thought, was the eventual establishment of a mass democracy to replace the bureaucracy.

Carrying Mao's portraits, waving Mao's Little Red Books, the Red Guards marched through city streets and countrysides in a "search and destroy" operation against all symbols of the "feudal past" and "bourgeois influences." Party officials were "arrested" and paraded through the streets, wearing dunce caps, to confess their "crimes" at mass rallies.

What the [People's Daily's] editorial had advocated, that "the masses of the people themselves are to take over the destiny of the socialist country, and manage themselves the cities, industry, communications and economy" has been realized. The revolutionary storm of January [1967] has in a short time [transferred power] from the hands of the officials to the hands of the enthusiastic workers. Society suddenly discovered that [people] not only could go on living without the officials, but could live better, develop with greater liberty and faster. . . . Without the officials and their apparatus, the forces of production were liberated; . . . coal was produced as usual . . . , communications carried on as usual . . . as the workers' enthusiasm for production and their [spirit of] initiative were greatly liberated.[7]

It was a moment of power and exuberation for the young people, and many excesses were committed. These excesses cannot and should not be condoned. The ultra-leftists were especially strong in a city like Shanghai, which they wanted to turn into a "Shanghai People's Commune." Mao Zedong, however, was having second thoughts. "Let us rather be more on the side of stability," he said. "Let us not change all the names. That would lead to the question about changing the form of government: the state system and its appellation. Are we going to become a Chinese People's Commune?"[8]

In February 1967, "revolutionary committees" were sent into cities and factories to take over the reins of government from the young leftists. But the experiment with mass democracy was not over yet. In many regions, armed conflicts took place in which the regular army either played a direct role or supported those who did—including arming radical workers and students. In August 1967, the ultra-leftists made another attempt to "communize" the entire country, but the loss of the Chairman's support doomed the movement, and their battle was lost to the revolutionary committees.

For their generation, what remained memorable and invaluable was the political consciousness developed during those years—to be subsequently transformed as they found themselves used and discarded and sent to the countryside. Some of these individuals said the following in a *dazibao* in 1974:

To say that the principal function of the Great Proletarian Cultural Revolution was to unveil and destroy the headquarters of Liu Shaoqi's capitalist headquarters, is not as good as to say it is to train the people and the masses to liberate their own revolutionary, democratic spirit. . . .

The freedom of speech, the freedom of publishing, the freedom of assembly, the freedom of association, which are all in the Constitution, and the freedom of "linking-up" [*cuan-lian*: literally, going around the country and joining up with other groups] which is not in the Constitution have all been put into practice. . . . This is a revolutionary gain never known to the Chinese people in the previous millennia.[9]

China's earlier "dissidents," including Li Yizhe (whose words are cited above) and Wei Jingsheng, all belonged to this group of Red Guards who learned by bittersweet experience what political participation means. With gradual maturation, they realized that mass democracy is at best capricious and irrational. Procedural norms and a rule of law are necessary, to prevent the excesses of a dictatorship as well as of a mass democracy.

Democracy and Rule of Law: The Dream for the Future

Until the events of April–May 1989, the world had presumed that, with few exceptions, the Chinese people are neither interested in, nor ready for, human rights and a democratic rule of law. When we dig into recent history, we find that this is not true. The Chinese people have long been hungry for a democratic rule of law, although they have not been able to discuss the subject in detail. In other words, we have many voices asking for democratic institutions and for the separation of powers. We have few specific proposals as to how this is to be put into effect in a country like China, with a huge peasant base.

In most cases, when people ask for the protection of their "democratic rights," they are just demanding the enjoyment of elemental *human rights*: above all, freedom from political persecution as well as from miscarriages of justice. Such were in part due to the caprice of the masses during the Cultural Revolution, and in part also due to the regime's preference for handing down severe penalties even for trivial offenses. Recently, an airport employee who cracked a joke about hijacking was reported to the judiciary and sentenced to serve three years. On hearing this sentence, he told the judge: "I was foolish to joke about hijacking. But your sentencing me to three years in prison is a worse joke: it makes a farce of justice."[10] This demonstrates how the rule of law now in force is far from one that incorporates the basic sense of fairness.

Interestingly, the best-known advocates of freedom and democracy were for a long time individuals from the grass roots: persons who had finished senior middle school or the equivalent, like the Li Yizhe trio, Yang Xiguang, and Wei Jingsheng. Intellectual leaders only became outspoken sometime later. This demonstrates the relative timidity of the leading intellectuals as well as the temerity of ordinary people. Besides, the desire for freedom and democratization is clearly not limited to university graduates.

Li Yizhe's work appeared in Guangzhou at a time when the country was being mobilized by the anti-Confucius, anti–Lin Biao campaign. It represented the work of three young men: Li Zhentian, Chen Yiyang,

Wang Xizhe (Wang became the best known of the group), under a composite name made up of one syllable from each of their names. All had been Red Guards. All had suffered imprisonment as ultra-leftists, and came out of it chastened and matured. Their sixty-seven-page *dazibao* was done with the permission of the provincial authorities (including that of Zhao Ziyang), and was completed in November 1974.

The authors offered their manifesto "On Socialist Democracy and Its Rule of Law" as a humble petition to the Fourth People's Congress, scheduled to meet soon. Using the language of the time, the authors described two headquarters: an *idealized* one, represented by Mao Zedong's "correct" line, and a *vilified* one, called the fascist line of the fallen Lin Biao and described as still being in power. Coming at a time when people were fatigued from the constant struggles of the Cultural Revolution and the chaos and disorder that accompanied these, their words made a lot of sense.

> In the recent years, policies have changed many times, even from morning to night . . . creating a confusion of thought in the people and doubt regarding the party. We think the Fourth People's Congress should once more explain the place of the party in the history of socialism, and realize what should have the form of law.[11]

The socialist rule of law is designed to replace the lawlessness and the miscarriages of justice committed during the Cultural Revolution. The authors of this *dazibao* actually wanted a restoration of the 1954 Constitution:

> Did not the Constitution of 1954 also state what the democratic rights of the people are? Has not Chairman Mao said many times: Without a broad people's democracy, the dictatorship of the proletariat cannot be firm? . . .
>
> The Fourth People's Congress must establish clear laws to punish those who transgress the law while knowing it, those who transgress the law while being in charge of it, who make up false accusations, take private vengeance through public means . . . , have private prisons, carry out numerous tortures, and have no regard for people's lives.[12]

As a matter of fact, the Fourth National People's Congress, in which the young people had placed their hopes, was to adopt a new constitution that abolished most of the citizens' rights and freedoms guaranteed by the earlier one of 1954, and even explicitly allowed the public security forces to make arrests without specific authorization! (It should be noted that for having published their *dazibao*, with official approval, the authors were punished as having "abused"[!] their constitutional right. As of September 1989, at least one of them was still under detention.)

Demands for democratization resurfaced toward the end of the Cultural Revolution. They were heard at the First Tian'anmen Incident (April 1976), and were quickly silenced. They were aired once more, especially through *dazibao* posted on the brick walls at a section of west central Beijing called Xidan (November 1978 to March 1979). John Fraser calls it the "Tiny Democracy Movement" in part to tease colleagues who were saying that it involved only relatively few people "who didn't represent the population as a whole." Fraser himself did some research on the effectiveness of such wall posters and was told that if one poster stayed for at least half an hour and was read by only a few individuals "within a few days anyone in Peking who wanted to know what was on it could find out." After all, "when the state controls all the principal forms of communication, unofficial lines work remarkably well." Besides, all over the country people can find out from the Voice of America broadcasts; they are also actively helped by intercity travelers and even by railway employees who take notes and circulate them. "You know, railway people are the messengers of China, especially if they are on a regular run to Peking."[13]

The Xidan democracy movement flourished during the so-called Spring of Beijing. One of its early spokesmen was Ren Wanding, an educated worker who organized a Chinese Human Rights' Alliance with a nineteen-point proclamation (1979) asking for guarantees to various freedoms and for political reforms: "to liberate thinking from the cage, to permit [the air of] freedom to permeate the country, and to allow the wise Chinese people to share in the treasures of humanity." Interestingly, this Alliance also pleads for the recognition of minority rights, and for giving "minority nationalities sufficient autonomy."[14] When the spring thaw was over, Ren was sentenced to four years' imprisonment. But Wei Jingsheng's case became much better known than Ren's.

When the Gang of Four fell in 1977, many people suggested ever so gently that there was really a fifth guilty party—the recently deceased Mao Zedong himself. When the policy of Four Modernizations was launched, some also hinted at a missing fifth modernization: that of the political system. The person who brought this need out into the open was Wei Jingsheng, a twenty-nine-year-old former soldier then serving as an electrician for the Beijing zoo. He and others took advantage of the brief thaw in political climate to call for freedom and democratization, including a national referendum to elect deputies to the National People's Congress as well as other leaders at all levels and in various areas.

Wei Jingsheng represented the impatience of a generation that found itself cheated by the Cultural Revolution and could not be satisfied with new slogans and a new mobilization, even for a goal called the Four Modernizations. He criticized Deng Xiaoping directly, for minimizing Mao Zedong's mistakes. He even challenged the legitimacy of Deng's rule, and called it a "new dictatorship." The events of 1989 have proved him right.

In his famous *dazibao*, Wei had this to say:

> The people need democracy. When they demand democracy, they simply demand that which originally belonged to them. Whoever dares to deny them democracy is nothing but a shameless bandit, even more despicable than the capitalist who robs the workers' sweat and blood. . . .
>
> The only reason we want to achieve modernization is to ensure democracy, freedom, and happiness for the people. Without this "fifth modernization" all other "modernizations" are nothing but lies.[15]

In October 1979, Wei Jingsheng was sentenced to fifteen years' imprisonment on trumped-up charges. A fellow victim was a young woman, Fu Yuehua, who had helped the peasants petitioning in Beijing in January 1979, against hunger and repression. She was kidnapped by security personnel, and then sentenced to imprisonment on unrelated charges. The new 1982 Constitution removed the "four freedoms," which previously included expressing opinions freely in *dazibao*.

If the Xidan democracy movement is relatively well known outside China, the parallel movement in Shanghai has been much less reported. Actually, the Forum for Democracy in Shanghai had gotten to work shortly after the first wall posters came up in Beijing (November 1978). Many of the activists were unemployed young people who had returned from the countryside, to which they had been exiled during the Cultural Revolution. The leader was Qiao Zhongling, allegedly an eloquent speaker who attracted thousands to the rallies at People's Square. He was later arrested.

By contrast with Wei Jingsheng and others, Fang Lizhi is a very different kind of democracy advocate in today's China. His participation, and the participation of other intellectual leaders, have transformed the Chinese dissident movement and given it much more intellectual sophistication. An astrophysicist, Fang was expelled from the Communist party for the first time during the Anti-rightist campaign (1957) and rehabilitated only after the Cultural Revolution. Among other things, he proposed to Communist officials to make public their own earnings and properties, and he insisted on freedom of the press as a precondition for political reform. Both of these points became incorporated in the students' demands in spring 1989.

After his second expulsion from the party in early 1987, Fang continued to speak out on sensitive issues. On January 6, 1989, he addressed an open letter to Deng Xiaoping, asking for the release of Wei Jingsheng and all other political prisoners in honor of the seventieth anniversary of the May Fourth Movement and the fortieth anniversary of the founding of the People's Republic. On February 13, 1989, thirty-three other intellectuals followed his example and supported this cause. This action in turn inspired a mass petition from Hong Kong that collected over 23,000 signatures from the colony and from the world. When they tried to submit this mass petition to Beijing, the Hong Kong delegation met with a most unwelcome reception, and the petition itself was confiscated by the customs authorities in Tianjin on March 28, 1989.[16] The granting of amnesties is actually well known in Chinese history. The one emperor who distinguished himself in committing atrocities without ever granting amnesties was again the notorious first emperor of Qin, China's ruthless unifier, who died in 210 B.C.

As the amnesty petitions manifest, the Chinese people want first of all the protection of their rights as human beings. Liu Binyan, a journalist who was expelled from the party about the same time as was Fang Lizhi, is eloquent about "being able to talk about freedom."

> Some of us are afraid to hear about freedom. This is very abnormal. The fear itself proves a problem, a very big mistake, perhaps the mistake of several decades. Did not the Communist party want to liberate the whole of mankind? What is liberation? Liberation is to let everyone get freedom. *The Communist Manifesto* speaks of freedom many times. Why is it that freedom is no longer talked about after our Liberation? Even happiness can no longer be talked about: any mention of happiness is to pursue the happiness of the bourgeois class. This is a tragedy, and also an irony. Thousands of people including myself entered the Communist party to make revolution on the inspiration of freedom and happiness; many people lost their lives [fighting for] these slogans.[17]

The Cultural Revolution's best-known victim was the former head of state, Liu Shaoqi. He died under detention, of abuse and disease, alone and unattended, without anyone daring to show kindness to this "capitalist roader" and "enemy of the people." The authors of the 1988 television series *River Elegy* describe the conditions of Liu's death and offer this comment:

> In this very dark and eerie room, the chairman of the Republic, who had personally presided over the promulgation of the Constitution [of the Republic] and the statutes of the party, was secretly imprisoned and

spent the last twenty-eight days of his life. When he died, the white hair on his head was fully a foot long.

When the law cannot protect an ordinary citizen, it will not be able to protect the chairman of the republic. Unless the structure of Chinese society undergoes reform, and Chinese politics, economics, culture and concepts are modernized, who can guarantee that tragedy will not be reenacted?[18]

Abuses of power in today's China have been such that the rule itself has been decried as "feudal," that is, pre-modern, or what characterizes "Oriental despotism." But the safeguards in the traditional political structure are no longer in force, including the civil service examinations that recruited an educated personnel for the bureaucracy. Today, it is usually through connections to the privileged few, the ruling elite, that entry into the bureaucracy or the leadership circle is achieved—regardless of merit. Traditional China also had an office called the censor, with the responsibility of blowing the whistle on the government, even of censuring the emperor. That is also gone.

Among those arrested after June 4, 1989, is Yu Haocheng, an editor belonging to the Ministry of Public Security, and publisher of the Chinese translation of Solzhenitsyn's *Gulag*. Appropriately, he had argued for human rights, and especially for "freedom from fear."

Socialist or Liberal Democracy?

The various spokesmen for democracy usually appear to be asking for a socialist democracy, although they insist that it be a *genuine* democracy, rather than one in name alone. Wei Jingsheng, for example, pleaded for the realization of a "true socialism" and the enforcement of socialist constitutional rights:

What is democracy? Genuine democracy means giving all powers to the workers' collectives. . . . What is genuine democracy? It is a system that allows the people to choose, at their own will, representatives who administer in the name of the people, in conformity with the people's will and interests. The people must retain the right to dismiss and replace their representatives at any time, to prevent them from abusing their powers and turning into oppressors.[19]

Fang Lizhi refers to the Chinese constitution as a feasible instrument for democratization—provided it is actually implemented.

The content of our constitution is all right. If we compare our constitution with that of the U.K. and U.S., we'll find little difference. The problem is that we have not seriously carried out the constitution in practice. For example, the constitution talks about the separation of the three powers, but actually the power is concentrated. I think the most conservative slogan of the reform of the political order is to seriously put the Constitution into practice.[20]

Fang demands that the members of the National People's Congress be truly elected representatives, although he does not require that these elections be direct or universal, only that they be really done according to the constitution. But he would like the membership of the Congress reduced from the unwieldy three thousand. And he scoffs at the artificial unanimity reached in the National People's Congress, especially as this is vaunted by one of its members, who even wrote an article for the *People's Daily* overseas edition, claiming it better to have a vote of "3,000 to 0" in the Chinese Congress, rather than "51 to 49," as might occur in the United States Senate!

Fang favors the separation of the three powers, seeing in this also a necessary condition for the success of democratization.

Legislative, judicial and executive powers can be separated, China should democratize. Democratic societies are pluralistic. A monolithic control necessarily builds up a despotic dictatorship.[21]

He admits, however, that such separation of powers is not easy to practice "in Eastern countries, even in advanced Oriental countries."

Su Shaozhi, the former head of the Institute for the Study of Marxism-Leninism and Mao Zedong Thought in the Chinese Social Science Academy, now in the West, still speaks of socialism with some hope and affection. He emphasizes that true Marxism is for the liberation of the total human being, both politically and economically. While judging the dominant ideology behind the present regime to be a mixture of "feudal despotism and Stalinism," Su describes the tragic disillusionment that occurred during the bloodbath on June 3–4, 1989: that unarmed civilians, even when shot by real bullets, thought these to be rubber bullets because they could not believe that the regime would want to kill its own people.[22]

In their speeches, Chinese intellectuals have expressed a strong attraction to one kind of socialist democracy: that found in Scandinavian countries. To the question "What is socialism?" Fang Lizhi answers by praising the social democrats of Northern Europe, who, he says, still believe in Karl Marx but prefer class harmony to class struggle as a means of overcoming social contradictions. He describes how they have successfully created societies with a narrow gap between the rich and the poor, with high social benefits and low unemployment figures.

Even when the present regime is condemned for its brutality, the dissidents have not usually spoken out against the Communist party in itself. Their silence is not just the result of fear of reprisals. While there exists a range of political preferences, Chinese dissidents would generally opt for a socialist model, like that found in Scandinavian countries, if they are given a choice. There appears to be a common conviction that one may yet return to the original inspirations of Marxism, that the party itself may yet be transformed. The young dissident Liu Xiaobo speaks of reevaluating Marxism, and reminisces about his own discovery of that ideology at age fifteen:

> It is hard for me to forget the excitement I felt when I read the *Communist Manifesto* for the first time. I was profoundly moved by the passion and self-confidence that permeate the whole book. . . . I particularly like the writings of the early Marx, which have a stronger philosophical overtone and an uncompromising rebelliousness.[23]

For practical purposes, the Scandinavian model is called "socialist democracy" here, in distinction to the American model of a "liberal democracy." But the choice is not necessarily between one or the other. Depending on popular mandate, a country may be governed at one time by a socialist party, and at another time by a different one. One question still requires an answer: Is a Western-style elective government possible in China, even if political circumstances permit it? Given the large number of illiterate peasants in the country, I suggest here that China look to India as a practical model, since India does have such a democracy, and it does seem to work—up to a point. In fact, there are many more centrifugal forces at work in the Indian subcontinent (languages, religions, ethnic groups) than on the Chinese mainland. The fact that China does not have a real democracy is due more to historical than to ideological reasons.

But the Chinese remain most concerned with political reforms going on in other communist countries. They have watched the democratization of governments in Yugoslavia, Hungary, Poland, and of course, the Soviet Union. When the students took over Tian'anmen Square at the time of the Gorbachev visit, it was not just for the sake of seizing an occasion to grab news headlines outside the country. It was also out of a genuine admiration for his initiatives, and a desire to make their own government emulate his moves. It appears that the regime itself was quite aware of all this, and continues to fear above all a repetition in China the experience of these East European countries.

During the April–May demonstrations in 1989, the human rights activist Ren Wanding made the proposal to use the country's university campuses as a base to recruit experts who represent popular opinion among teachers and others, and organize new citizens' committees to work in collaboration with the National People's Congress to undertake a thorough restructuring of the government. His ideas may appear naive, but deserve a hearing: "In Poland, the workers' union took the leadership; in China, it is entirely possible for the educated classes to take leadership."[24] He voices the people's preference for social and political pluralism with a multiparty system:

> The democracy movement of 1989 is the mid-wife for a new party. . . .
> Perhaps, the infant girl [called] democracy may be killed in its cradle, but she will definitely be born again in the next storm. I believe that the long-range goal of the Chinese democracy movement is the peaceful transformation of the Communist Party's monolithic socio-political structure and its replacement by a pluralistic socio-political structure.[25]

Ren was among the earliest to be arrested in the 1989 roundup of dissidents.

The problem with the Chinese Communist party is the common knowledge of corruption at the top, and now, of renewed repression. If the dramatic developments in Eastern Europe in 1989 provide any basis for judgment, the future of Communism in China will remain bleak or at best shaky.

Is Democratization Possible through a New Authoritarianism?

Besides such words as freedom and democracy, another political slogan that has been often aired in China during the past decade is that of a "new authoritarianism." The actual inspiration comes from the models offered by the Four Little Dragons just off China's coast: South Korea, Taiwan, Hong Kong, and Singapore. Envious of their economic prosperity and mindful of their despotic tendencies, China's rulers have been considering ways of learning from their experience. Reformist circles around the moderate leaders, first Hu Yaobang and then Zhao Ziyang, have especially studied this concept, distinguishing it from any "old" authoritarianism, that is, plain old despotism. To my knowledge, this "new" authoritarianism envisions basically a benevolent despotism, in looking to a strong leader to give the country the right direction it needs, and also to protect the individual freedom of the citizens.

The new authoritarianism reveals the people's malaise concerning the old despotism, to the extent that it persists today. Its basic proposal is to build a new society on the basis of the old, and it pins all its hopes on the initiative of the ruler.

China's proponents of this new authoritarianism see the separation of the economy from politics as the first step toward achieving modernization as well as democratization. In that sense, they too look forward to the realization of democracy as the final objective. Basically, these people see the country as going through a Brezhnev era like the Soviet Union's, and await their own Gorbachev to revitalize politics and bring about democratization.

Critics of this new authoritarianism have pointed out that countries with iron-fisted leaders and a successful economy are the exception rather than the rule. Besides, the Four Little Dragons are themselves moving toward democracy. (Here, the case of Taiwan is most striking.) The American scholar whose name has been associated with the theory of new authoritarianism is Samuel P. Huntington. Huntington believes in the importance of proper legal authority in democratic as well as authoritarian societies. He insists that there is no *necessary* connection between authoritarianism and economic prosperity—for there is plenty of evidence of impoverished countries under dictatorial regimes. He also believes that authoritarian regimes should permit early democratization to assure their own continuing stability. To use his words:

> In an established single-party system, as in a democratic, competitive party system, political stability is measured by the degree to which the system possesses the institutional channels for transforming dissenters into participants.[26]

The Tian'anmen Incident of 1989 has revealed that China will see no political change without the approval of its top leadership, and the full power of this leadership resides either in one man, as with Mao or Deng, or with a small group, which was the case before Deng perceived himself strong enough to assert total control. Any democratization in the future will only follow a "benevolent despotism," which is another name for a "new authoritarianism." At first sight, no despot may be willing to despoil himself of power. But a wise leader may realize change to be inevitable for the country's greater prosperity, and also for the survival of the government itself.

Envisaging Changes

In the final analysis, democratization is only possible in a favorable political climate, whether it is undertaken by the regime itself, or by an organized opposition. After the June crackdown on the mass demonstrations, the political climate in China is against democratization. If one is to rule out the possibility of a successful armed insurrection, this can only come from above, that is, from a regime more favorable to change than the one currently in power. What chances can we envisage for such a change to take place?

As already mentioned in the previous chapter: the octogenarian dictatorship cannot last forever; and when it goes, the charisma associated with these veterans of the Long March will also depart from the scene. A power vacuum will ensue, most probably with the army as arbitrator. Following upon a longer or shorter period of instability or anarchy, a new power will hopefully seek more rationalization as well as institutionalization. In that eventuality, are there lessons from the present that can be useful in the future?

At a conference in Quebec City, Canada (June 6, 1989), Wang Zhao-jun, from Beijing's *Chinese Journalism Press*, gave an excellent analysis of the three political alternatives open to the country—at least before June 4, 1989.[27] Depending on power alignments, Wang's insights may still be useful some time in the future:

- *the "bird-cage economy"*—A term invented by the hard-liner Chen Yun himself, this metaphor of a bird in the cage refers to the centrally planned economy preferred by himself and his protégé, Premier Li Peng. The four sides of the cage represent the Four Fundamental Principles: socialism, the Communist party, the People's Democracy (that is, the Democratic Dictatorship of the Proletariat), and Marxist-Leninism/Mao Zedong Thought. Chen argues that one should not smother the bird by holding it in one's hands; one should give it some space, but leave it in the cage. Although intended as a metaphor for an economic policy, it has clear political references.

- *a covert restructuralism*—This refers to the views of those members of the party led by Zhao Ziyang, and formerly under Deng Xiaoping himself. They represent varying degrees of openness, both for the economy and for the political structure. They had hoped to present themselves as orthodox, at the time when the students were making noises for democratic reform. They were against suppressing the protesters by violent means, but they were not the actual organizers of the student protests.

- *a Western-style liberal democracy*—This represents the deepest desire of the student movement, which unveiled its own statue of the Goddess of Democracy, modeled on the Statue of Liberty.

With the crackdown, the bird-cage economy has basically won the political struggle at the top echelon of power. And it has also lost the trust of the people and the country. Together with the economy, the people feel that they are the caged birds. At the present moment, the cage is indeed very small and tight. But even should it be made larger, the birds can never be content inside.

The covert restructuralists have lost their leader in Zhao Ziyang. It is not known whether he or his spirit may rise up once more from the ashes, or whether someone else may take over his mantle. But this group basically remains attached to Communist rule. Their plans may eventually become subject to the same twists and turns and periodic violence as the plans of their party comrades. With the radical disillusionment people are now suffering, can any restructuring serve to build up new hopes?

A Western-style liberal democracy, symbolized by the statue of the goddess, may one day serve as a real option—but not for some time, given the political realities. However, if a controlled economy and a market economy can be made into bedfellows, we may yet look forward to the co-existence of certain elements of a liberal democracy with other elements of Marxism. The pledges Beijing made to Hong Kong point in this direction (even if the regime's record lacks credibility). I am now referring to an eventual alliance between the covert restructuralists and the liberals. But when the day comes for a change of regime, the covert restructuralists will not be able to run a government without the help of the increasingly liberal-minded intellectuals, all the more as events in Eastern Europe are pointing to the Communist party's loss of credibility everywhere.

Will Democracy Come to China?

Just because the people desire democracy, it does not necessarily follow that they are ready for it, or that they will get it. So, are the Chinese people ready for it?

Speaking superficially, one may say no. In a huge population like that of China's, only two million attend universities, that is, 0.5 percent of the entire country. While the students and their urban supporters were demonstrating for freedom and democracy in the big cities, the peasants in the countryside were more preoccupied with the coming harvest. Many never heard about these demonstrations or of the crackdown. Had the regime decided to opt for democratization, would the illiterate or semiliterate peasants have been ready for it?

This is a serious problem for a pre-industrialized society. On the one hand, China's peasants had developed their political consciousness under the Communist government. With their support, Mao Zedong had won the party leadership and the Communist Revolution. And yet, even more than the urban dwellers, the peasants had suffered the changes of party line from land reform and distribution to communization to the present responsibility system under which the communes have once more been dismantled. Like peasants everywhere, their attachment is to the land, and to their freedom in the use of both the land and its produce. A capricious government cannot give them the assurance of this freedom.

But the 1989 democracy protests did not touch the peasants as a mass group. From all indications, the tragedy is all the more poignant as the students had never expected to lead a mass movement, nor can they be expected to do so successfully. Students can ignite the flame, but it has to be carried forward by other segments of society. The movement that responded to the students' call was mainly based in the urban centers, but a successful democracy movement will have to mobilize the entire society. Even with peasant discontent, such mobilization will remain difficult without proper organization and strategy.

At this stage, there is evidence of desire for real democracy, of readiness to sacrifice all for its attainment. But such desire is based more on the opposition to autocracy than on an understanding of the principles of democratic government, even on the part of the urban population that supported the student movement. China still has a long road to go if the vast country is to become a democracy with institutionalized and implemented procedural norms based on government by consensus.

Despite opposition to the present regime, democratization is still easier to achieve when it arrives through the collaboration of those in power, as is happening in the Soviet Union and Eastern Europe. It is to be hoped that, for their own salvation, the future leaders of China will move in that direction, even if the emotional current now prevalent runs against the entire Communist regime. One lesson from spring 1989 is that things could have turned the other way. Had Deng Xiaoping thrown his support behind the reformist group, China could be on the road to democratization.

An Agenda for the Future

In communist countries, where the regime undertakes the political education of the masses, it often awakens political consciousness as well as economic expectations without being able to satisfy such. The constitutional pledges to safeguard democratic rights have actually aroused a hunger and thirst that the powers that be are unable to satisfy. Instead, we see a regime creating an active volcano for itself, and then sitting upon it.

This is why there is hope that a new regime may actually do something about the situation, rather than continually fanning the hopes of the people, only to frustrate them at the same time.

The authorities' treatment of dissent has been erratic, sometimes loosening (fang), sometimes tightening (shou) the screws. The pattern may look inscrutable to the outsider, except that they usually follow what is felt to be expedient, and expediency frequently changes. Often, the treatment of dissent represents a compromise between the various factions, hard-liners and moderates. The authorities have usually hit hardest at the most powerless dissidents, men like Wang Xizhe and Wei Jingsheng, but have tolerated for a longer time the voice of a Fang Lizhi, even though he was more widely heard, because of his internationally recognized scholarly stature.

At the present moment, the faction in power has suppressed the voices of democratic reform, representing a middle ground between a totalitarian dictatorship exercising power in an arbitrary fashion and a Western-style liberal democracy. The "guns of June" have stifled the voices of reform and even eroded the middle ground itself. The dilemma now facing the government is between continuing with a hard-line dictatorship on the one hand, and alternatively permitting a complete overhaul of its own structure—in other words, a transformation into a genuine democracy.

There are allegedly over 40 million Communist party members. Of these, 50 to 70 percent, including many recruited during the Cultural Revolution, are illiterate or semiliterate. The problems involved in such a party's governing China are enormous. Added to this are problems compounded by party structure and tradition. Every communist country is a police state; every communist party is accustomed to habits of secrecy, having passed its formative years as an underground organization, without ever becoming adjusted to an above-ground status. But even if the party as a whole stands responsible for the mismanagement of the nation, for the unhappiness of the population, there remain in the party many individuals who have consciences and keen insight, and who know reform is imperative if the party is to survive.

However, if and when the moderates return, they will have to contend with stronger voices from the liberals. They will have to work toward a real compromise: both to guarantee and give real freedom to the people, and to introduce such structural changes as would enable the separation of powers, to prevent abuses of power, bureaucratic corruption, and to assure a proper political succession. This will be, in effect, a mixing of two models. To the extent that it must be a democracy without the dictatorship, it will mean the repudiation in all but name of class struggle, a much-abused part of Communist ideology.

Is such a repudiation possible? Stranger things happened when China first opened itself to the forces of market economy from the outside. Stranger things are happening today, in the Soviet Union and in East European countries. China's students and intellectuals have openly expressed their interest in Gorbachev's *glasnost* as well as in the political reforms now going on in Poland and Hungary. If the Soviet Union has the advantage of a supreme leader in favor of a certain measure of democratization, it also has the disadvantage of a countryside that has shown itself more difficult to mobilize than the Chinese countryside, and of a larger number of discontented ethnic groups, many of which want to secede. China has many problems of its own, and the army crackdown has resulted in even more. But even within the military there are clearly forces that did not favor the crackdown, that would opt for moderate reforms when an occasion presents itself. China must yet await such an occasion, presumably possible some time after Deng Xiaoping's demise.

And when that day comes, what kind of changes may we realistically look forward to?

I shall outline a few points that have been tossed around. I shall not dwell on reforms of the economic structures, though these are badly needed. I will proceed from the premise that without political reforms, economic reforms will not work. The political reforms needed are:

1. firm assurances for the protection of human rights (not just citizens' rights), together with freedom for the press, demonstrated among other things by the country's signing the United Nations Declaration of Human Rights and by amnesty granted to political prisoners;
2. recruitment of an independent bureaucracy, based on the merit principle, to remain independent of party connections and to incorporate adequate reform of the infrastructure;
3. restructuring of the National People's Congress, as well as the Political Consultative Conference (a "United Front" organization) into what should resemble two houses of a legislature;

4. reform of the People's Court, so that it should no longer function as the punitive arm of the Communist party, but become an independent judiciary;
5. the reform of the People's Office of the Ombudsman (*renmin jiancha yuan*), with supervisory authority over elections and the functioning of the bureaucracy;
6. reform of the education system, including improved remuneration for teachers and other professional personnel, to revive confidence in the usefulness of acquiring skills and culture;
7. introduction of real elections to national and provincial legislatures, through transformed national and provincial "people's congresses" and "political consultative conferences" or their counterparts;
8. a federal system of government, giving more and genuine autonomy to the provinces and especially to the so-called Autonomous Regions like Tibet and Xinjiang, and of course, Hong Kong; and
9. an economy made independent of politics through reform of the dual currency system and dual price structures, and serious incorporation of market principles.

This is a horrendous list, because the changes required are so comprehensive and numerous. But then, much the same is true of the East European countries. These needs are symptoms of the Communist disease.

Each of these points also raises other problems, because each will change the power structure—in effect granting power to those agencies that have so far only served as "cosmetics," while removing it from the entrenched few. How are elections to be held in such a vast country with so many illiterate peasants? How can a judiciary like the present one, accustomed to abusing citizens' rights, be reestablished to protect these very rights? Will not a federal government succumb to regional bosses like the erstwhile "warlords"?

Conclusion: The Outlook

All these and other questions are difficult to answer in detail. The best answer at present is to say: consider the alternative. The country will sink into a worse quagmire unless bold reform is to take place at the earliest possible moment. Besides, the Communist regime can redeem itself, in the aftermath of all the mistakes it has made, only by starting anew on a course of action that can restore confidence in government.

Of course, reforms cannot succeed without a reform of the Communist party itself, and the abolition of the present system of dual control—with the party placed above the government and its constitution, and with a paramount leader placed ultimately above the party. But then, with the examples of the Soviet Union, Poland, and Hungary, there is no reason why the Chinese Communist Party cannot reform, if it really wishes to survive and retain some usefulness. Had it done so earlier, it might have maintained more party monopoly. After the experience of the crackdown, the party would have to permit free elections and a multi-party system, when the moment for reform returns.

True, the future of reform in China will also hinge upon the success of the reforms in the Soviet Union and in Eastern Europe. At present, in spite of Gorbachev's tremendous popularity outside of the Soviet Union, he is finding it increasingly difficult to hold together a kind of coalition between hard-liners and reformers, and to make his *perestroika* produce results in a country accustomed to seventy years of a rigidly controlled economy and its concomitant results of the lack not only of consumer goods, but even of essential supplies. There is still the possibility of a hard-line comeback in that country, which will spell doom for more than reform in the Soviet Union. But the fact that the Soviet system has produced Gorbachev and his associates is a sign of hope for the world itself.

China is at present being ruled by a small group of octogenarians, the last remnants of the "heroic" first generation of the Chinese Revolution. But their generation of strongmen, and the charisma they possessed, will necessarily pass away. With a new generation of leaders, the country will do well to find, as Taiwan has been finding, a democratic rule of law in which the events of the future can be shaped. And there is actually no alternative, because no ruler can govern forever without the minimal consent of the governed. The night will yet be a long one, but dawn has to come.

> Man is born free; and everywhere he is in chains . . .
> The strongest is never strong enough to be always the master, unless he transforms strength into right, and obedience into duty.
> . . . from whatever aspect we regard the question, the right of slavery is null and void, not only as being illegitimate, but also because it is absurd and meaningless. . . . It will always be equally foolish for a man to say to a man or to a people: "I make with you a convention wholly at your expense and wholly to my advantage; I shall keep it as long as I like, and you will keep it as long as I like."[28]

■

What Now?

The quotation that follows is from a manifesto signed on May 19, 1989, by ten leading Chinese intellectuals, including Yan Jiaqi, a political scientist, and Su Xiaokang, a producer of *River Elegy* now living outside China:

> We, as intellectuals, in the name of our personal integrity and all our moral rectitude, with our body and mind, with all our dignity as individuals, solemnly swear never to retreat in the quest for democracy pioneered by the students with their blood and lives, never under any pretext to disengage ourselves out of cowardice, never to allow again the humiliations of the past, never to sell out our moral integrity, never to submit ourselves to dictatorship, never to pledge allegiance to the last emperors of the China of the eighties.[1]

The Chinese Self-Depreciation

Self-depreciation among the Chinese is not limited to intellectuals, but has been articulated best by this group. During the last decade, as intellectuals have reflected on the woes of the past, they have been saying especially two things:

1. intellectuals are a weak-kneed lot, inclined to pay homage to the authorities rather than speaking their minds for the well-being of the people; and
2. they are the products of a weak-kneed civilization, which as trained them to generations of hypocrisy and servitude.

The Ugly Chinaman by Bo Yang (alias Guo Yitong) highlights both views. Without pointing the finger particularly at intellectuals living under the Communist regime, Bo has made a sweeping critique of the group in general, for both past and present. He criticizes Chinese intellectuals as having weak character, and inclined to "worship power" as well as those in power. He describes Chinese culture as a conglomeration of "slave politics, abnormal morality, individualist life views, and utilitarian selfishness."

More than any other group, Chinese intellectuals consider themselves responsible for the conscience of the nation. More than any other group, they have been humiliated, forced to compromise. At this critical juncture in the nation's history, they have taken a stand to resist tyranny and to fight for freedom and democracy. They do this with full awareness of the bad name of intellectuals as a group, and of Chinese civilization as a legacy.

The brief manifesto of May 19 can serve as a response to the judgment that intellectuals are "weak-kneed." It expresses a firm intention on the part of the signatories to stand up to the dictatorial regime and continue to support the quest for democracy. But it is more than a political statement: it is a moral position as well, affirming the values that are being repressed, and renouncing cowardice and compromise. Coming from scholars and writers who have been both active and visible during the last decade, the statement is also an effort to turn a new page on the record of *intellectuals* living under the Communist regime.

This manifesto was written before the crackdown, but at a moment when certain premonitions were already evident. Only ten signed, a very small number; but given the extent of nationwide support the freedom and democracy movement received, we may be sure that thousands, perhaps millions, would have signed such a manifesto—all the more so after the massacre and on account of the massacre.

Actually, Chinese intellectuals have been overly-critical of themselves. With all the tragedies in this review of more recent history, one thing has come through: that the educated classes, both students and intellectuals, are not as weak-kneed as they sometimes make themselves out to be. Living under one of the world's most despotic regimes, they have time and again shown their courage as individuals and as a group, and (especially in the most recent incidents) they have, in turn, inspired the courage of the masses. For this, they are feared by the state, which knows that "the only privilege it cannot take away is that of thinking."[2]

Although *The Ugly Chinaman* by Bo Yang was published in Taiwan, and *River Elegy* was made on the mainland, they have initially elicited the same response from both sides of the Taiwan Strait, as simplistic, superficial culture-bashing efforts. Bo Yang's book is actually an echo (though an inferior one) of the sentiments of the writer Lu Xun (1881–1936), as expressed in his many works, especially *The Story of Ah Q*—a devastating satire that caricatures the Chinese national character through its depiction of a fictitious figure Ah Q, a man unable to face the facts about himself and the world, but who does not cease to deceive and congratulate himself on his own mistakes, ignorance, and cowardice.

Where *River Elegy* is concerned, an outsider's impression is that of a repetitious train of images bearing home an intense self-hatred, marked by the rejection of a backwater culture. Even more than *The Ugly Chinaman*, *River Elegy* hammers hard on the second point: that Chinese culture serves to shackle the people rather than to liberate them. This television series has been seen by millions of people already. Its central image is the Yellow River, which arises out of the great loess plateau of the country's northwest. The Yellow River is an ambivalent symbol, having nurtured the ancient civilization while also having devoured the inhabitants in its basin by periodically bursting its dikes. The producers are advocates of the point of view that the country should turn its back on the traditional agrarian culture and life-style symbolized by the river, and join the modern industrialized culture of the West, symbolized by the ocean into which the river eventually flows.

But there is the deeper political message contained in *River Elegy*. In retracing the source of the river, and its tortuous route into the ocean, the authors are also recalling the history of the Chinese Communist Party. History had exhibited a "human face" during its infancy in the northwest (the Yan'an period, 1937–45), just as the river serves a nurturing function in these upper reaches. Later on, however, it turned monstrous and tyrannical under the great leader Mao Zedong, just as the river becomes capricious in its course, often devastating the ancient capital of Kaifeng (where Mao's rival Liu Shaoqi died of abuse during the Cultural Revolution). A proper channeling of the river's waters into the ocean represents the country's opening to a world culture, to that which is beyond its own borders.

The message of both *The Ugly Chinaman* and *River Elegy* is that an important sector of Chinese intellectuals, especially on the mainland but also in Taiwan, is rejecting the ancient civilization that has so long been identified with China and its people. They consider this civilization to be a reflection of their own collective shortcomings and sufferings, and believe that national resurrection can only occur after a total sundering with the past. To use the stirring words of *River Elegy*: "The legacy of a great culture has become a great burden of culture; a great sense of cultural superiority has become a huge sense of cultural guilt."

I have referred to these two works because I find them symptomatic of much of the malaise now affecting China and the Chinese. A proud people, they are unburdening their Freudian complex regarding the culture that nourished them, and the party that also claims to have brought them out of the dark ages into light. I am not asserting, however, that all intellectuals agree in debunking traditional culture. There are definite nuances between various positions. It would be incorrect to say that all of them advocate a wholesale rejection of the cultural legacy. But all favor some kind of restructuring, or readaptation. Besides, there are also those who have changed with the wind and mouthed official slogans at every turn, especially during the Cultural Revolution. It is interesting to note that in the aftermath of the Tian'anmen Incident, those who have come out in favor of the official position have usually not published their names. Still, it is now feared that the government will take measures to *use* traditional Chinese culture, by blaming all who have criticized it as being unpatriotic. Critics have emphasized that Chinese self-deprecation is all the more remarkable at a time when the Japanese are showing renewed pride in their culture, which owes so much to that of China. A sense of collective achievement, on the part of the Japanese, who are also trying to attribute much of their modernizing effort to the earlier traditional culture, is missing in the case of the Chinese.

A more serious book than Bo Yang's is Wen Yuankai and Ni Duan's *Zhongguo guominxing gaizao* (The restructuring of the Chinese national character) (1988). A more objective account, it presents a few "good points" of the Chinese national character in about five pages, only to go on to fifty pages of "bad points," followed by five long chapters about how character can be changed and transformed. Among other things, it advocates the study of "the problem of the human being," including human essence and human values, the promotion of "a spirit of courage," putting emphasis of creativity and initiative in education, and encouraging ideas of democracy, freedom, and pluralism.

> To demand that human beings be regarded as human beings, is a demand coming from . . . self-respect. To awaken every person's self-respect is also to awaken the self-respect of an entire nation. . . .
>
> Only with freedom is the human being . . . not a slave. Only when each person is fully conscious of himself or herself as the master of the country, and not as the slave, can we enhance the sense of social responsibility (p. 232).

During the Cultural Revolution, outsiders have sometimes asked why China, unlike the Soviet Union, had no Sakharov or Solzhenitsyn. Since then, during the decade of openness, many Chinese intellectuals have borne witness to the desire for freedom and human rights. The events of June 3–4, 1989, tell us why we had not heard from them earlier, and why we might not hear from them again for some time. The Chinese Communist leaders, both Mao Zedong and Deng Xiaoping, are much more repressive than their contemporaries elsewhere—including Khrushchev and Brezhnev.

Is the Culture to Blame?

Is the age-old Chinese culture to blame for the ills of the Chinese people? Should Confucianism be condemned for the guns of June 1989? On first hearing, these questions seem unusual, as the culprit has been the Communist regime. On the other hand, some expatriates are saying that traditional culture—with its despotic tendencies, and Confucianism in particular as a philosophy that emphasizes vertical human relationships—should share the blame with Deng Xiaoping and Li Peng.

This association of the culture and the party, like that of the country and the party, appears at first sight unfathomable. Has not the party formally rejected the traditional culture, especially Confucianism, and embraced an alien ideology called Marxist-Leninism? If the party has made mistakes, why blame them on the old cultural legacy as a whole? Are not other Asia-Pacific regions, where traditional philosophy was never rejected, doing better socially and economically than Communist China?

And then one thinks of West Germany after the Second World War. As a people, the post-war Germans have probably done more soul-searching than any other nation on earth. They have had to answer some hard questions about Nazi Germany and its crimes. Why was Hitler permitted to rule as a despot without more active resistance on the part of the German people? Why were the Nazis allowed to exterminate the Jews? These questions were all the harder to answer as the Germans had the benefit of a Christian culture that taught love rather than hate, and a national tradition preferring freedom above all else. Nazism was not Christianity; it was as anti-Christian as Communism can be. But the assumptions behind the question are that those Christians among the population had not resisted Nazi tyranny sufficiently. The German national character took the blame for its respect for authority, its passiveness in the face of tyranny, somewhat as the Chinese intellectuals have been blaming their own national character for a habitual cowardice vis-à-vis political power, and their Confucian heritage for excessive respect for authority. However, let us pay attention: a Hong Kong paper *Ta Kung Pao* (October 7, 1989) reported on an address in Beijing by a former Soviet ambassador and China scholar, H. Federenko, on the opening day of an international conference on Confucius. In this address, he stated that this

Chinese philosopher deserves to be remembered for his teaching on humanity (*ren*) because he did not believe in killing people, whereas Stalin, who killed so many people, deserves to be forgotten.

For both Chinese and Germans, national character and traditional culture are only part of the story. There is also another important factor: the totalitarian regime, and this, according to Hannah Arendt, makes all the difference:

> No matter what the specifically national tradition or the particular spiritual source of its ideology . . . totalitarianism differs essentially from other forms of political oppression. . . . Wherever it rose to power, it developed entirely new political institutions and destroyed all social, legal and political traditions of the country. . . . [Totalitarian] governments . . . operate according to a system of values so radically different from all others, that none of our traditional legal, moral, or common sense . . . categories could any longer help us to come to terms with, or judge, or predict their course of action.[3]

While the German soul-searching had been over their collective guilt regarding the Jews, the Chinese intellectuals' self-probing had more to do with the ills of China as a country. Besides, the same German nation, divided between east and west, reacted differently to its own recent history. No public probing or soul-searching concerning the Nazi extermination of Jews took place in East Germany, as it did in West Germany. Besides, while West Germany prospered after the war, East Germany, under a Communist government, lagged far behind. The differences may be compared to those between mainland China, which is Communist, and Hong Kong and Taiwan, which are not. Taiwan has its own inferiority complex, due to its smallness next to the mainland, and its complicated international status as "Republic of China." Hong Kong has been a British colony, and fears the eventual reunion with the mainland. The people in Taiwan and Hong Kong have not experienced the same kind of self-probing as those on the mainland, presumably because their recent histories have been different.

It is also useful to compare briefly the situation of the Chinese with that of the Japanese. At the present moment, there are signs that the Japanese are elated not only with their economic success, but also with the feeling that their success is tied to a cultural, and even ethnic, superiority. For those who know history, such a phenomenon should be put in its place. After all, how did Japanese intellectuals feel immediately after the Second World War under American occupation? An eminent Japanese scholar, Maruyama Masao, is known for his criticism of traditional Japanese culture and thought, as well as of the emperor system, as impediments to true modernization. The English translation of his book, *Studies in the Intellectual History of Tokugawa Japan* (1974) has stirred up an intellectual debate in Western scholarly circles as well, although the reasons for Western scholars arguing for one position or the other are not the same as the reasons for his own compatriots who either agree or disagree with him. I am not mentioning his work here in order to give a detailed analysis. I do so to show that self-doubt, self-criticism, and even self-deprecation are found not only among today's Chinese. While opinions will always differ, and will always remain debatable, whoever may utter them, those scholars from Asian societies who are more ready to voice a critical opinion of their own traditions and societies often brave criticism themselves and deserve to be heard. This is also true (perhaps all the more true) of intellectuals from Islamic countries, facing such controversy as that which arose with Ayatollah Khomeini's condemnation of Salman Rushdie for his book *The Satanic Verses* (1989).

Besides, when we look at history, we cannot but acknowledge more rigidity and structure in traditional Japanese society, with its caste system and its privileged *samurai* class as well as with its outcast *burakumin*, than in traditional Chinese society before Communist rule. This can also be said of Korea, which traditionally had a *yanban* class, with privileges coming from birth not only in the right families, but also from the right mothers (rather than from concubines). In traditional China, no one was, at least in theory, excluded from the civil service examinations for reasons of birth. I mention these factors to highlight my argument that the recent and current situation in China cannot be blamed simply on Chinese culture, or the inherent problems within traditional Chinese society. To do this would be an oversimplification. Modern history has witnessed an extremely complex drama of human factors. As is already mentioned in this book, the Japanese War with China (1937–45) played a prominent role in permitting Communist takeover and Communist dominance, as did the Second World War in the case of many East European countries.

Americans, too, know what soul-searching means. They have the experience of having been stunned both by the Vietnam War and by Watergate, and generally by finding themselves no longer possessing the same political clout or leading edge in industrial technology. Americans know self-doubt, and exercise self-criticism. They see their nation as a great power, but wonder whether it is in decline, and why. Americans should be able to empathize with the Chinese, who know themselves to have been a great nation, but feel themselves alienated from a system that enslaves them.

Going Beyond Patriotism

Taken superficially, the message of *River Elegy* seems to recall the ravages of the past century and especially of the Cultural Revolution. On analysis, however, the message is not so simple. Something else comes through beyond the superficial self-hatred and the deprecation of Chinese culture. It is a desire to go beyond just "being Chinese."

For the past century, the nation has been moving from crisis to crisis. All that time, the people's energy has been repeatedly abused by the ruling powers in the name of patriotism. The Communists have been the worst transgressors. Time and again, one "great leader" after another has made serious mistakes, without consulting the people, but always forcing the consequences on them, with exhortations to patriotism.

An irony in Chinese language is that the modern term for "country" (*guojia*) frequently refers to the state as well. Loving one's country (*aiguo*) can easily be turned into loving one's government, loving the ruling party, loving the party leader. And the reverse is also true: opposition to leader, party, government, is considered treason, treachery.

In real life, however, the most unpatriotic have been the leaders themselves. Mao, an emperor in all but name, called himself *wu-fa wu-tian*, "a Buddhist monk under an umbrella"—the wordplay refers to a man with a shaved head, who covers himself from the skies, or, literally, "having neither hair (*fa*) nor Heaven (*tian*)." Since the word "hair" sounds like "law" (also *fa*), Mao acknowledged that he acted as an "outlaw," fearing neither the laws of man nor the laws of God. Deng likewise has shown himself "above the constitution." Having for an entire decade placed emphasis on the rule of law, he has permitted it to be suspended, with illegal house searches and kidnappings, with tortures and instant condemnations. His belated personality cult is placing him in the same category as Mao, the dictator.

But the people have finally discovered that such misguided patriotism is a poor substitute for food, and for freedom. The writer-soldier Bai Hua proclaims this in his filmscript, *Unrequited Love* (1980), describing an artist's love for his native land. Having chosen to return home from overseas to serve the country, he found himself a victim of the Cultural Revolution. His daughter would ask him this unanswerable question: "You have loved the country. Does the country love you in return?" The artist was to die while fleeing from persecution, frozen in the snow, his body curled up in the shape of a question mark.

Why?

According to communist ideology, human beings can only be acknowledged according to their "class nature." There can be no "human rights," because there can only be "class" rights, "political" rights. In the case of citizens of the People's Republic, whatever rights they have are allegedly bestowed on them by the state, and can be taken from them at any time. The party members, of course, have more rights. But fundamentally, the "paramount leader" alone has all the rights of a *pater familias*, including the power of life and death over all the party members and all the citizens.

From this brief explanation, we can understand "class struggle" as the defense of the rights of the proletariat against all others. And the proletariat has been identified with the ruling party, or the small circle within that party. But this is an unnatural ideology that serves only the interests of the despots. Traditional Confucian culture never condemned political despotism; instead, it insisted that the ruler be humane to keep the mandate of government, bestowed upon him by Heaven. When asked whether a minister might murder his king, Mencius had referred to the successful overthrow of the ancient Shang house by that of Chou, commenting that the last Shang ruler had forfeited his rulership by his vices, and no longer deserved the title of king: "I have heard of the killing of a mere fellow (the former king), but I have not heard of murdering a ruler."[4]

Mencius's words about the ruler-minister relationship may also be extended to the relationship between the ruler and the whole populace:

> If a ruler regards his ministers as his hands and feet, then his ministers will regard him as their belly and heart. If a ruler regards his ministers as dogs and horses, the ministers will regard him as any other man. If a ruler regards his ministers as dirt and grass, the ministers will regard him as a bandit and an enemy.[5]

In our introductory chapter, we quoted Wang Ruoshui's words about "the specter of humanism," given in the style of Karl Marx's opening statement in the *Communist Manifesto*. Liu Xiaobo, arrested June 1989, also emphasized the importance of "being human."

> In choosing between reviving the nation (nationalism) and liberating the human being ("personalism"; in Chinese, *gexing zhuyi*), our compatriots today who are resolved to modernize should first choose human liberation. The human being is the goal, the country is a means.[6]

People should not be forced, he says, to love "a country that dehumanizes him" and enslaves him. Instead, the recognition of the right to private ownership is a step forward toward recognizing human dignity and individual humanity.

This latest movement of student protest, backed by the urban masses, confirms what many dissidents have been saying all along: we want to be free human beings—not just "Chinese citizens," and we think we can be both. We want *human* rights, our *birthrights* as human beings, not just the so-called rights of citizens, which the state imagines it can freely give and just as freely take away.

True, "human rights" (*renquan*) is an imported term. But that does not mean there is no place for such a concept in China. Human beings usually know when they are dehumanized, that they deserve better, more humane treatment. The Chinese are no different.

Failing to find appropriate symbols of this deep human desire from traditional culture or from Communist ideology, the demonstrators set up a likeness of the Statue of Liberty, a gift from the people of the French Revolution to the people of the American. It asserts their belief in a universal value: that of *human liberty*, the natural freedom of human beings—even more than as the symbol of a liberal, Western, political idea. This statue was crushed by the tanks that rolled into Tian'anmen Square, but models of the same have quickly arisen in Hong Kong, Paris, and San Francisco, as the symbol of continued overseas Chinese support for the movement that was so brutally repressed.

What Now? The Path to Democracy

Who can say China is not ready for democratization when the student demonstrators ran their show better than the authorities ever did? For a brief interval on the world's stage, we saw discipline and organization, courage and initiative, creativity and spontaneity. The masses are not lacking in these either. They devised many ways to bar entrance to the soldiers and the tanks, to protect the peaceful and the innocent. It is reported that the crime rate dropped during the weeks of student demonstrations in Beijing.

For a brief interval, the residents of Beijing not only showed their unity of purpose, they also revealed the source of their unhappiness. The ill-trained service personnel in the stores and hotels, the poker-faced pedestrians, the state-controlled journalists accustomed to serving as mouthpieces for the party line—they all lifted their masks and became live *human beings*, supporting at great personal risk a movement that revealed the profound oppression under which all live, to plead for reforms that might transform all into *happy human beings*.

The discipline is there; the energy is there; the determination is there. What else can prevent the democratization?

The army, maybe. But suppose the army is brought over to the side of the people? That is not impossible, considering the hesitation on the part of many in the military to participate in the butchery. Consider the gripping image: the lone man facing the tanks—and the tanks hesitated, for about half an hour. The Hong Kong press described the man later as a nineteen-year-old student by the name of Wang Weilin. He has since been arrested; he was even paraded on television together with others and could have been executed according to the *ex post facto* decree regarding executions of those who obstruct military action. But the tank commander is reported to have also been reproved.

Of course, there is much that remains to be done, to pave the way to a real democratization. Things may get even worse before they get any better. But there should be support, not objection, on the part of the outside world for democratization in China. Such support can go a long way. The outside world, which has grown so much in its knowledge of conditions in China, should lend its active support to the Chinese democracy movement—as a movement of human beings seeking more *humanity* in their lives, and doing so peacefully.

One example of such support has been awarding the Nobel prize to the Dalai Lama for his peaceful protests against Chinese repression. This action is to be lauded, even if others had regarded the student leader Chai Ling (rumored to have been killed by the government) as a better candidate. The Dalai Lama has consistently praised the student movement of 1989 and mourned its tragic end. In a sense, he is also speaking for the silenced multitudes.

Fang Lizhi has insisted that democracy has no color line. There can be no "Chinese" democracy, as there is no "Chinese" physics. Democracy is a universal concept. We may add: so too are human freedom, human rights. Presumably, there will be a distinctive Chinese road to democracy, as there has been a distinctive American road to democracy, or Filipino road, or Korean, or Taiwanese. The important thing is that China must get on this road quickly, not only for the sake of her own people, but also for the sake of regional stability in Asia and peace in the world.

Let it not be forgotten: no matter what the differences, China still shares something very basic with the rest of the world. Like the rest of humanity, the Chinese also are people. They can laugh, and they can feel hurt, even when they seem to be repeating meaningless political slogans.

The Chinese want freedom and human dignity, and they also want to live! That the students crying "Freedom or Death" have been crushed by tanks does not mean they did not want to live. That the tanks came crushing on them does not mean Chinese culture does not value life. The worst mistake anyone can make while watching China is to assume the Chinese to be a "different kind" of humanity, whether the "new" humanity allegedly transformed by Mao Zedong (a repudiated model) or the "inscrutable," "old" humanity caricatured in Fu Manchu and others. To interpret China correctly, it is more important to have this sense of a common humanity than many years of studying Confucianism, Legalism, Marxist-Leninism, and Maoism. To understand how the Chinese feel, a little empathy goes a long way.

No revolution can succeed if undertaken by students and intellectuals alone. But what we witnessed in April to May 1989 was a mass movement that will live on in people's minds and hearts, to inspire them to continue with the peaceful struggle. Despite the bloodbath, the demonstrations of 1989 did not end in failure. What we saw of the crackdown was only the tip of the iceberg. The top leaders are too old; they have outlived their usefulness; they have lost contact with the masses; they cannot forever keep a lid on the population. The country, however, is ready for takeoff. This has to come.

It is indeed an irony that the people of China, in particular the residents of Beijing, surprised themselves that sleepless night on June 3–4, 1989. "We did not know we could be so brave," they are now saying in private. The human spirit is indomitable, even the human spirit of the Chinese people, burdened by self-doubt and self-deprecation. They have shown that they do not desire to remain in bondage to an all-powerful state machine. May one suggest that the Chinese national character may not be so bad after all?

In reflecting upon the backwardness of China and the defects of the Chinese national character, Fang Lizhi has also said:

> The Chinese nation has something very unique. There are what may be called defects. There are also what may be called advantages. It deserves to be criticized; it also deserves to be loved, after being criticized. [The writer] Lu Xun [has also] talked about how he wrote *The Story of Ah Q* with a love that follows a great hatred [for the Chinese people] and a hatred that follows a great love.[7]

Ya Ding, a young Chinese novelist in exile in Paris, who predicted the Tian'anmen crackdown in a novel he published the year before,[8] had this to say about the political situation in June 1989: "An old man is dying but a child is born." According to his explanation, the old man is the three-thousand-year-old civilization, based on submission to those in power, and the child is democracy. Ya Ding's 1988 novel was published in French: *Les Héritiers des sept royaumes* (The heirs of the seven kingdoms). The thirty-two-year-old author has been living in France since 1985. He observes:

> In China it has always been either dictatorship or anarchy. You take heed of the emperor but if there's no longer an emperor there can only be anarchy. Anarchy, however, is the best terrain for democracy.[9]

For many Chinese outside of the mainland, the opposition between past and future may be too stark. Theirs is the feeling that the three- (or four-) thousand-year-old civilization has contributions yet to make to the future, despite its shortcomings. An old man is dying, and a child is born—but the child is the issue of the old man. It represents hope: for a transformed future in which a proper reevaluation can also be made of the past. And it is to this brighter future that this book is dedicated.

Eastern Europe: Mirror Image for China?

As changes continue to sweep Eastern Europe, we see more and more a contrast of hope and freedom in one hemisphere and of fear and repression in the other. Why so? Is China on the whole similar to, or different from, the East European countries?

The cycle of dictatorship and demonstrations suggests similarity in the structures of repression as well as protest. In each case, there is popular discontent with a Stalinist leadership, corrupt to the core. We hear allegations of foreign bank accounts for Romania's former leader Nicolae Ceausescu as well as for the Chinese hard-liners; of many in the security forces of each, raised as orphans, trained to unquestioning obedience, and ready to kill their own people to protect the privileges of the few. On the other hand, we see young students and intellectuals in each hemisphere serving as the conscience of their nations while risking death in the forefront of dissent.

There are also differences, historical, cultural, and political, among the East European countries and between them and China. My own observation is that the varying outcomes of protest in Europe and China have less to do with culture than with the circumstances of politics, especially the stronger influence of Gorbachev in Europe and the staggering size of China as a geopolitical reality. In the long run, however, it is impossible for China to remain communist if the Soviet Union and Eastern

Europe change their course. This is because communism is even less part and parcel of Chinese culture and society (or of North Korea and Vietnam) than it is of the West, and because the legacy of communist rule has run contrary to human nature and genuinely human aspirations for freedom and democracy. When the time comes for more democratization, China will suffer because of its lower overall level of education as well as its inadequate industrial base, compared with those of the East European countries. But China is also favored because of the surprisingly entrepreneurial spirit of its people, including its peasantry, when compared, for example, to the relative inertia of the Soviet countryside. Besides, should China resume the road to reform, it can count on the experience accumulated during its twelve years of openness, as well as vast overseas Chinese investments and human resources, including those from Hong Kong, Taiwan, and Southeast Asia.

Will reform resume after more bloodshed, or will there be peaceful transition to a new generation of leaders? We do not know the answers to these questions. In the cases of East Germany and Czechoslovakia (two Soviet satellites), bloodshed was averted more by chance than by planning. In the case of Romania, even civil war and a tragic death toll could not restore the fortunes of a dictatorship formerly thought to be firmly entrenched. The Chinese leadership should learn from these examples to avoid further suppression of dissent by violence.

And what of the role of religion in politics and protest, East and West? The Christian churches have been strongly supportive of the politics of protest in Eastern Europe, but they have a much smaller constituency in China. It is doubtful that the traditional Chinese religions can stand up to the state in like manner. On balance, the protests in both East and West go deeper than discontent fostered by religion or the lack of religious liberty. They have been fueled by the absence of *human* liberty, the inhumanity of man for man, as backed by the state machine, its secret police, and its military technology. But the measure of religious liberty is itself a measure of human freedom and political liberation. Where religion was more tolerated, such as in Poland and Hungary, we also found an earlier start to democratization.

We have seen that the state machine, the secret police, and the military technology can all fail in the face of vast human protests. An alliance of fear is intrinsically vulnerable. And the worst systems can still produce intelligent and courageous individuals, whether as leaders or as dissidents. The revolution turned sour can be overthrown by its own children, reared on a revolutionary rhetoric of justice while witnessing hypocrisy and corruption. Karl Marx's call, "You have nothing to lose but your chains," will eventually achieve its goal of stirring the enslaved to shake off their shackles, especially those imposed by Communist dictatorships.

The year 1989 will go down as one of the great watershed years in history. Perceived for decades as a political fixture, state communism collapsed in Eastern Europe like a row of dominoes. It may not survive into the twenty-first century. The events of April–June 1989 in China have helped us to understand the events of fall and winter 1989 in East Germany, Czechoslovakia, and Romania. And the events in East Germany, Czechoslovakia, and Romania can in turn help us to understand China.

The lesson of 1989 is that hope can conquer fear.

Documents

Beijing Students' Alliance Statement[*]

To Our Compatriots in the Whole World
From the University Students' Autonomous Alliance of Beijing

What Really Happened in the Beijing Massacres

Only a month has elapsed since May 4, 1989, the seventieth anniversary of the May Fourth Movement, but the five-star national flag has once again been soaked in the blood of the patriotic democracy fighters in Beijing, the capital of the People's Republic of China. Blood has flowed everywhere on Chang'an Street; mourning tones are heard everywhere in Beijing. Since the Chinese nation has reached this moment of extreme danger, we wish to honor the democracy fighters who have been killed or wounded for the sake of the Republic, and to offer a serious announcement to the people of China and to the whole world.

Since April 15 [1989], young students themselves in Beijing have organized a large-scale patriotic democracy movement. In spite of prohibitions, these students in Beijing went to Tian'anmen Square on April 22 to participate in the memorial service in honor of Comrade Hu Yaobang. After the service, student representatives knelt in front of the Great Hall of the People to submit their petition, but were not received by any of the government officials.

On April 26, the *People's Daily* published an editorial that crudely judged the student movement to be a riotous uprising. The following day, to protest this malicious and inaccurate reportage by the *People's Daily*, the universities at the capital once more organized a demonstration that received the enthusiastic support of the masses at the capital. A million people took to the streets. Students and masses from different cities in the entire country rose in support, bringing the patriotic democracy movement to a climax.

Facing the people's outcries and the irresistible patriotic democracy movement, the government authorities used their customary tricks of doubletalk and delaying tactics and made efforts to split the movement. They did not hold dialogue with the real representatives of the students,

* This translation is based on the text included in a collection of selected source materials (Series One) on the Chinese democracy movement, published by the *October Review* in Hong Kong on June 25, 1989, pp. 22–23.

refused to respond to the conditions for dialogue, and intentionally caused social disorder. At the time, young students and the remarkable Beijing population manifested the greatest measure of self-control and discipline, defending the peace and unity of the city of Beijing even though the government paid no attention to the pleas of the young students and millions of people.

On May 13, the university students at the capital could no longer wait indefinitely, and organized a one-thousand-member hunger strike in an effort to continue the group petition. Within two days, the group increased to over three thousand. They received a strong response from various sectors of society and movements of support from the entire country. The popular masses urged the government in strong language to begin a dialogue with the students in a spirit of sincerity and equality, and to accept quickly the conditions of the hunger strikers.

On the dawn of May 19, Zhao Ziyang, Li Peng, and others finally appeared at Tian'anmen Square, visited the hunger strikers, and affirmed the students' patriotism, saying that the party's central [authority] had not judged the student movement to be a riot, and guaranteed that there would be no reprisals in autumn. However, that very evening, Li Peng and Yang Shaoqun assembled some Party, military, and political cadres at a meeting where the patriotic democracy movement was called a "riot," and where they also requested emergency action to stop this "riot."

The following day, the state council and the city government of Beijing declared martial law, as tens of thousands of soldiers reached the city suburbs. The military arrived, bringing with them a belligerent mood.

From the moment the military moved into Beijing, young students and Beijing residents rushed to every street intersection to talk to the soldiers about the affairs of state, and to cultivate fraternal feelings. After that, the disorder that the government had itself created in the city was quickly overturned, and the relations between the population and the army were good. The people of Beijing were able to live and work happily in an atmosphere of peace and stability in this beautiful ancient capital. According to news reports during those days, criminal and traffic incidents as well as fire alarms dropped measurably.

However, a conspiracy of violence was at that moment being organized and was aimed at the innocent students and people.

On June 2, speeding military vehicles killed three people and wounded one other person seriously at Muxidi, raising the curtain on the reactionary government's bloody crushing of the patriotic masses.

On the dawn of June 3, soldiers dressed in civilian clothes were seen on their way to the city center, and were stopped by residents and students. At Qianmen, Bukou, Xidan, and other areas, the soldiers used tear gas and rubber bullets, wounding many students and residents. At Liubukou, a seven-year-old child was trampled to death on the spot by soldiers.

On the evening of June 3, the troops that had as their vanguard armored personnel carriers, along with special police squads firing tear gas, invaded Tian'anmen Square from all sides, indiscriminately shooting the unarmed students and residents with machine guns and bayonet rifles along the way. Four hundred people were killed at the Muxidi area, as the troops were also shooting those people who were striving to save the wounded.

On the dawn of June 4, three armored personnel carriers heading southbound crashed into a public bus parked in the middle of the road at the Xidan intersection. Immediately after that, continued gunshots as well as moving vehicles could be heard coming from the direction of the Military Museum. According to students escaping from that area, many students and residents were killed or wounded between the museum and Xidan.

At 12:40 A.M., the troops first used a large amount of tear gas about five hundred meters away from Xidan, causing people who could hardly open their eyes to crouch on the ground. Just then, several cars started burning at the same time, obviously the work of undercover agents who wanted to use students as scapegoats and give the authorities an excuse for their violent crackdown.

At 12:50 A.M. on June 4, a large mass of special police forces crying "Smash them!" fired their guns ceaselessly at the unsuspecting and unarmed students and citizens on the streets. At once, rows of students and residents fell in pools of blood; dozens died instantly, hundreds were wounded, and among the dead were also passersby. Students and others who escaped into the smaller alleys were also shot by soldiers who discovered them. In the deep recesses of a small alley east of Xidan, one bullet injured four people at the same time. No one among the masses in the streets was exempt from the shooting, not even infants or the elderly.

Shortly after 1:00 A.M., a large military convoy of vehicles reached the Xidan intersection, while countless masses were watching quietly on the streets or near the entrances to the small alleys. But soldiers rushed over and shot at the masses, as rows of people fell down. The soldiers not only shot at the masses, but also chased after the citizens and students who were running away using all kinds of weapons, including police truncheons, whips, and guns. A student from the Second Foreign Language Institute of Beijing was badly hit in his legs. He reported that while several male students were rushing over to save a female student, a bullet flew over and instantly mowed down five students. After three hours, when the military had passed the Xidan intersection, survivors among the residents and students were rushing over to Tian'anmen Square, but found that the streets had been barricaded by soldiers who were shooting unhesitatingly at passersby, without letting people run away. Shots were especially dense where people were shouting slogans.

From 11:00 P.M. on June 3 to 6:00 A.M. on June 4, the sounds of machine guns and bayonet rifles were everywhere at Tian'anmen Square, Chang'an Street East and West, and near the Qianmen area. Wherever soldiers had passed, there were pools of blood and innumerable casualties, accompanied by the heartrending cries of people on the streets. Military vehicles were all over Tian'anmen Square and tanks were charging everywhere. According to an incomplete calculation, from 6:00 A.M. on there were over seven thousand wounded and over three thousand dead, although the massacre was still going on with growing casualties. Innumerable citizens and students had fallen in pools of blood, all of them unarmed, and with no way of resisting the gunfire. However, they had placed masks over their mouths, believing that soldiers would only use tear gas and shoot rubber bullets. The naive students and good citizens had never guessed that the Li Peng regime would be so heartless and inhuman. Those students and residents who fell at Muxidi died without even knowing that they had been shot by real bullets. According to the Li Peng regime, these innocent citizens . . . [ellipsis recorded in the text] earnestly desiring democracy were the so-called rioters.

Between June 3 and June 4, the bloody incidents caused by the government troops carrying out a mindless massacre against a defenseless people make up the real counterrevolutionary evidence of the illegal government. People throughout the world can never forgive Li Peng's reactionary government; the debt of blood must be repaid by blood.

What started on April 15 in Beijing was carried over into the whole country, and influenced the whole country. It was a great and patriotic democracy movement. Young students raised the banners of democracy, to fight for freedom, condemning dictatorship and despotism, opposing bureaucratic corruption and asking for a clean government. They represented the desires of a population of one billion; they echoed the wishes of a billion people. This movement inherited and developed the spirit of May Fourth, and opened a new page in the history of freedom and democracy in China. However, the small handful of anti-party, anti-people individuals led by Deng Xiaoping, Li Peng, and Yang Shangkun feared and hated this mass patriotic democracy movement. Paying no attention to the good of the country and the nation, and in order to protect themselves and the interests of a very small minority, they covered up the real facts, made up rumors, created incidents, and maligned the patriotic democracy movement as a riot, a counterrevolutionary riot. They persevered in their warnings and threats, using alternately hard and soft tactics, and then raised butchers' knives against unarmed students and residents, causing these world-shocking atrocities. The facts clearly reveal their most brutal and corrupt character, and prove forcefully that their regime is not at all a people's government, but rather the most cruel and despotic regime in the world. They also prove that the small clique around Deng Xiaoping, Yang Shaoqun, and Li Peng are the criminals of history, the scum of the nation, and the enemy of the people. The Fascist government has torn off its own hypocritical mask; the great dictator has revealed his ferocious face, as the land of China is shrouded by clouds of darkness and the city of Beijing is enveloped in a storm of blood. But history has also announced that the people will triumph, that freedom and democracy will triumph. We university students in Beijing will not shrink away from the forces of evil, but will struggle against them to the very end. We shall use our blood and our youth to announce to the people of China and the people of the world that we shall not cause shame to our predecessors of the May Fourth movement, and to the martyrs of the April Fifth incident [at Tian'anmen in 1976]; we shall not cause shame to our own times and our nation, to the spirit of democracy and freedom! At this moment of danger to our nation, we raise a plea to the people of the entire country to rise up in unison and overthrow the reactionary regime of Deng, Yang, and Li—the inhumane Fascist regime intent upon murdering our people, the dictatorship that tramples on the people's desires. We call upon all countries and peoples who love peace, liberty, and democracy to unite under the banners of peace, liberty, and democracy and to support the patriotic democracy movement of the Chinese students and people, to accuse the Chinese authorities of their Fascist atrocities, and to impose effective economic and diplomatic sanctions on the dictatorial regime of Deng, Yang, and Li, to make manifest the spirit of democracy and to open wide the road to human rights. People of China, people of the world: let us unite, fight for democracy and freedom, and overthrow dictatorships and Fascism. Long live democracy, long live liberty, long live the people!

The University Students' Autonomous Alliance of Beijing
June 4, 1989

Official Statement of the
Party Central and State Council*

To All Members of the Communist Party and
to the People of All Nationalities in the Entire Country

At present, the capital, Beijing, is in a grave situation. For over a month, a very small number of individuals with ulterior motives have been intent upon creating a riot. From the dawn of June 3, this riot developed into a shocking, violent counterrevolutionary uprising.

A very small number of violent elements stirred up some people who did not understand the real facts and created this violence. They barred the troops entering the urban areas and Tian'anmen Square from carrying out their duties under martial law, destroyed and burned over a hundred military vehicles and other public vehicles, scolded, beat and kidnapped cadres, warriors, armed police, and security police, and robbed these of their guns and bullets and other military equipment. They attacked Zhongnanhai, the Great Hall of the People, the Central Broadcasting and Television Building, the Security Offices, and other important departments, robbed stores, and burned police kiosks. They also brutally killed several dozen warriors of the Liberation Army and of the armed police, even hanging the corpses of the murdered warriors on an overpass railing. Their aim in this violent uprising was to overthrow the leadership of the Party, the system of socialism, and the Chinese People's Republic. They cried out in public such slogans as "Take up arms, overthrow the government!" and "Let us kill 470 million Communist Party members!" The plotters and organizers of this violent counter-revolutionary uprising are mainly a very small minority of people who for a long time have stubbornly insisted on capitalist liberalization and political conspiracy, people who have linked up with enemy forces over-seas and outside the county, people who have offered party and state secrets to outlaw organizations. Those who are committing acts of vio-lence such as beating, destroying, robbing, and burning are mainly unreformed elements that have been released after completing prison terms, political hooligans and gangsters, followers left behind by the

* Translated from the text published in the *People's Daily*, overseas edition, June 6, 1989.

Gang of Four, and other dregs of society. In short, they are reactionaries who hate the Communist Party and the socialist system. As everybody knows, for over a month the government has been practicing patience and self-control toward the riot caused by a very small minority who have been deceiving the masses, but this very small minority thought that the government was too weak and soft, and escalated their activities until they aroused a violent counterrevolutionary uprising.

Facing this grave situation, the People's Liberation Army troops that were enforcing martial law could no longer endure things, and began a bold measure of firmly putting down this violent uprising. To avoid hurting innocent people, urgent notices were issued from the afternoon of [June] 3rd on, counseling the big groups of students and citizens not to obstruct the activities of the troops enforcing martial law. In putting down [the uprising], the troops enforcing martial law did their utmost to prevent bloodshed. But the very small number of violent rioters acted as though they heard nothing, and madly attacked the troops enforcing martial law. In this situation, there were some casualties, but most were Liberation Army soldiers and armed police. This is not what we wanted to see. But without such action, the uprising could not have been put down, more bloodshed would have taken place, the republic that was established with the lives of millions of martyrs would have been overthrown, the results of socialist upbuilding and of ten years of reform would have been destroyed overnight, and the entire country would have been enveloped in a "white terror." Hence, boldly putting down this violent uprising was an upright action, in accordance with the interests of the people of the capital and the desires and basic interests of the people of the entire country.

Relying on the courageous struggle of the officers and soldiers of the People's Liberation Army and of the armed police enforcing martial law, and relying on the vast masses of the people and the support and coordination of the young students, we have won the victory in the first step in putting down the violent uprising. But we should observe soberly that the violent counterrevolutionary uprising is not yet completely over, that a very small number of violent elements are not ready to admit defeat. They will yet await an occasion to fight back, to create incidents. All Party comrades and our entire people should heighten their alertness, keep their eyes open, stay united, and struggle with them firmly till the bitter end in order to defend the Revolution and the results of upbuilding and reform. As long as they dare to continue making trouble, we shall struggle with them till the end. We have the direction of Marxism, we have the great people's democratic dictatorship, several hundred million Communist Party members, several million Liberation Army soldiers loyal to the Party and to the people, and we have the strong support of a vast number of workers, peasants, educated elements, and of the various democratic parties and of various sectors of patriotic people. We fully possess the strength and the confidence to conquer them thoroughly, to overcome this violent uprising completely.

All members of the Communist Party, vast masses of the people, and all patriotic individuals should support the summons of the Party and the government, distinguish right and wrong, consider the situation as a whole, and act quickly, coming forth to struggle firmly against the very small minority of people who created violence, and not do anything to the contrary. You should believe in the Party and the government's ability to stop this violent uprising. Communist Party members must set a good example and serve as people's models. The vast numbers of cadres and workers should keep to their duties, work for production, protect supplies, and defend positively social order and normal discipline in society. All levels of organization in the Party and the government should strengthen positive channeling and work on political thought, patiently instruct the young students and the vast masses, not easily believe in or spread rumors, and not carry on any form of "linking up," in order to struggle to keep stability and create a calm and good social environment, pressing forward in the task of upbuilding and of reform in unity.

Party Central and State Council
June 5, 1989

Deng Xiaoping's Address[*]

To commanders above the corps level of the marital law enforcing troops.

You comrades have been working hard.

First of all, I'd like to express my heartfelt condolence to the comrades in the People's Liberation Army (PLA), the armed police and police who died in the struggle; and my sincere sympathy and solicitude to several thousand comrades in the army, the armed police and police who were wounded in the struggle, and I want to extend my sincere regards to all the army, armed police and police who participated in this struggle.[**]

I suggest that all of us stand and pay a silent tribute to the martyrs.

I'd like to take this opportunity to say a few words. This storm was bound to happen sooner or later. As determined by the international and domestic climate, it was bound to happen and was independent of man's will. It was just a matter of time and scale. It has turned out in our favor, for we still have a large group of veterans who have experienced many storms and have a thorough understanding of things. They were on the side of taking resolute action to counter the turmoil. Although some comrades may not understand this now, they will understand eventually and will support the decision of the Central Committee.

The April 26 editorial of the *People's Daily* classified the problem as turmoil. The word was appropriate, but some people objected to the

---

[*] Delivered on June 9, 1989; published in the *People's Daily* (overseas edition), June 28, 1989, and in a book entitled *Deng Xiaoping tongzhi lun gaige kaifang* (Comrade Deng Xiaoping on Reform and the Open Policy), Beijing, Renmin, 1989). This standard translation is published in *Beijing Review*, July 10–16, 1989, vol. 32, no. 28. Since its publication, this address has been made the basis of political study and discussion sessions all over the country. The official version of the 1989 Tian'anmen Incident is based on his speech, including the assertions that the demonstrations represented "turmoil" (*dongluan*) which later developed into a rebellion or "violent uprising" (*baoluan*) (or what is given in the statement as "counterrevolutionary rebellion") against the government, that the military acted only in self-defense, and that no blood was shed at Tian'anmen Square itself. Deng also discloses that the government had expected popular disturbances, that there had been initial disagreement regarding how to respond to the demonstrations, and that the older comrades had played a preponderant role in the decision-making that followed. In presenting this official translation of the document, the author of this book has added some footnotes for explanatory purposes only.

[**] The armed police are themselves actually a contingent of the Chinese armed forces.

word and tried to amend it. But what has happened shows that this verdict was right. It was also inevitable that the turmoil would develop into a counter-revolutionary rebellion. We still have a group of senior comrades who are alive, we still have the army, and we also have a group of core cadres who took part in the revolution at various times. That is why it was relatively easy for us to handle the present matter. The main difficulty in handling this matter lay in that we had never experienced such a situation before, in which a small minority of bad people mixed with so many young students and onlookers. We did not have a clear picture of the situation, and this prevented us from taking some actions that we should have taken earlier. It would have been difficult for us to arrive at a conclusion on the nature of the matter had we not had the support of so many senior comrades. Some comrades didn't understand this point. They thought it was simply a matter of how to treat the masses. Actually, what we faced was not just some ordinary people who were misguided, but also a rebellious clique and a large number of the dregs of society. The key point is that they wanted to overthrow our state and the Party. Failing to understand this means failing to understand the nature of the matter. I believe that after serious work we can win the support of the great majority of comrades within the Party.

The nature of the matter became clear soon after it erupted. They had two main slogans: to overthrow the Communist Party and topple the socialist system. Their goal was to establish a bourgeois republic entirely dependent on the West. Of course we accept people's demands for combating corruption. We are even ready to listen to some people with ulterior motives when they raise the slogan about fighting corruption. However, such slogans were just a front. Their real aim was to overthrow the Communist Party and topple the socialist system.

During the course of quelling the rebellion, many comrades of ours were injured or even sacrificed their lives. Some of their weapons were also taken from them by the rioters. Why? Because bad people mingled with the good, which made it difficult for us to take the firm measures that were necessary.

Handling this matter amounted to a severe political test for our army, and what happened shows that our People's Liberation Army passed muster. If tanks were used to roll over people, this would have created a confusion between right and wrong among the people nationwide. That is why I have to thank the PLA officers and men for using this approach to handle the rebellion.

The PLA losses were great, but this enabled us to win the support of the people and made those who can't tell right from wrong change their viewpoint. They can see what kind of people the PLA are, whether there was bloodshed at Tian'anmen, and who were those that shed blood.

Once this question is made clear, we can take the initiative. Although it is very sad that so many comrades were sacrificed, if the event is analyzed objectively, people cannot but recognize that the PLA are the sons and brothers of the people. This will also help people to understand the measures we used in the course of the struggle. In the future, whenever the PLA faces problems and takes measures, it will gain the support of the people. By the way, I would say that in the future, we must make sure that our weapons are not taken away from us.

In a word, this was a test, and we passed. Even though there are not so many veteran comrades in the army and the soldiers are mostly little more than 18, 19 or 20 years of age, they are still true soldiers of the people. Facing danger, they did not forget the people, the teachings of the Party and the interests of the country. They kept a resolute stand in the face of death. They fully deserve the saying that they met death and sacrificed themselves with generosity and without fear.

When I talked about passing muster, I was referring to the fact that the army is still the people's army. This army retains the traditions of the old Red Army. What they crossed this time was genuinely a political barrier, a threshold of life and death. This is by no means easy. This shows that the people's army is truly a Great Wall of iron and steel for the Party and country. This shows that no matter how heavy the losses we suffer and no matter how generations change, this army of ours is forever an army under the leadership of the Party, forever the defender of the country, forever the defender of socialism, forever the defender of the public interest, and they are the most beloved of the people.

At the same time, we should never forget how cruel our enemies are. For them we should not have an iota of forgiveness.

The outbreak of the rebellion is worth thinking about. It prompts us to calmly think about the past and consider the future. Perhaps this bad thing will enable us to go ahead with reform and the open-door policy at a more steady, better, even a faster pace. Also it will enable us to more speedily correct our mistakes and better develop our strong points. I cannot elaborate on this today. I just want to raise the subject here.

The first question is: Are the line, goals and policies laid down by the Third Plenum of the 11th Central Committee, including our "three-step" development strategy, correct? Is it the case that because this riot took place there are some questions about the correctness of the line, goals and policies we laid down? Are our goals "leftist"? Should we continue to use them for our struggle in the future? These significant questions should be given clear and definite answers.

We have already accomplished our first goal of doubling the gross national product. We plan to use 12 years to attain our second goal of doubling the GNP.* In the 50 years after that, we hope to reach the level of a moderately developed country. A two-percent annual growth rate is sufficient. This is our strategic goal.

I don't believe that what we have arrived at is a "leftist" judgment. Nor have we set up an overly ambitious goal. So, in answering the first question, I should say that our strategic goal cannot be regarded a failure so far. It will be an unbeatable achievement for a country with 1.5 billion people like ours to reach the level of a moderately developed nation after 61 years.

China is capable of realizing this goal. It cannot be said that our strategic goal is wrong because of the occurrence of this event.

The second question is this: Is the general conclusion of the 13th Party Congress of one focus (refers to making economic development the nation's central task) and "two basic points" correct? Are the two basic points—upholding the four cardinal principles (that is, keeping to the socialist road and upholding the people's democratic dictatorship, leadership by the Communist Party, and Mao Zedong Thought) and persisting in the policy of reform and opening up—wrong?

In recent days I have pondered these two points. No, we haven't been wrong with the four cardinal principles. If there is anything amiss, it's that these principles haven't been thoroughly implemented; they haven't been used as the basic concept to educate the people, educate the students and educate all the cadres and Party members.

The crux of the current incident was basically the confrontation between the four cardinal principles and bourgeois liberalization. It isn't that we have not talked about such things as the four cardinal principles, worked on political concepts, and opposed bourgeois liberalization and spiritual pollution. What we haven't done is maintain continuity in these talks. There has been no action and sometimes even hardly any talk.

The fault does not lie in the four cardinal principles themselves, but in wavering in upholding these principles, and in the very poor work done to persist in political work and education.

---

* Deng Xiaoping speaks of "doubling" and "redoubling," terminology taken from contract bridge, at which he is an avid player.

In my Chinese People's Political Consultative Conference talk on New Year's Day 1980, I talked about "four guarantees",* one of which was the "enterprising spirit of hard struggle and plain living." Hardworking is our tradition. Promoting plain living must be a major objective of education and this should be the keynote for the next sixty to seventy years. The more prosperous our country becomes, the more important it is to keep hold of the enterprising spirit. The promotion of this spirit and plain living will also be helpful for overcoming corruption.

After the People's Republic was founded we promoted plain living. Later on, when life became a little better, we promoted spending more, leading to wastage everywhere. This, in addition to lapses in theoretical work and an incomplete legal system, resulted in backsliding.

I once told foreigners that our worst omission of the past ten years was in education. What I meant was chiefly political education, and this doesn't apply to schools and students alone, but to the masses as a whole. And we have not said much about plain living and the enterprising spirit, about what kind of a country China is and how it is going to turn out. This is our biggest omission.

Is there anything wrong with the basic concept of reforms [viz., *perestroika*] and opening up [viz., *glasnost*]? No. Without reforms and opening up how could we have what we have today? There has been a fairly satisfactory rise in the standard of living, and it may be said that we have moved one stage further. The positive results of ten years of reforms must be properly assessed even though there have emerged such problems as inflation. Naturally, in reform and adopting the open policy, we run the risk of importing evil influences from the West and we have never underestimated such influences.

In the early 1980s, when we have established special economic zones, I told our Guangdong comrades that on the one hand they should persevere with reforms and opening up and on the other hand they should deal severely with economic crimes and carry out ideological and political education.

Looking back, it appears that there were obvious inadequacies; there hasn't been proper coordination. Being reminded of these inadequacies will help us formulate future policies. Further, we must persist in the coordination between a planned economy and market regulation. There cannot be any change in this policy.

* These refer to (1) unswervingly implementing the Party's political line; (2) maintaining a political situation of stability and unity; (3) carrying forward the enterprising spirit of hard struggle and plain living; (4) training a contingent of cadres who adhere to the socialist road and have professional expertise.

In the course of implementing this policy we can place more emphasis on planning in the adjustment period. At other times there can be a
little more market regulation so as to allow more flexibility. The future
policy should still be a marriage between the planned economy and
market regulation.

What is important is that we should never change China back into a
closed country. Such a policy would be most detrimental. We don't even
have a good flow of information. Nowadays, are we not talking about the
importance of information? Certainly, it is important. If one who is
involved in management doesn't possess information, he is no better
than a man whose nose is stuffed and whose ears and eyes are shut.
Again, we should never go back to the old days of trampling the economy
to death. I put forward this proposal for the consideration of the Standing Committee. This is also an urgent question, a question we'll have to
deal with sooner or later.

In brief, this is what we have achieved in the past decade: Generally,
our basic proposals, ranging from a developing strategy to policies,
including reforms and opening up, are correct. If there is any inadequacy,
then I should say our reforms and opening up have not proceeded
adequately enough. The problems we face in implementing reforms are
far greater than those we encounter in opening our country. In political
reforms we can affirm one point: We have to adhere to the system of the
National People's Congress and not the American system of the separation of three powers. The U.S. berates us for suppressing students. But
when they handled domestic student unrest and turmoil, didn't they
send out police and troops to arrest people and cause bloodshed? They
were suppressing students and the people, but we are putting down a
counterrevolutionary rebellion. What qualifications do they have to criticize us? From now on, however, in handling such problems, we should
see to it that when a trend occurs we should never allow it to spread.

What do we do from now on? I would say that we should continue,
persist in implementing our set basic line, principles and policies. Except
where there is a need to alter a word or phrase here and there, there
should be no change in the basic line or basic policy. Now that I have
raised this question, I would like you all to consider it seriously. As to
how to implement these policies, such as in the areas of investment, the
manipulation of capital, etc., I am in favor of putting the emphasis on
capital industry and agriculture. In capital industry, this calls for attention to the supply of raw materials, transportation and energy; there
should be more investment in this area for the next 10 to 20 years, even
if it involves heavy debts. In a way, this is also openness. Here, we need

to be bold and have made hardly any serious errors. We should work for more electricity, railway lines, highways and shipping. There's a lot we can do. As for steel, foreigners estimate we'll need some 120 million tons a year in the future. Now we turn out some 60 million tons, half of what we need. If we were to improve our existing facilities and increase production by 20 million tons we could reduce the amount of steel we need to import. Obtaining foreign loans to improve this area is also an aspect of reform and opening up. The question now confronting us is not whether the policies of reform and opening up are correct or not or whether we should continue with these policies. The question is how to carry out these policies, where do we go and which area should we concentrate on?

We have to firmly implement the series of policies formulated since the Third Plenary Session of the Eleventh Party Central Committee. We must conscientiously sum up our experiences, persevere in what is right, correct what is wrong, and do a bit more where we lag behind. In short, we should sum up the experiences of the present and look forward to the future.

That's all I have to say on this occasion.

Deng Xiaoping
June 9, 1989

■

Notes

Introduction: On Being Human and Being Chinese

Wang Ruoshui's essay, from which the epigraph and the passage quoted on p. xx are taken, appeared first in the *People's Daily* in March 1983. It was written in honor of Karl Marx's death centenary. According to my information, it was published despite government prohibition, mainly because the order forbidding the publication arrived too late to stop the print. For this, he was removed from his office as deputy editor-in-chief. The essay was later published together with other writings under the title *Wei rendaozhuyi bianhu* (In defense of humanism) (Beijing: Renmin, 1987), which is the edition I consulted. Wang was expelled from the party in 1988.

1. The Event

A Note on Sources: The event of April–June 1989 in Beijing has been well documented all over the world in print and picture. Besides the books, newspapers, and newsmagazines referred to at the end of my Chronology of Events and following the introduction, and in the notes to this chapter, I have also synthesized the information from Chinese-language sources, including several books since published on this subject, one of which is Han Shanbi, ed., *Lishi de changshang* (The wound of history) (Hong Kong: East & West Culture, 1989), vol. 1. For the account in this chapter, the following Chinese-language daily newspapers have been especially useful: *Ming Pao Daily, Shun Po, Sing Tao Daily, Wen Hui Daily,* all from Hong Kong; *China Times Daily, China Times Express, United Daily,* all from Taiwan. For the story of the student demonstrations and the crackdown, I have also consulted articles from the following newsmagazines: *Asiaweek* (English and Chinese editions), *Cheng Ming, Hong Kong Economic Journal Monthly* (Shun Bao Monthly) (especially the June 1989 issue), *Ming Pao Monthly* (especially the May and June issues, 1989), *The Nineties, Pai Hsing Semi-Monthly* (especially May 16, 1989), *Tide Monthly,* all from Hong Kong; and *China Spring 73* (June 1989), from New York.

Besides the news reports mentioned in the text, English-language sources include these recent works by eyewitnesses: *Beijing Spring,* photographs by David and Peter Turnley, text by Melinda Liu (New York: Stewart, Tabori & Chang, 1989); *Crisis at Tiananmen,* by Yi Mu (San Francisco: China Books & Periodicals, 1989); *June Four: A Chronicle of the Chinese Democratic Uprising,* by the photographers and reporters of *Ming Pao* News, translated by Zi Jin and Qin Zhou (Fayetteville: University of Arkansas Press, 1989); *Massacre in Beijing,* by the editors of *Time* Magazine, with an introduction by Nien Cheng (New York: Warner Books, 1989); *Tiananmen Diary: Thirteen Days in June,* by Harrison E. Salisbury (Boston: Little Brown, 1989); *Tiananmen: Rape of Beijing* by Michael Fathers (New York: Doubleday/Anchor, 1989); *Tiananmen Square,* by Scot Simmie and Bob Nixon (Vancouver: Douglas & McIntyre, 1989).

There are also the printed transcript from ABC News, "The Koppel Report: Tragedy at Tiananmen: the Untold Story" (June 27, 1989); and Nicholas D. Kristoff's

English-language China Update feature article in *The New York Times Magazine*, November 12, 1989.

1. This is taken from Fang's 1985 speech, "On Reforms," given in a collection of his addresses, *Yanlun zaibian* (Hong Kong: Shuguang, 1988) p. 13.
2. Andrew Spano, in *Sunday Morning Post*, Hong Kong, May 28, 1989.
3. Professor Ruth Hayhoe spent the month of May 1989 visiting Chinese campuses and circulated a written account of her experiences in a letter dated 22 June 1989. As of July 1989 she is cultural attaché at the Canadian embassy in Beijing. This excerpt is printed with her permission.
4. *The Sunday Morning Post*, Hong Kong, May 28, 1989. The seven octogenarians are, in alphabetical order: Bo Yibo (born 1907), Chen Yun (born 1905), Deng Xiaoping (born 1904), Li Xiannian (born 1909), Peng Zhen (born 1902), Wang Zheng (born 1908), Yang Shangkun (born 1907).
5. *Asiaweek*, English edition, June 2, 1989.
6. See note 3 above.
7. David Aikman, *Maclean's*, June 19, 1989, p. 15.
8. Ibid.
9. Chai Ling's testimony was published in *Sing Tao Daily*, June 11, 1989.
10. *Newsweek*, June 19, 1989, p. 22.
11. Ibid.
12. Ibid.
13. *Time*, June 19, 1989.
14. The eyewitness was Jennifer MacFarlane, in *Newsweek*, June 19, 1989.
15. Ibid.
16. I spent April to June 1989 in Taiwan, as visiting professor at Tsing Hua University, and am quoting from a conversation.
17. *Newsweek*, June 19, 1989.
18. Ibid.
19. Harrison Salisbury, *Tiananmen Diary* (Boston: Little Brown, 1989), p. 56. For the situation in Hong Kong, consult Frank Ching, "Red Star over Hong Kong," *World Policy Journal* (Fall 1989): 657–63.

2. Through Western Eyes

The epigraph is taken from Harold R. Isaacs, *Images of Asia* (New York: Capricorn Books, 1958), p. 66.

1. Michel Oksenberg, "Confession of a China Watcher," *Newsweek*, June 19, 1989, p. 30. On the subject of the China-watchers' self-reproach, consult an article published in the Chinese language *China Times Weekly*, June 19, 1989, pp. 54–58.
2. Ross Terrill, *800,000,000: the Real China* (New York: Dell, 1971), p. 24.
3. Simon Leys, *The Burning Forest* (New York: Henry Holt, 1985), p. 113.
4. John Fraser, *The Chinese: Portrait of a People* (London: Collins, 1980), p. 301.
5. *The New York Times*, June 27, 1989.
6. Deng Xiaoping's speech of June 9, 1989, has been published in *Deng Xiaoping Tongzhi lun gaige kaifang* (Deng Xiaoping on reform and openness) (Beijing: Renmin, 1989), p. 119. See also the English translation provided in this book.
7. Yang Nung and Lai Shi, "Zhongguo zhengju de yuce" (A prognosis of the political situation in China), *China Spring*, July 1988, p. 32.
8. *The New York Review of Books*, February 24, 1972.
9. *University of Toronto Bulletin*, June 26, 1989.
10. Fraser, p. 257.

3. The Dictator and His Tabula Rasa

The epigraph comes from Mao Zedong (April 1958); see *Peking Review,* June 10, 1958. This journal is now called *Beijing Review.*

A Note on Sources: A new English-language volume that has just appeared in print is Roderick MacFarquhar, Timothy Cheeck, and Eugene Wu. *The Secret Speeches of Mao Zedong* (Cambridge, MA: Harvard University Press, 1989). It presents Mao's unedited words from the "Hundred Flowers" to the "Great Leap Forward," that is, 1957–58.

For China under Deng Xiaoping, I have consulted also Mineo Nakajima, *Junen ato no Chugoku* (China after ten years) (Tokyo, 1985).

1. *Wen Wei Po,* Hong Kong, June 11, 1989.
2. Wei Jingsheng's statement is translated in Simon Leys, *The Burning Forest,* p. 230.
3. *The People's Daily,* September 15, 1986.
4. Robert Jay Lifton, *Revolutionary Immortality* (New York: Random House, 1968), p. 7.
5. Ibid., pp. 4–5.
6. *Sunday Morning Post,* Hong Kong, May 28, 1989.
7. Consult Mao's letter to Jiang Qing, see L. Ladany, *The Communist Party of China and Marxism, 1921–1985* (London: Hurst, 1988), p. 362.
8. Consult Chow Tse-tsung, *The May Fourth Movement: Intellectual Revolution in Modern China* (Stanford: Stanford University Press, 1960), pp. 239–40.
9. Nien Cheng, *Life and Death in Shanghai* (London: Collins, 1984), p. 661.
10. George F. Will, in *Newsweek,* June 19, 1989.
11. *Zhongguo minyun yuanshiliao jingxuan* (Hong Kong: October Review, 1989), p. 68. This is a volume of primary materials on the democracy movement.
12. This is taken from Wang's speech in 1987. See the collection of his addresses, *Yanlun zaibian* (Hong Kong: Shuguang, 1988), p. 136. The book is a collection of selected speeches by Fang Lizhi, Liu Binyan, and Wang Rowang, published in 1987 by the government for use at "criticism sessions," and reprinted in Hong Kong in 1988.

4. Chinese Communism: Old Wine in New Bottles?

The epigraph, like other quotations from Mao in this book, is taken from Stuart R. Schram's *The Political Thought of Mao Tse-tung* (New York: Praeger, 1969). This piece is from the report "On the New Stage," and is in Schram, p. 172.

1. Consult Karl A. Wittfogel, "Social Revolution in China," in Eugene Kamenka, ed., *A World in Revolution?* (Canberra: Australian National University, 1970), pp. 42–44.
2. Benjamin I. Schwartz, *Chinese Communism and the Rise of Mao* (Cambridge, MA: Harvard University Press, 1951), pp. 192–99.
3. Mao Zedong, "The Greatest Friendship" (1953), in Schram, p. 429.
4. *New Youth (Xin Qingnian),* vol. 4, no. 4.
5. Schwartz, pp. 202–4.
6. This is adapted from Mao Zedong's "A Single Spark Can Start a Prairie Fire" (1930) in *The Selected Works of Mao Tse-tung* (Beijing: Foreign Languages Press, 1967), vol. 1, p. 124. What these words tell us of the primacy of keeping initiative and mobility in warfare comes from the ancient text, Sunzi's *The Art of War,* from which Mao Zedong has often quoted.

7. The quotations in this book from the *Analects* and *Mencius* are adapted from the English translations in James Legge, *The Chinese Classics* (Oxford, Clarendon: 1861–72), vols. 1–2.

8. For Liu Shaoqi, I consulted his *Selected Writings* (*Liu Shaoqi xuanji*), a Chinese edition published in Tokyo, 1967. The English translation is taken from the standard translation, *How to Be a Good Communist* (Beijing: Foreign Languages Press, 1951). Liu Shaoqi quotes from *Analects* 2:4 on p. 9.

9. Liu Shaoqi, p. 24.

10. *Laozi*, ch. 80. English translation is taken from D. C. Lau, *Lao Tzu: Tao Te Ching* (Penguin Books, 1963), p. 142.

11. *Laozi*, ch. 17, from Lau, p. 73.

12. Ibid.

13. The quotation from *Han Feizi* (Sect. 5) is taken from the translation by Burton Watson, *Han Fei Tzu: Basic Writings* (New York: Columbia University Press, 1964), pp. 17–18.

14. Mao Zedong, "Reform in learning, the Party and Literature" (1942), in Schram, p. 179.

15. Franz Schurmann, *Ideology and Organization in Communist China* (Berkeley: University of California Press, 1968), p. iii.

16. William Hinton, *Fanshen: A Documentary of Revolution in a Chinese Village* (New York: Vintage Books, 1966), p. vii.

17. *The Nineties*, September 1989.

18. Mao Zedong, "On the People's Democratic Dictatorship" (1949), in Schram, p. 300. Benevolent government is the hallmark of Confucian political theory; Mao's admission that the Communist state represents violence rather than benevolence proves that he does not consider his government to be influenced by Confucianism.

19. Karl A. Wittfogel, *Oriental Despotism: A Comparative Study of Total Power* (New Haven: Yale University Press, 1957), pp. 125–26.

20. Ibid., p. 123.

21. Wittfogel, "Social Revolution in China," in Kamenka, p. 51.

22. Deng Xiaoping's words are given in Tao Kai et al., *Zouchu xiandai mixing* (Abandoning modern superstitions) (Hong Kong: Joint Publishing, 1989), p. 45. This book especially reports on the debates regarding practice as the criterion for truth. According to this book, these words of Deng's are also in Deng's Selected Writings. I have not however found them in *Deng Xiaoping Wenxuan* (Selected writings of Deng Xiaoping) (Hong Kong: Joint Publishing, 1983).

23. Hu Yaobang's words are found in Tao, et al. p. 49.

24. Tao et al., pp. 96–97.

25. Tao et al., p. 109.

26. Tao et al., p. 110.

27. Tao et al., p. 119.

28. For Liu Xiaobo's views, see *Ming Pao Monthly*, August 1989, p. 36. On this point, I find his position and that of many other dissidents rather biased and not based on real historical knowledge.

29. This is taken from an earlier interview of Bao by Zhang Jiefeng, in *Pai Hsing*, July 1989, p. 21.

30. The final quotation is from Lucian W. Pye, *China: An Introduction* (Boston: Little, Brown, 1972), pp. 357–58.

5. Student Protests in Modern Chinese History

The epigraph is taken from Liu Yizheng's article in *Xueheng* 42 (1925).

A Note on Sources: For education in the People's Republic, I relied on Yao Robing, *Zhongguo jiaoyu: 1949–1982* (Education in China: 1949–1982) (Hong Kong, 1985) and an article by Lu Junfu on problems in mainland China's education, in *Ming Pao Monthly* 282 (June 1989): 52–56.

1. I refer here to Professor Tsuchida Kenjiro, of Waseda University, Tokyo.
2. *Mencius* 6B:15. The English translation is adapted from James Legge, *The Chinese Classics* (Oxford: Clarendon, 1892), vol. 2, p. 447.
3. Liu Yizheng's article was published in *Xueheng* (1925).
4. Chen Duxiu is quoted in Chow Tse-tsung, *The May Fourth Movement*, p. 20.
5. Roderick MacFarquhar, *The Hundred Flowers* (London: Atlantic Books, 1960), p. 20.
6. Ibid., p. 95.
7. Ibid., p. 168.
8. Ibid., p. 170.
9. Ibid.
10. For the 1986 student protests, there is an eyewitness account about the event in Shanghai, *China Spring* 64 (1988): 6–14.
11. Wei Jinsheng's 1975 *dazibao* is translated in Simon Leys, *The Burning Forest*, p. 238.

6. Is There Religious Freedom in China?

The epigraph is taken from Mao Zedong, "On the New Democracy" (1940). See *Selected Works of Mao Tse-tung*, vol. 2, p. 381.

A Note on Sources: There are many brochures, newsletters, and periodicals that give news about Christianity in China, often published by church-related agencies. I am familiar with the National Council of Churches of Christ's *The People and Church in China* (1982), and with the following newsletters and periodicals: Maryknoll's *Mission Forum*, the National Council of Churches' *China Notes* (New York), Joseph J. Spae's *China Update*, the United Methodist Church's *China Talk* (Hong Kong), the Canadian Council of Churches' *China and Ourselves*, the Graduate School of Theology's *China and the Church Today* (Hong Kong), and the German-language *China Heute* published by *Monumenta Serica*. I have also found in China some numbers of Chinese-language religious periodicals published by Protestants, Catholics, and Buddhists and intended for internal circulation.

The Institute for the Study of World Religion at the Chinese Social Science Academy publishes journals that circulate outside as well: the *Shijie zongjiao yanjiu* (Studies on world religions) and the *Shijie zongjiao ziliao* (Materials on world religions). The former features articles dealing more with religions in China, the latter concerns itself more with developments outside China. Both include news of conferences on the subject of religion. The latter also presents book reviews.

1. Richard C. Bush, Jr., *Religion in Communist China* (Nashville, TN: Abingdon Press, 1970), p. 111.
2. A rather recent book with a lot of information about the Catholic Church in China is Jean Charbonnier's *Guide to the Catholic Church in China* (Singapore, 1986).
3. Bush, p. 257.
4. Donald E. MacInnis, *Religious Policy and Practice in Communist China* (New York: Macmillan, 1972), p. 292.
5. Ibid., p. 336.
6. *The Constitution of the People's Republic of China* (Beijing: Foreign Languages Press, 1983), p. 32.
7. *Red Flag* (June 16, 1982), vol. 6, no. 12.

8. Ren Jiyu, *Zhongguo zhexueshi* (A history of Chinese philosophy) (Beijing: Renmin, 1979), vol. 1, p. 75.
9. There are many books on Jews and Muslims in China, some of which I include in the source bibliography at the end of this book. A recent account of *The Jews of Kaifeng* written from the Jewish viewpoint, is published by the Beth Hatefutsoth, the Nahum Goldman Museum of the Jewish Diaspora (Tel Aviv, 1984) on the occasion of an exhibition of documents, photographs, and other items.
10. For Manicheans in China, I consulted Samuel N. C. Lieu, *The Religion of Light* (Hong Kong: Hong Kong University, 1979).
11. There are many books on Chinese Jews and Chinese (and Tibetan) Buddhism, although the experience of Tibetans as well as Muslims under Communist rule is little known outside the country.
12. Liu Xiaobo, p. 36.
13. *China Spring Digest,* March/April 1987. (An English edition of *China Spring.*)
14. Fang Lizhi, *Zanmei wozhu zhihou* (After praising my lord) (Hong Kong: Ming Pao Publishing, 1988), p. 5.
15. *China News Update,* August 1989. This is a Presbyterian newsletter published in New York.

7. The Two Tian'anmen Incidents: 1976 and 1989

The epigraph is taken from *He shang* (River Elegy), published in Hong Kong (Joint Publishing, 1989), see page 7. For the translation into English of the verses quoted, I am indebted to an article by Frederic Wakeman, Jr., "All the Rage in China," *The New York Review of Books* (March 2, 1989). Wakeman calls the work *River Dirge*.

1. *He shang* is a television series prepared by intellectuals like Su Xiaokang and Wang Luxiang, and produced in June 1988 by China Central Television, with an entirely Chinese narration. The script has been published in book form in Hong Kong.
2. For the 1976 Tian'anmen Incident, I have consulted the following eyewitness accounts:

   [Gao Jie and others,] *Deng Xiaoping fuchu neimu* (The inside story of Deng Xiaoping's restoration to power) (Taipei: *China Times* publication, 1977), pp. 77–84.

   Li Yizhe. *Guanyu shehui zhuyi de minzhu yu fazhi* (On socialist democracy and its rule of law), edited by Qi Hao (Hong Kong: Bibliothèque Asiatique, 1977). Although this book gives Li as its author, it is actually a compilation including materials on the 1976 Tian'anmen Incident.

   Naka Kunihito, *Ten'anmon jiken* (The Tian'anmen Incident) (Tokyo: Bungei shunju, 1979), chaps. 3–4.

   Okada Takahiro, *To Shohei no Chugoku* (Deng Xiaoping's China) (Tokyo: Nihon keizai shinbunsha, 1979) chap. 2.

   Tao Kai, Zhang Yide, Dai Qing et al., *Zouchu xiandai mixing* (Abandoning modern superstitions) (Hong Kong: Joint Publishing, 1989). This book deals mainly with the Debates on the Norm of Truth, but includes materials as well on the 1976 Tian'anmen Incident.

   Yan Jiaqi et al., *Siwu yundong jishi* (The facts about the April Fifth Movement) (Beijing: Renmin, 1979).
3. For the 1976 Tian'anmen Incident, consult *The People's Daily,* November 21–22, 1978, which includes poems like this one. Consult also Naka Kunihito, *Ten'anmon jiken,* p. 95.
4. For the 1989 Tian'anmen Incident, Chen Xitong's very long official report was reproduced in the U.S. edition of the Chinese-language *World Journal,* July 7–8, 1989.

5. For Deng Xiaoping's June 9, 1989, address, consult the English translation of the text, included in this book.
6. For Michel Oksenberg, see *Newsweek*, June 19, 1989.
7. This came from Jay Mathews's article in the *Seattle Times*, May 28, 1989.
8. Ibid.
9. Tao Kai, p. 142.
10. *He-shang*, p. 111.
11. *Deng Xiaoping lun gaige kaifang* (Deng Xiaoping on reform and open policy) (Beijing: Renmin, 1989), p. 6. This small book includes Deng's address of December 13, 1979, as its first selection, and his speech to the martial law troops on June 9, 1989, as its final selection. There is a tragic irony in the implied contradiction between some of his words uttered at the beginning of his regime, and others pronounced after the June 1989 crackdown. Deng was willing to use democratization to promote his own power, but turned against it out of fear of losing power.

8. What of Moral Legitimacy?

The epigraph is taken from *Mencius* 4B:3; Legge, p. 318.

1. John Locke, *Two Treatises of Goverment* (Cambridge: Cambridge University Press, 1988), Treatise 2, chap. 4, p. 283.
2. *Mencius* 5A:5; Legge, p. 357.
3. For Xunzi, see sect. 9; in Burton Watson, trans., *Hsün Tzu: Basic Writings* (New York: Columbia University Press, 1963), p. 40.
4. *Han Feizi*, sect. 7; consult B. Watson, trans., *Han Fei Tzu: Basic Writings*, p. 30.
5. *Han Feizi*, sect. 49; Watson, trans., *Han Fei Tzu: Basic Writings*, p. 103.
6. This is from a 1985 address. See Fang Lizhi, *Minzhu bushi shiyude* (Democracy is not granted from above) (Hong Kong: Zhongguo Xiandaihua xuehui, 1987), p. 113.
7. *The Constitution of the People's Republic of China.*
8. Ibid.
9. MacFarquhar, pp. 87–88.
10. Ibid., p. 94.
11. Li Yizhe, *Guanyu shehuizhuyi de minzhu yu fazhi* (On socialist democracy and its rule of law) (Hong Kong: Bibliothèque Asiatique, 1977), p. 94. The English translation was done by myself.
12. Where criminal law is concerned, I consulted Jerome Alan Cohen, "The Criminal Process in China," in *Soviet and Chinese Communism: Similarities and Differences*, edited by Donald W. Treadgold (Seattle: University of Washington Press, 1967).
13. For Wei Jinsheng, see Leys, *The Burning Forest*, pp. 230, 229–30.
14. For Ren Wanding, see *Ming Pao Monthly*, July 1989.
15. For Wei Jingsheng, see Leys, *The Burning Forest*, p. 226.
16. This is taken from *Zhongguo minyun yuanzhiliao jingxuan* (Selected documents on the Chinese democracy movement), p. 37.
17. These words come from Victor Orban, and are quoted by Miklos Haraszti in an op-ed article in *The New York Times*, July 2, 1989. The article is interestingly entitled: "In Making Democracy, Stir Often, Do Not Boil." This is especially significant in the light of later demonstrations, especially in October–December 1989, in many Eastern European countries, especially East Germany and Czechoslovakia.
18. Karoly Grosz is also quoted by Miklos Haraszti. See ibid.
19. Ibid.
20. Harlan W. Jencks, in *The New York Times*, June 20, 1989.

9. Will "Mr. Democracy" Come to China?

The epigraph is taken from Li Yizhe, p. 115.

A Note on Sources: The quotations from Li Yizhe's *dazibao* (1974), given in the epigraph and elsewhere, are translated from the Chinese *Guanyu shehui zhuyi de minzhu yu fazhi* (On the socialist democratic system and its rule of law). This book remains a good source for the earlier democracy movement.

For the Xidan movement, besides the works already mentioned elsewhere, I have consulted materials published in Hong Kong, including reprints of articles published in underground journals or as wall posters, for example, *Zhongguo dixia kanwu* (Chinese underground journals) (Hong Kong, [1979]). Wei Jingsheng's writings in Chinese are collected in *Tanso yu Wei Jingsheng* ("Exploration" and Wei Jingsheng) (Taipei: Youshi, 1983). I also consulted Liu Shengji, *Beijing zhi chun* (The Spring of Beijing) (Taipei, Youshi, 1984); Andrew Nathan, *Chinese Democracy* (New York: Knopf, 1985); James D. Seymour, ed., *The Fifth Modernization: China's Human Rights Movement 1978–79* (New York: Human Rights Publishing Group, 1980). For the parallel movement in Shanghai, I consulted Anne McLaren's article in *China in the Seventies: Australian Perspectives,* edited by Stephen Fitzgerald and Pamela Hewitt (Canberra, Australian National University, 1980).

For later developments, a new work is Orville Schell, *Discos and Democracy* (New York: Doubleday/Anchor, 1989). Part 3 presents a profile of the three dissidents associated with the 1986–87 movement: Fang Lizhi, Liu Binyan, and Wang Ruowang.

1. Benjamin I. Schwartz, pp. 88–90.
2. This is taken from Deng Xiaoping's address to the Third Plenum (December 1978). See *Deng Xiaoping tongzhi lun gaigi kaifang* (Comrade Deng on reform and open policy) (Beijing: Renmin, 1989), p. 8.
3. Ibid.
4. English translation in Leys, p. 229.
5. *The Constitution of the People's Republic of China,* p. 6.
6. English translation in Leys, p. 227.
7. For Yang Xiguang, see Li Yizhe, p. 130.
8. For Mao Zedong's eventual opposition to the establishment of the Shanghai Commune in January 1967, see Li Yizhe, pp. 13–14.
9. This comes from Li Yizhe's *dazibao,* ibid., pp. 78–79.
10. *Cheng-ming,* May 1988.
11. Li Yizhe, p. 95.
12. Ibid., pp. 96–97.
13. John Fraser, p. 309.
14. James D. Seymour, ed., *The Fifth Modernization: China's Human Rights Movement 1978–79* (New York: Human Rights Publishing Group, 1980).
15. English translation in Leys, p. 227.
16. For petitions of amnesty in favor of political prisoners, I have consulted articles in *China Spring* 71 (April 1989); *Dongxiang* 55 (April 1989).
17. For Liu Binyan, as for Wang Ruowang and Fang Lizhi, there is a collection of their words provided by the government for criticism sessions. The edition I used is Fang Lizhi, Liu Binyan, and Wang Ruowang, *yanlun zaipian* (Hong Kong: Shuguang, 1988), pp. 78–79.
18. *He shang,* p. 93.
19. English translation in Leys, pp. 233–34.

20. Quotations from Fang Lizhi are taken from *Minzhu bushi shiyude* (Democracy is not granted from above) (Hong Kong: Zhongguo Xiandaihua xuehui, 1987), p. 113.

21. Ibid., p. 150.

22. Su Shaozhi, quoted in the Chinese-language *World Journal*, September 8, 1989.

23. This is quoted in an article by Zeng Huiyan, *Cheng-ming*, August 1989, p. 43.

24. *Ming Pao Monthly*, July 1989, p. 49.

25. Ibid., p. 48.

26. Samuel P. Huntington, "Social and Institutional Dynamics of One-Party Systems," *Authoritarian Politics in Modern Society*, ed. by Clement H. Moore, and Samuel P. Huntington (New York: Basic Books, 1970), p. 44.

27. Wang Zhaojun spoke to the Canadian Asian Studies Association meeting at Laval University, Quebec City, on June 6, 1989.

28. Jean-Jacques Rousseau, *The Social Contract and Discourses* (London: J. M. Dent, 1982), Book 1, chaps. 1 and 3, pp. 165, 168.

What Now?

A Note on Sources: For this chapter, even more than for the others, the books consulted are especially those that are now banned in mainland China. Reports are that there is a list of the names of over fifty authors whose works are now prohibited. In this book, I have usually quoted those writers who are now either in exile or under arrest.

It is symptomatic of the malaise in the country that one recent series of publications is called "China Disease Series" (Journalism Press). It includes Lu Wa et al., *Beiju xingbie* (The tragic sex) (1988), on the exploitation of women today; Su Xiaokang et al., *Wutobang ji* (Dirge to utopia) (1988); Wang Yubo's *Da fanlung, xiao fanlung* (Big cage, small cage) (1989), an indictment of "feudal" vestiges in today's China.

1. The statement of the ten intellectuals is given in *China News Analysis*, No. 1387 (June 15, 1989), p. 9.

2. *Bai Hua jinzuo xuan* (Recent works by Bai Hua), edited by Bi Hua and others. (Hong Kong: Tiandi, 1981), p. 18.

3. Hannah Arendt, *Totalitarianism*, Part 3 of *The Origins of Totalitarianism* (New York: Harcourt, Brace & World, 1968), p. 158.

4. *Mencius* 1B:8.

5. *Mencius* 4B:3.

6. *Ming Pao Monthly*, May 1989, p. 40.

7. Fang Lizhi's statements have been published in *Zanmei wozhu zhihou*. In this case, see his letter from Japan (1981), on p. 33.

8. The Reuters News report on Ya Ding is given in *The Korea Times*, Seoul, June 10, 1989.

9. Ibid.

Sources

Some English-language Books Consulted

There are many excellent books in Western languages on Chinese history in general and the Communist Revolution and the People's Republic of China in particular. I am only listing a few that I have actively consulted in the writing of this book, and others that may be useful to a wide reading public. I am not listing any articles from newspapers and journals, as there would be too many, and I am not relisting every book mentioned in the text or in the notes.

Amnesty International. *China: Violations of Human Rights: Prisoners of Conscience and the Death Penalty in the People's Republic of China.* London: Amnesty International, 1984.

Arendt, Hannah. *Totalitarianism.* New York: Harcourt, Brace & World, 1951.

Barnard, A. Doak. *Communist China and Asia.* New York: Vintage Books, 1960.

Bell, Daniel. *The End of Ideology.* New York: Free Press, 1962.

Brown, G. Thompson. *Christianity in the People's Republic of China.* Atlanta, GA: Friendship Press, 1983.

Bush, Richard C., Jr. *Religion in Communist China.* Nashville, TN: Abingdon Press, 1970.

Charbonnier, Jean. *Guide to the Catholic Church in China.* Singapore: China Catholic Communication, 1986.

Ch'en, Jerome. *Mao and the Chinese Revolution.* London: Oxford University Press, 1965.

Ching, Frank. *Hong Kong and China: For Better or For Worse.* New York: Asia Society, 1985.

Ching, Julia. *Confucianism and Christianity: A Comparative Study.* Tokyo: Kodansha International, 1977.

Chow Tse-tsung. *The May Fourth Movement: Intellectual Revolution in Modern China.* Cambridge, MA: Harvard University Press, 1960.

Chu, Michael, S. J., ed. *The New China: A Catholic Response.* New York: Paulist Press, 1977.

de Bary, W. Theodore. *The Liberal Tradition in China.* New York: Columbia University Press, 1983.

Fairbank, John K. *The United States and China.* Cambridge, MA: Harvard University Press, 1971.

Feuerwerker, Albert, ed. *Modern China.* Englewood Cliffs, NJ: Prentice-Hall, 1964.

Fitzgerald, C. P. *China: A Short Cultural History.* London: Cresset Press, 1961.

Fitzgerald, Stephen, and Pamela Hewitt, ed. *China in the Seventies: Australian Perspectives.* Canberra: Australian National University, 1980.

Fraser, John. *The Chinese: Portrait of a People.* London: Collins, 1980.

Frolic, B. Michael. *Mao's People: Sixteen Portraits of Life in Revolutionary China.* Cambridge, MA: Harvard University Press, 1980.

Goldman, Merle. *China's Intellectuals: Advise and Dissent.* Cambridge, MA: Harvard University Press, 1981.

Hinton, William. *Fanshen: A Documentary of Revolution in a Chinese Village.* New York: Vintage Books, 1966.

Isaacs, Harold R. *Images of Asia: American Views of China and India* (originally published under the title *Scratches on Our Minds*). New York: Capricorn Books, 1958.

Kamenka, Eugene, ed. *A World in Revolution.* Canberra: Australian National University, 1970.

Kennedy, Paul. *The Rise and Fall of the Great Powers.* New York: Random House, 1987.

Küng, Hans; and Julia Ching. *Christianity and Chinese Religions.* New York: Doubleday, 1989.

Ladany, Laszlo. *The Communist Party of China and Marxism, 1921–1985.* [London:] Hurst, 1988.

Lau, D. C., trans. *Lao Tzu: Tao Te Ching.* Harmondsworth, England: Penguin Books, 1963.

Lazzarotto, Angelo S. *The Catholic Church in Post-Mao China.* Hong Kong: Holy Spirit Study Centre, 1982.

Levenson, Joseph R. *Confucian China and its Modern Fate: A Trilogy.* Berkeley, CA: University of California Press, 1968.

Leys, Simon. *The Burning Forest.* New York: Henry Holt, 1985.

————. *The Chairman's New Clothes.* London: Allison & Busby, 1977.

Lifton, Robert J. *Revolutionary Immortality: Mao Tse-tung and the Chinese Cultural Revolution.* New York: Random House, 1968.

MacFarquhar, Roderick. *The Hundred Flowers.* London: Atlantic Books, 1960.

MacInnis, Donald E. *Religious Policy and Practice in Communist China.* New York: Macmillan, 1972.

Maruyama Masao. *Studies in the Intellectual History of Tokugawa Japan.* Princeton, NJ: Princeton University Press, 1974.

McWhirter, Norris, and Ross McWhirter. *Guinness Book of World Records, XX ed.* New York: Bantam, 1977.

Meisner, Maurice J. *Mao's China and After.* New York: Free Press, 1986.

Merwin, Wallace C., and Francis P. Jones, ed. *Documents of the Three-Self Movement.* New York: National Council of the Churches of Christ in the U.S., 1963.

Metzger, Thomas A. *Escape from Predicament: Neo-Confucianism and China's Evolving Political Culture.* New York: Columbia University Press, 1977.

Nien Cheng. *Life and Death in Shanghai.* London: Collins, 1984.

Nathan, Andrew J. *Chinese Democracy.* New York: Knopf, 1985.

Orr, Robert G. *Religion in China.* New York: Friendship Press, 1980.

The Constitution of the People's Republic of China. Beijing: Foreign Languages Press, 1983.

Pye, Lucian W. *China: An Introduction.* Boston: Little, Brown and Company, 1972.

Robinson, Joan. *The Cultural Revolution in China.* Harmondsworth, England: Penguin Books, 1969.

Salisbury, Harrison E. *Tiananmen Diary: Thirteen Days in June.* Boston: Little, Brown, 1989.

Schell, Orville. *Discos and Democracy: China in the Throes of Reform.* New York: Doubleday, 1989.

Schram, Stuart R. *The Political Thought of Mao Tse-tung.* New York: Praeger, 1969.

Schurmann, Franz. *Ideology and Organization in Communist China.* Berkeley, CA: University of California Press, 1968.

Schwartz, Benjamin I. *Chinese Communism and the Rise of Mao.* Cambridge, MA: Harvard University Press, 1951.

Seymour, James D., ed. *The Fifth Modernization: China's Human Rights Movement 1978–79.* New York: Human Rights Publishing Group, 1980.

Solomon, Richard H. *Mao's Revolution and the Chinese Political Culture.* Berkeley, CA: University of California Press, 1971.

Spae, Joseph J. *Church and China: Towards Reconciliation*. Chicago, 1980.

Spence, Jonathan B. *Gate of Heavenly Peace: China and Its Revolution, 1895–1980*. New York: Penguin Books, 1982.

Terrill, Ross. *800,000,000: the Real China*. New York: Dell, 1971.

Treadgold, Donald W., ed. *Soviet and Chinese Communism: Similarities and Differences*. Seattle: University of Washington Press, 1967.

Treadgold, Donald W. *The West in Russia and China: Religious and Secular Thought in Modern Times*, vol. 2. Cambridge: Cambridge University Press, 1974.

Wakeman, Frederic, Jr. *The Fall of Imperial China*. New York: Free Press, 1975.

Watson, Burton, trans. *Han Fei Tzu: Basic Writings*. New York: Columbia University Press, 1964.

Werner, E. T. C. *Myths and Legends of China*. London: Harrap, 1924.

White, Lynn T., III. *Policies of Chaos: the Organizatinal Causes of Violence in China's Cultural Revolution*. Princeton, NJ: Princeton University Press, 1989.

Wickeri, Philip L. *Seeking the Common Ground: Protestant Christianity, the Three-Self Movement and China's United Front*. Maryknoll, NY: Orbis Books, 1988.

Some Books in Asian Languages Consulted

Many books listed are now proscribed in China. Newspaper and journal articles consulted are not listed, as there are too many.

Bai Hua. *Bai Hua jinzuoxuan* (Selected works of Bai Hua). Hong Kong: Tiansi, 1981.

China Times Reporters. *Beijing Xueyun Wushixi* (Fifty days of student movement in Beijing). Taipei: *China Times*, 1989.

Deng Xiaoping. *Deng Xiaoping tongzhi lun gaige kaifang* (Deng on reform and open policy). Beijing: Renmin, 1989.

Fang Lizhi. *Minzhu bushi shiyu de* (Democracy is not given from above). Hong Kong: Zhongguo Xiandai hua xuihui, 1987.

———. *Zanmei wozhu zhihou* (After praising my lord). Hong Kong: Ming Pao Publication, 1988.

———. Liu Binyan and Wang Rowang. *Yanlun zaibian* (Collected sayings). Hong Kong: Shuguang, 1988.

[Gao Jie and others] *Deng Xiaoping fuchu neimu* (The inside story of Deng Xiaoping's restoration to power). Taipei: *China Times*, 1977.

Gao Zao and Yan Jiaqi. *Wenhua geming shinianshi* (Ten years of cultural revolution). Tianjin: Renmin, 1986.

Gu Changsheng. *Chuanjiaoshi yu jindai Zhongguo* (Missionaries and modern China). Shanghai: Renmin, 1981.

Han Xanbi. *Lishide Changshang* (The wound of history), vol. 1. Hong Kong: East & West Culture, 1989.

Jin Guantao and Liu Qingfeng. *Xinsheng yu weiji* (Prosperity and crisis). Changsha: Hunan Renmin, 1984.

Jin Yaoji. *Zhongguo minzhu zhi kunju yu fazhuan* (The difficult situation of democracy in China and its development). Taipei: *China Times* Publication, 1985.

Li Yizhe. *Guanyu shehui zhuyi de minzhu yu fazhi* (On the socialist democracy and rule of law). Hong Kong: Bibliothèque Asiatique, 1976.

Lin Yusheng et al. *Wusi: Duoyuan de fansi* (The Fourth of May: reflections). Hong Kong: Joint Publishing, 1989.

Liu Shengji. *Beijing zhi chun: 1978–79* (The Beijing spring: 1978–79). Taipei, 1984.

Ma Tong. *Zhongguo Yisilanjiaopai menhuan suyuan* (On the origins of Chinese Muslim sects). Ningxia: Renmin, 1986.

Naka Kunihito. *Ten'anmon jiken* (The Tian'anmen incident). Tokyo: Bungei shunjū, 1979).

Nakajima Mineo. *Junen ato no Chugoku* (China after ten years). Tokyo, 1985.

Okada Takahiro. *To Shohei no Chugoku* (Deng Xiaoping's China). Tokyo: Nihon Keizai Shinbun Sha, 1979.

Pan Guangdan. *Zhongguo jinnei Yutairen de ruogan lishi wenti* (Some historical questions about the Jews in China). Beijing: Beijing University Press, 1983.

Ren Jiyu, ed. *Zhongguo zhexueshi* (History of Chinese philosophy) (1979), 4 vols. Beijing: Renmin, 1963–79.

Shao Yuming. *Ershi shiji Zhongguo Jidujiao wenti* (Problems of twentieth-century Chinese Christianity). Taipei: Zhengzhong, 1980.

Su Xiaokang et al. *He shang* (*River Elegy*). Produced in June 1988 by China Central Television. Accompanying text published in Hong Kong: Joint Publishing, 1988.

———. *Wutobang ji* (Dirge to Utopia). Beijing: Journalism Press, 1988.

Wang Ruoshui. *Wei rendaozhuyi bianhu* (In defense of humanism). Beijing: Renmin, 1987.

Wen Yuankai and Ni Duan. *Zhongguo guominxing gaizao* (The Restructuring of the Chinese national character). Hong Kong: Shuguang, 1988.

Yao Robing. *Zhongguo jiaoyu: 1949–1982* (Education in China: 1949–1982). Hong Kong: Huafeng, 1985.

Zhongguo dixia kanwu (Chinese underground journals). Hong Kong, [1979].

Zhongguo shibao (*China Times*), ed. *Deng Xiaoping fuchu neimu* (The Inside story of Deng Xiaoping's re-emergence). Taipei: *China Times*, 1977.

Newspapers and Newsmagazines Consulted

Citations of material quoted from newspapers and newsmagazines in English or other non-Chinese languages are usually given in the individual chapters, while information from Chinese-language sources is usually synthesized in the reporting presented in this book. The following is a selected list of Hong Kong–based English-language news sources consulted, mass-circulation Chinese-language newpapers consulted, and Chinese-language newsmagazines consulted. (Many Hong Kong papers have U.S. and Canada editions.)

Hong Kong–based English-language news sources

The Asian Wall Street Journal, which appears six times a week
Asiaweek
China News Analysis, a bimonthly
The Far Eastern Economic Review, a weekly
The South China Morning Post, which appears six times a week
The Sunday Morning Post

Chinese-language newspapers

From mainland China (both are official news organs)
The Guangming Daily, the paper for intellectuals
The People's Daily, especially the overseas edition

From Hong Kong
The Ming Pao Daily, a favorite paper of the intellectuals
Shun Po (*Hong Kong Economic Journal*), also considered to be the intellectuals' paper, with in-depth analyses of economic news

The Sing Tao Daily, a powerful paper with American and Canadian editions
Ta Kung Pao, a leftist paper, based in Hong Kong
The Wen Hui Daily, the best known leftist paper in Hong Kong

From Taiwan
The Central Daily, the official paper of the government
The China Times Daily, the second largest privately owned newspaper in Taiwan
The China Times Express, its evening edition
The United Daily, the largest mass-circulation privately owned paper in Taiwan

Chinese-language newsmagazines

From mainland China
Outlook Weekly, an official magazine aimed at the overseas readership.
Red Flag

From Hong Kong
Asiaweek. The Chinese edition usually has fuller reports than its English edition.
Business Weekly, founded in 1987
Cheng Ming. It claims to have confidential sources from within China, carries many exposé articles, and is especially feared on the mainland.
China Monthly (only a few issues from the early 1980s consulted)
Chung Pao Monthly. It has Taiwan connections.
Dong Xiang, a monthly related to the weekly *Cheng Ming*
Emancipation Monthly. It focuses on mainland news, with exposés, but is less known than *Cheng Ming.*
Hong Kong Economic Journal Monthly (Shun Bao Monthly), a substantial magazine with specialist contributions
Ming Pao Monthly, an intellectual's monthly
The Nineties, a monthly, the successor to the earlier *The Seventies*
Pai Hsing Semi-Monthly. It has good articles on student demonstrations.
The Perspective, a monthly with frequent business and finance exposés
Tide Monthly, another comprehensive magazine founded in March 1987
Wide Angle, a wide-circulation monthly
Also: The Hong Kong–based *October Review* has published a special series of primary source materials collected from the April–June democracy movement.

From Taiwan
China Times Weekly, related to *The China Times Daily*

From North America
China Spring, a New York–based monthly published by mainland students overseas who formed the *China Democracy Alliance* with a few retrospective issues in English translation. It is especially considered contraband literature on the mainland and in Taiwan. It had, for a time, an English-language edition in *China Spring Digest,* but this has lapsed.
The Voice of China. This independent monthly, focusing on mainland news, moved its base from New York to Toronto, but has ceased publication.

Index